Springer Series on Behavior Therapy and Behavioral Medicine

Series Editors: Cyril M. Franks, Ph.D., and Frederick J. Evans, Ph.D.

Advisory Board: John Paul Brady, M.D., Robert P. Liberman, M.D., Neal E. Miller, Ph.D., and Stanley Rachman, Ph.D.

Joseph R. Cautela, Ph.D., is Professor of Psychology and Director of the Behavior Modification program at Boston College. He is a past president of the Association for Advancement of Behavior Therapy and has authored six books and more than 80 articles in the field of behavior therapy. Professor Cautela has been a consultant to the Veteran's Administration and in various institutional settings such as psychiatric and medical hospitals and juvenile detention centers. He has supervised the clinical training of doctoral students and has been in private practice for more than 30 years. In addition, Dr. Cautela has been the primary developer of the field of covert conditioning.

Albert J. Kearney, Ph.D., received his degree in counseling psychology from Boston College in 1976. He has worked as a psychologist for public and private schools and in private practice. Currently, he is affiliated with the Maynard, Mass., Public Schools and the Behavior Therapy Institute of Sudbury, Mass. Dr. Kearney has consulted to various hospitals, schools, and mental health agencies, and has lectured on behavior modification at several colleges. He is a past president of the New England Society of Behavior Analysis and Therapy. A veteran marathon runner, Dr. Kearney has a special interest in sports psychology.

The Covert Conditioning Handbook

Joseph R. Cautela, Ph.D.
Albert J. Kearney, Ph.D.

Foreword by Joseph Wolpe, M.D.

SPRINGER PUBLISHING COMPANY
New York

Springer Publishing Company, Inc.
536 Broadway
New York, New York 10012

86 87 88 89 90 / 5 4 3 2 1

Library of Congress Cataloging-in-Publication Data

Cautela, Joseph R.
    The covert conditioning handbook.

    (The Springer series on behavior therapy and
behavioral medicine; v. 17)
    Bibliography: p.
    Includes index.
    1. Behavior therapy. 2. Imagery (Psychology)—
Therapeutic use. I. Kearney, Albert J. II. Title.
III. Series.
RC489.B4C38 1986   616.89'142   85-26161
ISBN 0-8261-4730-5

Printed in the United States of America

To Leo Reyna and Joseph Wolpe,
and to Catherine V. Kearney

Contents

Foreword

My personal and professional relationship with Joseph Cautela began 20 years ago when he attended the first June Institute for training in behavior therapy in the Department of Psychiatry at the University of Virginia. He stood out as an exceptionally knowledgeable member of the group, with an unusual ability to get to the heart of clinical problems. Unlike anybody else, he would often put forward innovative ideas for treatment tailored to the special circumstances of particular patients. It was a further manifestation of this inventiveness that he developed the major subcategory of behavior therapy that was to be called *covert conditioning*. Its first implementation was the mode of aversion therapy that he labeled *covert sensitization*. This has been widely used because it combines convenience with efficacy. Over the years, always attentive to basic principles of learning, Cautela has ingeniously expanded the applications of covert conditioning, and has attracted ever-growing interest from both clinicians and researchers.

It is particularly appropriate for Cautela and Kearney to have undertaken the much-needed task of bringing together in a systematic way the extensive literature that now exists in the field of covert conditioning. The book integrates a vast range of findings in a very logical way. A careful analysis of the import of each contribution is always provided, including in each case a commendable degree of recognition of the point of view of the contributor.

I am sure that this book will bring covert conditioning to the attention of a large new audience. At the same time, it will illuminate the field for those already working in it and will greatly facilitate future research.

Joseph Wolpe, M.D.
Professor of Psychiatry
Temple University Medical School and
Medical College of Pennsylvania

Preface

Wolpe's desensitization procedure (1958) is probably the most widely investigated therapeutic strategy in the history of psychology. While there is some controversy as to the nature of the viable factors in desensitization, the overwhelming evidence is a testimony to the efficacy of the procedure in treating maladaptive avoidance behaviors. If maladaptive approach behaviors such as smoking and alcoholism have anxiety components as antecedent conditions, it should follow that desensitization would also be somewhat effective in modifying maladaptive approach behaviors.

In 1966 the senior author was treating two clients, one of whom exhibited excessive eating and the other a high amount of alcoholic drinking. The behavioral analysis revealed the relevant antecedent conditions, and the client was desensitized to these stimuli. Even though desensitization appeared successful, the eating and drinking continued at almost the same rate. It then occurred to the senior author that if desensitization was not successful in eliminating the behaviors, perhaps it was due to the excessive number of neutral stimuli that became associated with the eating and drinking. According to Hull (1952), stimuli that are present when a drive is evoked and reduced can assume the properties of a secondary drive. This meant that a great many stimuli could have the power to evoke the approach behavior. Even if most of these stimuli could be discovered, the task of desensitizing clients to them could take an enormous amount of time. It seemed reasonable to assume that consequences were also contributing to the occurrence of the maladaptive approach behaviors. Finally, it was concluded that if an imagery procedure could affect antecedent conditions, then perhaps imagining aversive consequences could affect the target behavior. In the first two articles on covert sensitization (Cautela, 1966, 1967) a clear conceptualization of covert conditioning and its operant analogue had not yet been developed.

The possibility of utilizing imagery to increase the probability of particular behaviors led to the development of covert reinforcement. It seemed reasonable to assume that if behavior could be reduced by imagining aversive consequences, then perhaps behaviors could be increased by having a client imagine pleasant or reinforcing consequences. The successful clinical application of covert reinforcement led to the conceptualization of the covert conditioning model and its operant basis.

The term *covert conditioning* is a rubric for a number of procedures and a set of assumptions. Covert conditioning can be defined as the modification of a behavior by imagining particular consequences to influence the behavior in the desired direction. The target behavior is also usually imagined preceding the imagined consequences. Originally the term *covert conditioning* referred only to imagining both the target behavior and the consequence. Later the term was broadened to include instances in which the target behavior was conducted in vivo and only the consequence was imagined.

Acknowledgments

The authors wish to express their thanks to those individuals who have contributed in a variety of ways to the completion of this book. We are especially grateful to Julie Cautela, Anne Kearney, and Pat Tahan for their careful reading of the manuscript in various stages of preparation and for their many helpful suggestions which followed; to Katherine L. Kearney for her assistance in organizing the bibliography; and to Dorothy Burke, Laurel Delaney, and Catherine V. Kearney, who did most of the typing and word processing without which this work could not have been completed.

I

A Review of
Covert Conditioning

1

Covert Conditioning: Definitions and Assumptions

Background

In order to facilitate an understanding of covert conditioning within the behavioral context, it will be helpful to begin with a discussion of a few relevant background concepts.

Behavior

Although some authors, such as Catania (1979), are understandably reluctant to define behavior, others have offered various definitions. According to Reynolds (1968):

> Behavior refers to everything that organisms do. Most behavior, such as the dog's running to the kitchen, can be seen. Some behavior, such as speaking, may only be heard. Other behavior, such as thinking, is ordinarily accessible only to the organism that does the behaving. (p. 5)

White (1971) begins his lengthy definition by referring to behavior as, "The dependent variable in the science of behavior. Any activity of an organism . . . " (p. 12). Sulzer and Mayer (1972) define behavior as "any observable and measurable external or internal act of an organism" (p. 288).

An important element in common among these and many other definitions of behavior is the inclusion of events which take place within the body of the organism. Skinner (1963) has argued:

An adequate science of behavior must consider events taking place within the skin of the organism, not as physiological mediators of behavior, but as part of behavior itself. It can deal with these events without assuming that they have any special nature or must be known in any special way. The skin is not that important as a boundary. Private and public events have the same kind of physical dimensions. (p. 953)

Internal events, as will be seen shortly, are the realm of covert conditioning. Covert conditioning involves the manipulation of covert (internal, private) behavior (acts) of the organism to modify both covert behavior and external behavior. While some students of human behavior would question the validity of including private or covert behaviors in an analysis of behavior, we agree with the position of Glenn (1983), who has written, in a discussion of verbal behavior:

Some of the events involved in those functional relations may be private, but that does not take them out of the realm of a functional analysis. A private event is an empirical event if potentially detectable as functionally related to a response or to the stimulating environment. (p. 47)

Imagery

John B. Watson, the father of American behaviorism, was of the opinion that the investigation of private events did not help in understanding and predicting the behavior of organisms. Although he did not deny the existence of private events, he held the opinion that their lack of public observability made it impossible to consider them objectively. From Watson's point of view, private events were therefore not appropriate phenomena for scientific research (Watson, 1913).

The reluctance of most behaviorists to accept imagery as a viable construct continued until Joseph Wolpe's publication of *Psychotherapy by Reciprocal Inhibition* in 1958. In this landmark book, Wolpe described the development of systematic desensitization. In systematic desensitization, imagery is used as a practical means of exposing clients to anxiety-evoking stimuli. The popularization of systematic desensitization in the United States introduced the use of imagery to a large part of the American psychological community.

The decades that followed the appearance of *Psychotherapy by Reciprocal Inhibition* saw the development of several more imagery-based behavior therapy techniques. Along with systematic desensitization and covert conditioning procedures, other imagery-based behavior therapy techniques were devised, including emotive imagery

(Lazarus & Abramovitz, 1962) and implosive therapy (Stampfl & Levis, 1967).

In addition to the learning-theory based uses of imagery, proponents of cognitive therapy, such as Mahoney (1974) and Meichenbaum (1974), have made some use of imagery. They emphasize covert verbal behavior within the context of a social learning or social psychology model. Concepts such as expectation and attitude are particularly important within this model. Some of the similarities and differences between covert conditioning and cognitive behavior therapy will be discussed later.

Operant Conditioning

Operant conditioning emphasizes the influence of the environment on behavior. From an operant point of view, most behavior is seen as a function of events following the emission of a response. Since people are always in some kind of internal environment and overt environment, their environments are constantly influencing their behavior, and they are constantly learning, unlearning, and relearning different things. Although our environments usually influence our behavior in random, unplanned, inefficient ways, every environmental event that impinges on the organism does affect behavior. Therefore, behavior modification occurs constantly, whether systematically planned or not.

For the most part, environmental events within cultures tend to operate on the members of that culture in such a way that the majority of its members behave in ways reasonably consistent with the predominant values in that culture. From time to time, however, individuals learn behaviors which are maladaptive because they are detrimental to the individual and/or the culture. These behaviors are shaped, strengthened, and maintained by environmental events.

In behavior modification, principles of operant conditioning are often used in planned, directed ways to efficiently bring about desired changes in behavior. A survey conducted by Wade, Baker, and Hartmann (1979) revealed that procedures based on operant conditioning principles are used by a greater percentage of behavior therapists than any other procedures.

Operant conditioning, which Reynolds (1968) defines as "a process in which the frequency of performance of a bit of behavior is modified by the consequences of the behavior" (p. 1) includes five basic operations. Two of the five operations (positive reinforcement and negative reinforcement) strengthen or increase the frequency of the target behavior. The other three operations (extinction, punishment, and response cost) weaken or decrease the frequency.

Positive Reinforcement. If the immediate consequences of a behavior involve the addition of a stimulus to the situation, and this results in the behavior's being more likely to occur in the future, we say that positive reinforcement has occurred. The identification of the reinforcing stimulus also involves a decrease in behavior when the assumed reinforcing stimulus no longer follows the behavior. The consequence usually, but not always, is considered something pleasurable or rewarding to the organism being reinforced. For example, if we tell a joke and the consequence is that the listener laughs, chances are we are more likely to tell the same joke again.

In positive reinforcement, as with the operant conditioning operations, the timing of the consequences is critical. For example, if, in attempting to positively reinforce a particular response, the reinforcement is delayed after the emission of the target behavior, the wrong behavior might erroneously be reinforced.

Negative Reinforcement. Negative reinforcement is another operation by which behavior is increased. Catania (1979) defines negative reinforcement as follows: "When a response terminates or prevents an aversive stimulus and the response thereby becomes more probable, the stimulus is called a *negative reinforcer* and the operation is called *negative reinforcement*" (p. 104).

There are two forms of negative reinforcement. According to Reynolds (1968):

> Two paradigms in which aversive stimuli increase or maintain responding are escape and avoidance. In *escape*, a response terminates an aversive stimulus *after* the stimulus has begun; the organism cannot avoid the beginning of the aversive stimuli. In *avoidance*, a response avoids or postpones the beginning of the aversive stimulus. Escape and avoidance sometimes occur in combination. Thus, between presentations of the aversive stimulus, responses postpone its start; once it has started, responses terminate it. (p. 103)

In other words, if a particular behavior is followed by the cessation of a stimulus usually labeled aversive, and the frequency of that behavior increases, negative reinforcement has occurred. An example we are all familiar with is the buzzer apparatus connected to seat belts in automobiles. The buzzer emits an aversive noise from which we can escape by fastening the seat belt. The purpose of this arrangement is to make it more likely that riders will wear seat belts. Since, in this example, we escaped from an ongoing aversive stimulus, we label it an example of escape conditioning, the first of the two subtypes of negative reinforcement mentioned above. Sometimes, as in the case of seat belts, the aversive stimulus can be avoided by performing the target behavior (buckle seat belt) before the aversive stimulus begins. This second kind of negative reinforcement is called avoidance conditioning.

Extinction. The extinction procedure results in a decrease in the frequency of the target behavior. In extinction, the reinforcer, which has been maintaining the target behavior, is withheld. If, in the example of positive reinforcement used above, the listeners do not laugh at our joke, chances are we will be less likely to tell the same joke again in the future. It is crucial to remember that different people are reinforced by different stimuli in different situations. Laughter, or what may at first glance appear to be the obvious reinforcer, may not in fact be the reinforcing consequence. This should be considered both when choosing idiosyncratic reinforcers to use in positive reinforcement and when attempting extinction.

Once the reinforcing stimulus is identified and withheld, we do not always see an immediate decrease in the rate of the target behavior. Sometimes there is an extinction burst. The extinction burst is a temporary increase in the rate of behavior at the beginning of the extinction procedure. This state of affairs is sometimes discouraging to individuals attempting to implement an extinction program for the first time. If they are unfamiliar with the phenomenon of the extinction burst, then they may assume that either the procedure is incorrectly applied or extinction does not work. Mistakenly thinking they could be strengthening the maladaptive behavior, they hurry to "return things to normal" by reinstating the previous conditions. Instead of improving the situation, however, they are now reinforcing a higher rate of behavior than when the extinction program started. Also, because the target behavior has now been reinforced intermittently, it will be more difficult to extinguish in the future.

Another possible effect of extinction is extinction-produced aggression. The aggression may be directed toward either the individual withholding reinforcement or significant others (Azrin, Hutchinson, & Hake, 1966).

Punishment. If the presentation of a stimulus immediately follows the performance of a target behavior and the probability of the target behavior decreases, then punishment is said to have occurred. It should be noted that punishment does not occur unless the target behavior is decreased. Common examples would include a parent's spanking a child who is caught playing with matches or a teacher's reprimanding a student for talking in class.

Although punishment can effectively suppress behaviors, there are potential side effects which should be kept in mind when considering the use of punishment. One of the most important of these is the possibility that the individual who is administering the punishment will acquire similar aversive qualities in the view of the person being punished, thereby making it more difficult for that individual to use other forms of control effectively.

Two guidelines for effective administration of punishment should be emphasized. First, the punishing consequence should follow the target behavior immediately. Second, the punishing consequence should be aversive enough to result in discomfort or avoidance behavior. Use of too weak an aversive stimulus may result in habituation to that stimulus. This can lead to an inoculation or desensitization-like situation as the aversive stimulus is gradually strengthened in an effort to increase the effectiveness of the punishment, and the organism habituates to the increasing strength.

Response Cost. The third operation used to reduce the rate of the target behavior is response cost. In response cost the performance of the target behavior is followed by the removal of a usually reinforcing stimulus, but not the stimulus which has been maintaining the target behavior (Kazdin, 1972). For example, a teenager might lose the use of the family car for a week as a consequence of staying out too late at night.

Fines and loss of privileges are other common examples of response cost, which may be the predominant means of control in our culture. Although rarely labeled response cost, examples of this "common-sense" method of control abound (e.g., Jungemann, 1981, p. 168).

In considering the difficulty of effectively using aversive control (punishment and response cost), one should keep in mind (1) that most of our legal system is based on the attempted use of these operations and (2) the level of success of that system.

Modeling. Modeling, or observational learning, involves the imitation of behavior which an observer witnesses being performed by others. Although the processes involved in modeling are still being debated, Bandura (1969) has summarized the major behavioral explanations of the modeling phenomenon. He proposes a contiguity theory of modeling. Observation results in verbal and imagery coding of the relationship between the model and environmental events. In his discussion Bandura distinguishes between acquisition and performance of behavior. For example, an individual might observe a new dance step for the first time. Prior to the observation our observer would not have been able to perform the novel dance step. Now, once the behavior has been acquired through observation, the observer can and will perform the dance step when properly motivated. However, the actual performance may not take place for months, if ever.

The modeled incident may also be thought of as a discriminative stimulus which signals the observer that this behavior, in this situation, will be reinforced. When the conditions are sufficiently similar, that is, when the discriminative stimulus is presented at some time in the future, it will occasion the performance of the novel response which is consequently reinforced. An operant analysis of modeling might reveal that this comes about because the observer has been differentially reinforced, most likely on an intermittent schedule, for matching the behavior of others. Infants and young children typically receive a great deal of reinforcement from family members and other adults for imitating the behavior of others. As the child grows older, some of the imitations inevitably appear "less cute" and fewer responses are reinforced. This natural thinning of the reinforcement schedule continues, and the effectiveness of the specific behavior in bringing about a reinforcing consequence plays an ever-increasing role in the maintenance and shaping of the response.

It is important to note that the modeling phenomenon is not restricted to either live models or the visual modality. Movies, videotapes, audiotapes, books, and storytelling are all examples of effective ways in which models are presented symbolically. According to Bandura (1969), while symbolic modeling is effective, it is less effective than in vivo modeling.

Bandura (1965) showed that the consequences experienced by the models play an important part in whether or not the observed behavior is later performed by the observer. Perhaps modeling should not be thought of as a distinct, independent, learning procedure, but rather as one process through which the five basic operations of operant conditioning are delivered to the organisms.

Although model-observer similarity has been shown to be important, Bandura (1969) also cited evidence of the effectiveness of models with high prestige and status. He attempted to reconcile this apparent discrepancy by suggesting that observers who are bright, confident, and intelligent will tend to respond more to idealized models.

Lowe (1978, pp. 33–34) summarized several important criteria for effective models:

> The model should be seen by the observer as a person whom the observer has the capacity to emulate either in the present or in the future . . . . The

model should possess attributes which the subject admires . . . . The model should be seen as competent or capable of becoming competent in regard to the behavior being demonstrated . . . . The model should be similar in age and sex to the subject . . . and in initial response to the behavior being demonstrated . . . . The model should display gradually increased coping behavior relevant to the behavior to be modified rather than display initial mastery . . . and finally, the model should be reinforced for displaying the desired behavior . . . .

Defining Covert Conditioning

The term *covert conditioning* refers to both (1) a theoretical model and (2) a set of behavior therapy procedures which emphasize the use of imagery but also include covert vocal behavior. In clinical and experimental applications of covert conditioning, the individual is asked to imagine engaging in the target behavior. This scene is immediately followed by a scene in which the individual imagines a consequence designed to alter the strength and/or frequency of the target behavior.

In the past decade there has been considerable controversy about the notion of self-reinforcement (e.g., Goldiamond, 1976a, 1976b; Mahoney, 1976; Thoresen & Wilbur, 1976). The central point of the controversy seems to be whether or not an individual can reliably determine whether or not the criteria for reinforcement have been met (i.e., when the stimulus follows the response it increases the strength of the response, and when the stimulus is removed it weakens the response) and then effectively reinforce his or her own behavior. In the case of covert conditioning the client initially makes the reinforcing response in response to the therapist's instructions. Although it is the client who actually makes the reinforcing response, it is the therapist who initially determines whether or not a given criterion has been met.

In self-control applications of covert conditioning, clients may not always administer consequences appropriately, but when they do, it changes the target behavior in the intended direction. Since a consequence is defined in terms of the effect it has on the behavior it follows, the reinforcing quality of a self-delivered consequence can be empirically determined. Therefore, when a client covertly performs the target behavior and the scene of that behavior is reinforced by a second scene, it is covert self-reinforcement. Only the covert behavior has to increase for it to be considered self-reinforcement; however, it follows from the interaction hypothesis (see below) that changes may also be observed in the corresponding overt behavior.

Covert conditioning can also take place outside of the laboratory or therapy room. Just as overt events are constantly influencing each other in a nondirected, random, unplanned, natural occurrence of operant conditioning, haphazardly shaping our overt behavior, the same holds true for covert events. In other words, whether we plan it or not, like it or not, or even admit it or not, covert conditioning, like operant conditioning, is always going on. Thoughts, images, feelings, and other covert events are constantly interacting with one another, thereby influencing both the future likelihood and the form of covert behavior.

Assumptions

In the course of the development of covert conditioning procedures, the assumptions upon which it is based have also evolved. Stated in various forms, the number of these assumptions has ranged from a low of 2 (Scott & Rosenstiel, 1975) to a high of 10 (Cautela & McCullough, 1978). In some cases the evolution of the assumptions resulted from the increasingly available information about psychological processes in general and from further experience with and theorizing about covert conditioning in particular. The change in conceptualization of covert sensitization from possibly a form of contiguity conditioning to an analogue of operant conditioning is a case in point. In other cases, some of the assumptions are clarifications, corollaries, or logical conclusions drawn from one or more of the other assumptions. The number of assumptions has grown to expand the model to explain more phenomena, for example, organic illness.

The theoretical development of covert conditioning first involved three basic assumptions. These assumptions are the homogeneity assumption, the interaction assumption, and the learning assumption.

Homogeneity Assumption. Others have referred to the homogeneity assumption as the continuity assumption (Mahoney, 1974) and the assumption of functional equivalence (Day, 1969). It is shared by several others who have developed procedures involving the manipulation of covert events according to learning principles (e.g., Homme, 1965; Stampfl & Levis, 1967; Wolpe, 1958).

According to the homogeneity assumption, all categories of behavior (including the three categories of covert behavior mentioned above—

thoughts, images, and feelings) obey the same laws and are subject to the same parameters. Conditioning, as it has been demonstrated in animals and in humans, takes place in a similar manner in our covert processes. Just as we are likely to return to a restaurant where we enjoyed a good meal, a pleasant daydream of a long awaited vacation is likely to occur again. The same parameters that influence overt behavior influence covert behavior; for example, learning becomes stronger as the number of overt and covert trials increases. Intermittent reinforcement strengthens resistance to extinction in both overt and covert processes. Support of this functional equivalence comes from evidence which suggests that repeated imagery can have habituation effects similar to repeated presentation of external stimuli (Drummond, White, & Ashton, 1978; Yaremko & Butler, 1975; Yaremko, Glanville, & Leckart, 1972).

This assumption of homogeneity has heuristic value since it is parsimonious (does not involve assuming two qualitatively different kinds of behavior, but only one kind of behavior obeying the same laws). It also allows the generalization of empirical evidence derived from overt behaviors to covert behaviors.

The assumption that covert and overt behaviors are influenced by the same laws has been held by learning theorists such as Homme (1965), Hull (1943), Mahoney (1970), Mahoney, Thoresen, and Danaher (1972), Pavlov (1927), and Skinner (1953, p. 257). Also, there is ample experimental evidence to support this assumption (Ascher, 1973; Ascher & Cautela, 1972; Bauer & Craighead, 1979; Epstein & Petersen, 1973; Kazdin, 1974b; May, 1977; Miller, 1935; Roberts & Weerts, 1982; Schwartz & Higgins, 1971; Wade, Malloy, & Proctor, 1977).

Although covert and overt processes share important and similar properties in explaining, maintaining, and modifying behavior, we do not assume that covert responses correspond to the real world any more than do overt responses; that is, we do not assume that our sense modalities register photocopies of the real world. An excellent review and discussion of the functional equivalence of images and external physical objects is provided by Finke (1980). Cautela and Baron (1977) and Cautela (1980) also discuss this and other assumptions in greater detail.

Interaction Assumption.   The second assumption, the interaction assumption, states that all categories of behavior interact both with each other and with the environment and that the manipulation of one category of events can influence events in other categories in a predictable manner. More specifically, not only do overt and covert behavior obey the same laws, they also interact with each other according to these laws. For example, leaving a restaurant and saying covertly, "I really enjoyed that restaurant" will increase the probability of going to the same restaurant again. The more we pair going to the restaurant with covert expressions of approval, the stronger the response strength of the overt behavior of going to the restaurant will be.

This assumption, which underlies several approaches to therapy including systematic desensitization (Wolpe, 1958), rational-emotive therapy (Ellis, 1962), rational restructuring (Davison, 1966; Mahoney, 1974), and multimodal therapy (Lazarus, 1976), is supported by a wealth of studies demonstrating the effectiveness of a variety of behavioral techniques, involving the use of imagery, in changing overt behavior.

Carney and Hong (1982) demonstrated that facial EMG could reliably identify when subjects were visualizing covert sensitization scenes as opposed to when they were either visualizing pleasant scenes or were in a resting state. Schuele and Wiesenfield (1983) found that negative self-statements and corresponding imagery were accompanied by greater levels of cardiac and respiratory arousal than were neutral self-statements and associated imagery.

McMahon and Hastings (1980) have cited additional evidence that imagined events can lead to the same peripheral physiological effects as a perceived overt event, thereby supporting the hypothesis that covert psychological events can influence covert physiological events. They also propose that imagination of stressful events could have pathogenic effects similar to actual stressors, that is, covert behavior can produce organic dysfunction. Davidson and Schwartz (1977) present evidence that imagery behavior can influence the activity of both the CNS and the peripheral nervous system. Pavlov demonstrated that the digestive system could be influenced by conditioning (1927). It follows from the interaction hypothesis that various biological systems are susceptible to conditioning influences including the circulatory, hormonal, and immune systems.

In a series of studies, Ader and his colleagues demonstrated that the immune system could be influenced by classical conditioning (Ader, 1980). The usual procedure is to pair a neutral stimulus (distinctly flavored drinking solution) with an immunosuppressive drug. When conditioned animals were injected with antigens, their immunosuppressive response was shown to be attenuated. Similar results have been replicated in other laboratories (Rogers, Reich, Strom, & Carpenter, 1976; Wayner, Flannery, & Singer, 1978).

Ader considers an antigen to be an unconditioned stimulus and the production of antibodies to be an unconditioned response. He also assumes that when a neutral stimulus is paired with the production or suppression of antibodies, that neutral stimulus can become a conditioned stimulus influencing the production or suppression of antibodies (Ader, 1980). He further implies that psychosocial stimuli can act as conditional stimuli affecting the immune system. These studies and implications have far-reaching effects (e.g., the immune system is affected by learning). Ader's success in conditioning the immune system gives further support to the interaction assumption by demonstrating that overt physiological events can influence covert physiological events.

That covert and overt events can occur concomitantly does not preclude the possible validity of the interaction assumption. The distinction among the various categories of behavior is an artificial one for convenience sake. All organismic inputs and outputs are physiological events. It follows then that when we talk about psychological or covert events influencing physiological or overt events, we are simply talking about one category of physiological events influencing another class of physiological events.

Learning Assumption. The third assumption, the learning assumption, is that all categories of behavior respond similarly to the laws of learning, for example, heart rate, or galvanic skin response, or imagery may be reinforced or punished (Ascher & Cautela, 1972, 1974; Cautela, Walsh, & Wish, 1971; Scott, Blanchard, Edmundsen, & Young, 1973; Weiss & Engel, 1971). We also hold that other parameters of learning, such as resistance to extinction and intermittent reinforcement, apply to all categories of behavior.

If we take a methodological deterministic position, we must assume that there are laws governing learning even though we have not discovered the precise nature of these laws. While covert behavior is assumed to have both classical and operant components, to date covert conditioning has emphasized the covert analogue of operant conditioning procedures. There are a number of studies that indicate that the same learning variables that influence overt events influence covert events (Ascher, 1973; Ascher & Cautela, 1972; Baron, 1975; Cautela et al., 1971; Tondo & Cautela, 1974).

Covert classical conditioning is also subsumed under the covert conditioning model. Although it is a relatively unexplored area, Yaremko and Werner (1974) have provided some evidence to support the notion of covert classical conditioning. They conducted an experiment with four groups. Subjects in the first group received one overt pairing of a tone (CS) followed immediately by an electric shock (US). They then were instructed to imagine 10 more trials of this pairing. Subjects in the second group also received the overt pairing, but their 10 imagery tones and imagery shocks were imagined in random order. Remaining subjects received a single trace conditioning trial in which 12 seconds elapsed between the end of the tone and the beginning of the shock. Subjects in the third group then imagined the same imagery pairings as subjects in the first group while the fourth group of subjects imagined the CS and US in random order. After imagery all subjects received 10 overt CS exposures while their GSR was measured. The results " . . . show that groups which imagined paired stimuli were more responsive than their unpaired controls" (p. 218). The fourth group, which received neither real nor imagery trials, showed the least learning and quickest extinction. This finding is consistent with a covert classical conditioning explanation.

Behavioral Classification Assumption. There are three general classes of behavior. The first, *overt behavior*, is simply an external act or response of an organism. Most people would agree that external observable responses, such as running, writing, or brushing one's teeth, are examples of behavior. These overt behaviors involve observable responses influenced by external and internal stimulus input.

A second class of behavior is comprised of *covert physiological behavior*. Covert physiological behavior, or internal responses of the organism, encompasses all physiological behavior which occurs in or under the skin, such as circulation, nervous system activity, glandular secretions, and so forth. The individual is aware of some of these processes and unaware of others. Usually, these internal processes are not readily observable to other people. However, through the use of various forms of physiological instrumentation, some of them may be observed and measured. (See Hefferline & Perera, 1963, for one of the earliest demonstrations of the use of overt stimuli in the conditioning of covert physiological behavior.) It seems likely that as more sensitive and sophisticated equipment is developed, the realm of observable covert physiological behaviors will expand, that is, more currently unobservable behavior will become observable.

These internal processes are assumed to interact according to the same laws of learning that influence other classes of behavior. W. Horsley Gantt termed this process *autokinesis* (1976, p. 258). According to Gantt, conditioning takes place in the organism independent of external stimulation.

The third class of behavior is *covert psychological behavior*. Covert psychological behavior consists of thoughts, images, and feelings. Thoughts can be defined as subvocal speech, talking to oneself, or covert vocal behavior (sounds). Images can be defined as making responses similar to those that are made to particular external stimuli in the absence of those stimuli or "what we see with our eyes closed." Feelings are physiological states that are concomitant with particular overt behaviors labeled by the verbal community as emotional. Feelings involve internal sensations which one learns to experience in response to correlated thoughts and images from which various emotional states are inferred.

Covert psychological responses are assumed to occur concomitantly with a physiological event. Until more advanced instrumentation is developed in this area, however, we must rely on the individual engaging in covert psychological behavior to also observe these behaviors and report them to external observers.

Organic Events Assumption. A fifth assumption of the covert conditioning paradigm is that the three classes of behavior mentioned above (overt, covert physiological, and covert psychological) are all organic events. The classification of behaviors into three categories is merely a convenience to describe different categories of organic events. When we talk about psychological events influencing organic events, we are not saying that there are different levels of behavior interacting with each other, nor are we saying that some events are organic and others are not. We are saying that all the classes of behavior are organic events that influence each other in a predictable manner according to the laws of learning.

Skinner (1953) states:

> One important sort of stimulation to which the individual may possibly be responding when he describes unemitted behavior has no parallel among other forms of private stimulation. It arises from the fact that the behavior may actually occur but on such a reduced scale that it cannot be observed by others, at least without instrumentation. This is often expressed by saying that the behavior is "covert." (p. 263)

While all three general classes of events are in some manner observable, the current distinction among them is based on to whom and in what manner they are observable. In actuality, within the responding organism, this distinction is an artificial one. As improvements continue to be made in instrumentation, it seems likely that events which at present are only observed through self-report procedures will be observable through artificial extensions of the senses of the external observer. Again according to Skinner (1969), in writing about covert responses,

> The stimuli they generate are weak but nevertheless of the same kind as those generated by overt responses. It would be a mistake to refuse to consider them as data just because a second observer cannot feel or see them, at least without the help of instruments. (p. 242)

Continual Plastic Nervous System Assumption. A sixth assumption assumes a continual plastic nervous system. In other words, experiences (including covert events) can influence anatomical and chemical changes in the central nervous system. This applies to adults as well as children and is consistent with recent evidence presented by Rosenzweig and Bennett (1980) that new connections can be formed in the adult nervous system.

Universal Influence of Consequences Assumption. Assumption seven is that consequences influence all classes of behavior simultaneously. If, for example, a child is reinforced in the midst of a temper tantrum, not only is the child's overt motor behavior reinforced but so might be the thoughts, images, feelings, and physiological responses that may be occurring. Not all systems and organs, however, condition at the same rate or to the same extent. Gantt (1976) referred to this difference as *schizokinesis.*

Mostofsky (1976, pp. 249–267) has reported evidence of operant conditioning influencing several physiological processes, including neural activity, heart rate, skin temperature, and pain. Weiss has commented that when one is reinforcing or establishing contingencies to behavior, he may be affecting the brain catecholamines (Seligman & Weiss, 1980, p. 483).

Nondirected Covert Conditioning

Covert conditioning, which occurs in response to intentional systematic, sequential, therapeutic instructions, directed either by the therapist or by the client in the form of self-control application (see section on self-control, p. 80), is referred to as directed covert conditioning. As mentioned earlier, random (not planned) overt events constantly influence behavior. Such is also the case with covert events. Although individuals experiencing these covert events may very well be unaware of their effect, these events still operate to influence behavior. Covert conditioning which is not intentionally directed is referred to as nondirected covert conditioning. Day-dreaming about eating a piece of pizza at home in the refrigerator and how delicious it would taste is an example of nondirected covert conditioning. Nondirected covert conditioning is, of course, subject to the interaction assumption. Through the interaction of events within or between different levels of behavior, many adaptive behaviors are learned and strengthened. A worker might practice or rehearse in imagination several different ways of asking her boss for a raise and her best guess as to the probable consequence of each. As the worker covertly tries out various approaches, in a covert trial-and-error process, her plan is shaped by the imagined consequences. Finally, she chooses a particular approach and attempts it overtly. Whether or not the worker's overt performance and its consequences coincide with the covert version depend to a large extent on additional factors, both overt and covert. It may turn out that the plan is never attempted. Beginning to implement the plan may evoke a prohibitive level of anticipation of aversive stimuli; environmental conditions may be arranged in such a way that the worker does not engage in assertive behavior.

As suggested earlier by Binder (1975), maladaptive behavior can also develop in a similar way. The same processes operate to influence behavior, whether adaptive or maladaptive. Covert behaviors may be modified by randomly occurring events, the results of which may be a maladaptive or even bizarre behavior. A possible scenario for the development of a dog phobia follows.

A young child who has never been close to a dog before starts to happily approach a strange dog. The child's mother notices what is happening and, being unsure of the strange dog, snatches her child away saying, "Be careful, Billy, stay away from strange dogs. They might bite you." Billy then reviews, in imagination, the event which has just taken place and adds the potential consequence described by his mother—being bitten by a dog (nondirected covert sensitization). Thus we have Billy imagining approaching a strange dog and being bitten.

The next time Billy hears or sees a dog, perhaps on television, he recalls and rehearses the unpleasant dog-related experience. After a few nondirected covert conditioning trials and no overt exposure to dogs, Billy's parents are bewildered when, several months later, while visiting Aunt Mary, her friendly old dog, Fido, walks in and Billy begins crying and shaking and runs away.

Inappropriate behavior can also be rehearsed without the naturally occurring aversive consequences. For example, a youngster might chase a rolling ball into a busy street or onto thin ice, thinking only of successfully retrieving the ball (naturally occurring, nondirected covert reinforcement). A student might tear up a poor report card without experiencing covert behavior of the additional aversive consequences from teachers and parents. One child, seeing a second child with a desired toy, might hit the child and try to take the toy away, in spite of the presence of both sets of parents. Although there can be other explanations of these individual instances of behavior, a lack of consideration of potential aversive consequences is often labeled a lack of impulse control.

Expectancy and Placebo Effects

The placebo effect is receiving increasing attention due to its importance in evaluating particular treatment procedures and because of speculation that the placebo effect may be mediated by certain neurochemical changes in the brain. For example, after reviewing recent research, Cautela and Kearney (1984) speculated that when a placebo has some effect in reducing pain, endorphine secretion may occur. These secretions may be elicited by the placebo instructions.

Levine, Gordon, and Fields (1978) studied the effect of naloxone (an opiate blocker) on dental postoperative pain to examine the hypothesis that endorphines mediate placebo analgesia. Subjects given naloxone along with a placebo reported significantly greater pain than those given only placebos. Prior administration of naloxone had reduced the probability of a positive placebo response. Additionally, naloxone produced no further increase in pain levels reported by subjects classified as placebo nonresponders (i.e., subjects who did not exhibit a placebo effect). One could speculate that the neurochemical changes and some of the accompanying overt behavioral changes may also be influenced by covert conditioning factors. Expectations produced by the placebo instructions could influence the individual to engage in anticipatory imagery concerning outcome or contingencies. For example, if an individual is given a placebo to reduce pain, perhaps the person imagines that the pain is not experienced in the usually painful situations (covert extinction), and the individual also imagines doing reinforcing activities as a result of imagined pain reduction (covert positive reinforcement).

It seems likely then that nondirected covert conditioning may, in some instances, contribute to the placebo effect or "nonspecific factors" in treatments that sometimes appear to have a greater effect than can readily be explained. If a client expects a given treatment to work, it seems logical to expect the client to engage in covert behavior about the treatment from time to time. That covert behavior may include images of the client's receiving the treatment, engaging in the new behavior, and experiencing the positively reinforcing natural consequences of the new appropriate behavior. In other words, the client is self-administering nondirected covert positive reinforcement trials with the image of getting well serving as the reinforcer.

On the other hand, a client who does not expect a treatment to work and rehearses scenes of the treatment's not having any effect is engaging in nondirected covert extinction. These processes may not only contribute to the effectiveness (or ineffectiveness) of psychological treatments, but of drugs and other medical treatments as well. According to the covert conditioning model, then, when individuals have expectations, they have some anticipatory imagery in the form of nondirected covert conditioning concerning outcome (contingency) and behavior is affected. We should add that there is no reason to assume that covert behavior which occurs in nonwaking states (e.g., dream images) should have any different influence on behavior than covert behavior which occurs in the waking state.

Nondirected covert conditioning may also be a factor contributing to the paradoxical effects of drugs observed from time to time. Psychotropic drugs sometimes produce a paradoxical effect rather than the intended effect (Kornetsky, 1976, p. 13). In certain cases, using drugs to decrease violent behavior results in an increase in the behavior. Perhaps these patients imagine hitting and being violent and getting desired results such as avoidance by others (covert negative reinforcement).

Covert Conditioning and Cognitive Therapy

Since both covert conditioning and cognitive therapy involve the manipulation of covert behavior, it is relevant to compare these approaches.

The issue of the efficacy of cognitive therapy will not be discussed here. The reader is referred to other reviews, such as those of Miller and Berman (1983) and Latimer and Sweet (1984). Before the question can be addressed, the term *cognitive therapy* should be clarified together with a discussion of some issues. Some authors would hold that any therapeutic approach which attempts to manipulate or modify covert processes to achieve behavior change should be included under the rubric of cognitive therapy (Wilson & O'Leary, 1980). According to this view, systematic desensitization, implosive therapy, and covert conditioning would be cognitive therapies. On the other hand, there are authors who hold that cognitive therapy has distinctive features to distinguish it from the aforementioned approaches (Beck, 1976; Mahoney, 1974; Wilson & O'Leary, 1980).

Covert conditioning, systematic desensitization, and implosive therapy have two features not shared by the cognitive strategies espoused by Beck (1976), Ellis (1979), Mahoney (1974), and Meichenbaum (1977). Covert conditioning, systematic desensitization, and implosive therapy all assume that covert behavior obeys the same laws that govern the interaction between the overt behavior of the organism and the external environment (the homogeneity assumption). Therapists who adhere to the covert conditioning model also assume that the laws are the laws of conditioning. These therapists also focus on the manipulation of imagery. Cognitive therapists do not assume the homogeneity assumption. They do not view conditioning as playing a central role in behavioral change. The emphasis of cognitive therapy is on the manipulation of thoughts or ideation as the major therapeutic strategy.

While prominent cognitive therapists share the above characteristics, they differ in the degree to which behavioral procedures such as relaxation, in vivo desensitization, and overt reinforcement are utilized. On one end of the continuum is Beck, who, while he advocates the use of other behavioral procedures as a valuable adjunct to cognitive therapy, usually does not include the strategies to any appreciable extent in his treatment descriptions.

On the other end of the continuum are Wilson and O'Leary, who advocate that cognitive therapists should not ignore the greater efficacy of behavioral procedures (1980, p. 282).

Somewhere in between, in order of increasing acceptance of the importance of traditional behavioral procedures for behavior change, are Ellis, Meichenbaum, and Mahoney.

The essential assumption of cognitive therapy that distinguishes it from the other therapies is that maladaptive ideation causes and maintains behavior disorders. Therefore, therapeutic strategies must aim at changing irrational beliefs (Beck, 1976; Ellis, 1970). The various strategies utilized are verbal persuasion (Ellis, 1970), problem solving (Beck, 1976), self-instructional training (Meichenbaum, 1977), and cognitive restructuring (Wilson & O'Leary, 1980, pp. 249–268).

The theoretical underpinnings of cognitive therapy appear to be those borrowed from social psychology. Client attitudes, beliefs, and expectations are explored and manipulated, but emphasis is not on the reality of the external environment but on the perception of the external environment. Misperception of the external environment results in behavioral and emotional disturbances. Cognitive therapists maintain that behavior therapy is effective insofar as it modifies faulty beliefs, attitudes, or expectations. Bandura's self-efficacy theory (1977) postulates that any treatment is effective insofar as it increases the client's expectancy that he/she can cope with threatening situations.

Bandura also holds that, while maladaptive thinking can cause and maintain behavior disorders, the best approach for modifying behavior disorders involves direct behavioral intervention. Bandura creates a curious paradox for himself in espousing different theoretical underpinnings for ideology and treatment. Covert conditioning, as previously stated, postulates the homogeneity assumption along with operant conditioning as the primary bases of behavior. Covert conditioning bridges the gap between radical behaviorism and cognitive therapy. While covert conditioning focuses on the manipulation of imagery and cognitive therapy emphasizes the modification of thought processes, both covert conditioning and cognitive therapy acknowledge the importance of all covert events for behavior change. Both covert conditioning and cognitive therapy assume that an important element of behavior change is the manipulation of covert behavior. Covert conditioning holds that the manipulation should follow conditioning procedures based on operant conditioning. Covert conditioning assumes that manipulation of covert behavior is often (not always) necessary for behavior change but it is not always sufficient. Cognitive therapy has contributed new strategies for behavior change and has helped mandate that radical behaviorism expand its investigations to include the causal relationships between covert and overt behavior.

2

Covert Conditioning Procedures, Part I

In the next two chapters preliminary steps leading up to the use of covert conditioning will be described, the seven covert conditioning procedures will be reviewed, examples will be given, and common features will be discussed.

Preliminary Steps

Behavior Analysis

When covert conditioning is employed (as in the use of any behavior therapy technique), a thorough behavior analysis is conducted (Cautela & Upper, 1975). There are 10 major steps (listed below) in conducting a behavior analysis. While it can be said that behavior therapy is constantly in progress during all phases of assessment and treatment, most of these steps should be taken prior to introducing specific behavioral techniques. Some of the later steps obviously cannot be taken until the formal program is underway.

Operationalize the Target Behavior. Operationalize means to describe the problem in terms of the specific behaviors involved. Self-reports of the client or observations of others which use labels such as depression, hyperactivity, or aggression are operationalized into behaviors subsumed under those labels. A label such as aggression can be quite misleading since it often means different things to different people. For example, a referral of a child exhibiting excessive aggressiveness may result from calling classmates names or from attacking schoolteachers with a knife. Both extremes of behavior have been labeled aggression. Since the term *aggression* has no commonly accepted objective parameters to delineate the behaviors which it is supposed to describe and/or explain, it can and does suggest different things to different people. A speaker may intend to tell a listener about an aggressive (name-calling) child. Based on the label, the listener may think he/she clearly understands what that aggressive child is like (a knife wielder). In fact, a serious miscommunication has taken place because of the use of a misleading label which, at best, provides us with little or no useful information.

Establish a Baseline. Establishing a baseline usually involves record keeping to gather information about the frequency and/or duration of the target behavior. The baseline is taken prior to beginning any formal intervention. This provides a reference point for evaluating the treatment plan once it is begun. By comparing changes in the rates of behavior from the pretreatment stage to the treatment stage, it can be determined whether the treatment is improving the situation, having no effect, or making matters worse. If the treatment effects are not acceptable, the treatment will, of course, have to be modified. In most instances, event-sampling and/or time-sampling procedures can be used as necessary to assist in the obtaining of baseline data.

Look for Antecedents. Antecedents are environmental events which precede the target behavior. It is important to remember that, consistent with the assumptions mentioned earlier, the environment does not end at the surface of the skin. Covert behaviors, both physiological and psychological, may serve as stimuli to elicit or occasion other behaviors. This is often the most difficult step in a behavioral analysis. Identifying the antecedent events is equally important in dealing with both classically conditioned responses and operant behavior.

Determine the Consequences. This is the third and usually most important element of the core of a behavior analysis. The core consists of determining what has been called the ABCs of behavior: the antecedents, the specific behaviors, and the consequences of the problem behavior. Consequences involve what occurs immediately after the target behavior. A delay in looking for consequences can result in identifying the wrong consequence.

In looking for consequences it is crucial to remember that most behavior is influenced by its consequences on an intermittent schedule. For example, some instances of the behavior are reinforced while others are not. Some behaviors which have been in an individual's repertoire for a relatively long time are maintained by such a lean reinforcement schedule that it may seem impossible to identify the effective reinforcers. It may even appear that there is no reinforcement at all. As is the case with antecedents, covert events may function as important consequences and must be considered. The experience of the clinician in dealing with similar problems can aid in the identification of relevant consequences.

Identify the Setting. Where and under what circumstances does the target behavior occur most and least often? The setting is a special type of antecedent, and it is helpful to think of it apart from other behavioral events. For example, does smoking behavior occur most often in one's automobile, but never in the kitchen? In identifying the most favorable setting for the emission of a particular behavior, one may also identify a stimulus which signals to the organism that a given behavior will be reinforced. This is called a discriminative stimulus (S^D). We say that an S^D occasions the occurrence of a behavior. (The symbol S^Δ represents a stimulus which indicates that a given behavior will not be reinforced.) When we refer to the fact that a behavior occurs under certain stimulus conditions and not others, it is called stimulus control. For example, a hospitalized patient may have a high rate of seizures in the presence of some staff but not others.

Note the Time. What time of day (or week, month, etc.) does the behavior occur and not occur? If we can determine the times of occurrence of the target behavior, we can more easily specify what other events are occurring at these high and low probability times and thereby identify possible antecedents and consequences.

Identify Positive Reinforcers and Aversive Stimuli. Events that are reinforcing or aversive in one situation may not be so in another. For example, an individual might usually be reinforced by a chicken salad sandwich, but not right after Thanksgiving dinner. Since events are ultimately defined as reinforcing or punishing based on their effect on behavior, there is no foolproof way of making this determination in advance. There are, however, several ways in which this can be attempted.

We can simply ask the client what he or she thinks will be reinforcing or aversive. A clinical interview can be assisted by a number of forms such as the Reinforcement Survey Schedule (Cautela

& Kastenbaum, 1967) and Aversive Scene Survey Schedule (Cautela, 1977a, 1981b), which have been developed to aid in this process. Depending on the client's needs, these forms may be completed alone or with the help of the therapist.

Given the opportunity, we might directly observe the client ourselves, particularly in free-choice situations, in hopes of discovering what activities and objects attract or repulse the client. Along these lines, the Premack Principal (Premack, 1959) may be employed. According to the Premack Principal, high probability behaviors can serve as reinforcers to increase the frequency of lower probability behaviors. For example, a chain smoker who keeps putting off doing her income taxes may make access to a cigarette contingent upon completing a certain amount of work on taxes. On the other hand, requiring a child to brush his/her teeth after every piece of candy he eats may reduce the amount of candy eaten.

Occasionally reinforcer sampling may be used to "prime the pump" by introducing the clients to possible reinforcers with which they are unfamiliar. In reinforcer sampling (Ayllon & Azrin, 1968) the client is exposed to a potential reinforcer so that he/she might have an opportunity to experience its potentially reinforcing qualities. This is the procedure that is used when consumers receive free samples of new products through the mail or in supermarkets.

Another approach is to ask others who are well acquainted with the client to list what is reinforcing or aversive to the client. The opinions and observations of significant others are, however, sometimes inaccurate and should be verified by other means, such as those above.

Plan and Implement the Program. Planning the behavioral treatment program involves determining, with the client, appropriate treatment goals. Determining the goals includes choosing what behaviors to modify. In addition, means of working toward those goals must be selected. The choice of procedures should also involve the client to the extent the client is capable of being involved. A major advantage of behavior therapy is, of course, the variety of behavioral procedures available for the treatment of client complaints. One of the most salient factors which must be considered in planning the course of treatment is the probability of success of a given treatment package. Nor should the reality of the client's day-to-day environment be overlooked.

Choosing the appropriate covert conditioning procedure for a client depends upon several factors:

1. A general rule of thumb, as in the case of all behavioral procedures, is to use the least aversive covert conditioning procedure wherever possible. Accordingly, covert reinforcement, the self-control triad, and covert modeling are preferred over the other procedures, which have aversive components.
2. The face validity of a covert conditioning procedure varies from client to client. Some clients view the covert sensitization procedure as a logical extension of punishment, but have difficulty viewing covert reinforcement as a logical extension of overt positive reinforcement.
3. If the person is engaging in maladaptive approach behavior, such as exhibitionism, and he/she is in danger of going to prison if caught again, then an aversive procedure such as covert sensitization or covert response cost should be used immediately for rapid behavior change.
4. Some clients find covert modeling more appropriate either because of very strong anxiety or inability to perceive themselves as performing the target behavior.
5. Covert sensitization and covert negative reinforcement are rarely used or employed with children because of their aversive nature and because of the likelihood of the children's lack of participation in these procedures. In general, we have found covert modeling the procedure of choice with children.
6. Every aversive covert conditioning procedure is always accompanied by covert positive reinforcement for the antagonistic behavior.

It is beyond the scope of this book to discuss the many treatment procedures, in addition to covert conditioning, available to the behavior therapist. We feel, however, that covert conditioning procedures have a useful place in the treatment of a wide array of behaviors, which will be discussed more fully later. Implementation of covert conditioning procedures will be discussed in detail beginning in the next section.

Monitor the Program. This step is ongoing, extending throughout the assessment, baseline, specific interventions, and follow-up stages. Once a treatment program is begun, the effectiveness of that program must be determined. This is usually done through a continuation of the baseline procedure set up earlier.

Evaluate and Adjust the Program. If the program is not working satisfactorily, earlier steps of the behavior analysis should be repeated.

Perhaps the correct reinforcers maintaining a maladaptive behavior were not identified. Perhaps the treatment package attempted was not practical. No matter what treatment originally appears to be the method of choice, it may be necessary to adjust the application of it or even try a totally new approach.

Rationale for Covert Conditioning

If, as a result of the behavior analysis, covert conditioning appears to be an appropriate part of the treatment package, the rationale for covert conditioning should be discussed with the client and some introductory instructions given. The following is an example:

> Your behavior occurs because it is maintained by the environment. Whenever you perform that behavior, it is rewarded or punished by other people. There are many studies that indicate that if the consequences of behavior can be manipulated, then the behavior can be increased or decreased in frequency. We have found that just by having people imagine they are performing certain behaviors and then imagine particular consequences, behavior can change in a similar manner. I am going to have you imagine certain scenes and ask you to imagine you are really there. Try not to imagine that you are simply seeing what I describe; try to use your other senses as well. If in the scene you are sitting in a chair, try to imagine you can feel the chair against your body. If, for example, the scene involves being at a party, try to imagine you can hear people's voices, hear glasses tinkling, and then smell the liquor and food. Now remember, the main point is that you are actually there experiencing everything. You don't merely see yourself there, but you are actually there. (Cautela & Bennett, 1981, p. 194)

Imagery Assessment

After the rationale and general imagery instructions are given, it is helpful to assess the client's imagery ability. It is important to note that in order to be effective the client must not only be able to experience the scenes clearly but must also experience the affective state which the overt counterpart of the scene would elicit.

Imagery assessment enables the therapist to determine what imagery skills to emphasize with the client during imagery training. In actual practice, both imagery assessment and imagery training are ongoing and highly interrelated. Asking the client to rate such factors as scene clarity, scene pleasantness or unpleasantness, and length of time to produce the scene provides the therapist with valuable information. In assessing the client's imagery it is also helpful to ask the client questions about the contents of the various scenes. Kazdin (1978) recommends instructing the client to narrate aloud the scenes being experienced as an aid to ongoing assessment. Since many stimuli which may be used in covert conditioning are perceived predominantly through a single modality (e.g., food-taste, music-hearing), assessing the client's responsiveness in the various sense modalities must not be overlooked. Instruments such as the Covert Conditioning Survey Schedule (CCSS) and Imagery Survey Schedule (ISS) (Cautela, 1977a) are particularly helpful in imagery assessment.

Besides relying on self-reports of imagery, the therapist should also observe the client's overt nonverbal behavior during imagery. If, for example, there is a happy, relaxed expression on the client's face while a covert sensitization vomiting scene is supposedly being practiced, something is likely to be amiss. If a client with a fear of bees appears tense and perspires while reporting visualizing a bee scene, it seems more likely that the scene actually is taking place than if the client is displaying a big smile. On the other hand, behavior such as smiling and licking one's lips would be appropriate if the client were supposed to be visualizing a reinforcing scene of eating an ice cream cone. It can also be helpful to ask the client details about the scene. What was the beach like? What was your mother wearing? If the client is visualizing him/herself walking into a bar, we might ask what is to the right and look closely to see if the client's eyes move to the right.

The importance of ongoing imagery assessment must be emphasized. Once a client has achieved high-quality imagery, it does not necessarily follow that all subsequent imagery experiences will be of the same high quality. For example, a client's ratings of image clarity may vary by as much as 50 percent from one session to the next. While some of this variability may be attributable to problems with observer (client) reliability, several other factors can contribute to this situation. Some of these factors include events outside of the therapy session which have impact on the client's level of anxiety, depression, or reinforcement. Also, the client may be having trouble adjusting to new scenes or getting bored with scenes that have been overused. In addition, there may be changes in the therapist's behavior such as change of voice or lack of enthusiasm. Therefore, the therapist must be sure to monitor the client's imagery during every session in which imagery is employed.

Imagery Training

The particulars of imagery training will vary from client to client. With all clients, however, it should be stressed that they not see themselves in the scenes as if they were watching themselves in a movie or on videotape, but rather they should imagine that they are actually in and experiencing the situation described. Sometimes this distinction can be made clear to clients by telling them that in the scene they can look down and see their arms, legs, and fronts of their bodies, but cannot see their faces or backs. The term visualization, which is often used in the imagery literature, has, unfortunately, sometimes been misleading in giving the impression that only the visual modality should be used. Actually, as many additional sense modalities as are appropriate should be involved, such as hearing, smelling, tasting, touching, and kinesthetic perceptions.

Kearney (1976) used a system of successive approximations in an imagery training procedure to involve five sense modalities. The subjects began by visualizing themselves sitting alone in an empty movie theater. Various familiar objects (e.g., exit signs, clocks) in the theater were described. Then the auditory modality was added as background music began playing in the imagined theater. Visual action and additional sounds were introduced as more people started to file into the theater. Touch came through the feeling of the arms of the chair, and finally the smell and taste of popcorn rounded out the five commonly used senses.

Applications of covert conditioning usually involve sets of two scenes: a scene of the target behavior and a scene of the consequences of that behavior. It is important that the client be able to shift quickly from the behavior to the consequences, and this process may take some practice. During the early stages of imagery training, it is important to choose scenes that the client can visualize relatively easily. The ISS is also helpful in identifying the useful elements of scenes to include in future scenes to increase their effectiveness.

In order to allow the client to concentrate on the scenes as much as possible, the client is asked to communicate to the therapist by signaling with a raised index finger. The signal is usually used to indicate that the client has clear imagery, but it may be used to give a yes/no answer to any question asked by the therapist.

The client is asked to close his or her eyes and imagine the target behavior scene described by the therapist. When the scene is clear, the client signals the therapist by raising the index finger. Then the therapist asks the client to imagine the desired consequences. When the consequent scene is clear, the client again signals with the index finger.

The client is next asked to visualize the scene alone, without the assistance of the therapist. Any difficulties that might arise are discussed. The client is asked if the scene was clear and what feeling it elicited. (For example, if an alcoholic is being treated with covert sensitization, could the glass of whisky and the barroom be clearly imagined, and could the vomit actually be seen, smelled and felt?) If there is any difficulty, the scene may be repeated by the therapist in greater detail.

Besides signaling scene clarity, the raised right index finger is also used by the client to signal the end of the scene. The therapist then uses the words "shift" or "reinforcement"* to notify the client to change from the scene of the target behavior to the scene of the consequence. This change of scenes should be completed within a few seconds. Some clients may need to practice the scene shifts several times in order to accomplish them quickly.

Covert Conditioning Procedures to Increase Response Probability

In the pages that follow, seven covert conditioning procedures are described and examples are given of each. The examples chosen are relatively simple for explanatory reasons. Covert conditioning has been successfully used in a number of very complicated situations, some of which will be referred to later.

Covert Positive Reinforcement

There are three ways in which a reinforcing stimulus can be presented:

1. It can be presented overtly, being transmitted to the central nervous system by means of sense organs.
2. It can be presented directly to the central nervous system without use of the external sense organs (Olds, 1956).

---

*Wish, Cautela, and Steffen (1970) found that the word "reinforcement" alone, without a following scene, can have reinforcing properties. Therefore, experimental studies usually use the word "shift" and clinical applications of covert positive reinforcement use "reinforcement."

3. It can be presented covertly by instructing the client to initiate mediational processes such as thinking or imagining.

Covert positive reinforcement (CPR; Cautela, 1970b) is a technique in which the individual reinforces himself/herself in imagination immediately after performing the desired behavior in real life or in imagination. CPR is used to increase the strength and/or frequency of a given behavior. Unlike systematic desensitization, the use of CPR is not limited to decreasing avoidance behaviors, but is also used to increase appropriate behaviors. While the use of relaxation training and a hierarchy can be helpful in implementing CPR, they are not necessary.

In implementing CPR, clients are instructed to imagine scenes in which they are performing the behaviors to be increased. In order to be maximally effective, the reinforcing scene should be clearly visualized within five seconds after visualizing the scene to be reinforced. One pair of target and reinforcing scenes is referred to as a single trial. An intertrial interval of at least one minute is recommended in order to avoid inhibition of reinforcement (Pavlov, 1927) and too rapid a growth of inhibitory potential (Hull, 1943).

Since CPR items are usually presented in temporal sequence, a chaining procedure has been very effective in clinical applications. The first scene trial (target behavior followed by reinforcing scene) is presented by the therapist. Next, the client practices the same scene trial without the therapist's assistance. Then the second scene trial is taught by the therapist and practiced by the client. This is followed by the client's practicing scene trials one and two in order. Scene trial three is introduced by the therapist, practiced by the client, and added to the chain for the client to practice. This process continues until the logical hierarchy is completed. This process and the roles of the therapist (T) and client (Cl) are represented schematically in Table 2-1.

Table 2-1. Sequence of CPR Scene Presentation

Scenes directed by:	T[a]	Cl	T	Cl	Cl	T	Cl
Scene trial:	S_1[b]	S_1	S_2	S_2	$S_{1,2}$	S_3	S_3

[a]T—Therapist; Cl—Client; S—Scene.
[b]The subscript indicates which scene or scenes are being practiced.

For example, the following scene trial sequence might be developed for a client with a fear of flying in airplanes. Step one, the therapist directs the client to imagine buying the tickets for the flight. (This and all target scenes are followed by reinforcing scenes.) Step two, the client practices the same scene trial (buying the tickets plus reinforcing scene) without the aid of the therapist. Step three, the therapist directs the client to imagine packing a suitcase. Step four, the client, without therapist assistance, imagines packing the suitcase. Step five, the client imagines buying the tickets, then packing the suitcase on his/her own. Step six, the therapist directs the client to imagine leaving the house to go to the airport. Step seven, the client imagines (unaided) leaving the house to go to the airport. Step eight, the client imagines buying the tickets, packing the suitcase, and leaving for the airport, all without the assistance of the therapist. In step nine the therapist adds the next scene and this process repeats itself until, eventually, all the scenes are practiced, in order, by the client without therapist direction.

Although treatment is begun on a continuous reinforcement schedule, the client is soon put on an intermittent schedule. Normally the client is asked to practice a number of trials (for example, 2 sets of 10 trials) each day between sessions.

Learning theory basis. Considered the covert analogue of overt positive reinforcement, CPR is designed to work according to operant conditioning principles. Accordingly, the frequency and strength of the response is seen as a function of its consequences. In the CPR procedure as in the overt positive reinforcement procedure, a response is followed by a reinforcing stimulus (a person or scene) which results in an increase in response probability.

Conceptualization of CPR as a covert analogue of operant conditioning allows us to draw upon the vast wealth of the operant literature (as is the case with the other covert conditioning procedures) for support and direction.

Cl	T	Cl	Cl	...	T	Cl	Cl
$S_{1,2,3}$	S_4	S_4	$S_{1,2,3,4}$	...	S_n	S_n	$S_{1,2,3\ldots n}$

Example.   The following is an example of how CPR was used to
help prepare a doctoral candidate for a last chance at his qualifying
examinations. Although he was a good student, he had previously
failed the exam three times, due to excessive anxiety. Notice that,
instead of presenting an anxiety hierarchy, a logical, temporal
sequence was used.

> Close your eyes and try to relax. I want you to imagine you are sitting down
> to study, and you feel fine. You are confident, and you are relaxed. I know
> you may be anxious here, but try to imagine that when you are about to
> study [S^D] you are calm and relaxed [R], as if you were acting a part. Start.
> [When the S raises his finger, the therapist delivers the word, "Rein-
> forcement," which, in this case, signals the image of skiing down a
> mountain feeling exhilarated] [S^{R+}]. Practice this twice a day and just
> before you study. Now let's work on the examination situation. It is the day
> of the examination, and you feel confident. ("Reinforcement.") You are
> entering the building and go into the classroom. ("Reinforcement.") You sit
> down and kid around with another student who is taking the exam.
> ("Reinforcement.") The proctor comes in with the exam. ("Reinforce-
> ment.") You read the questions, and you feel you can answer all of them.
> ("Reinforcement.")
>   Now let's do that again. This time you look the questions over and you are
> not sure about one question, but you say, "Oh, well, I can still pass the
> exam if I flunk this one question." ("Reinforcement.") All right, this time
> you look over the exam, and you can see two questions about which you are
> in doubt, and you say, "Well, I can still pass this exam if I take my time and
> relax. ("Reinforcement.") (Cautela, 1970b, p. 39)

Applications.   CPR, which is probably the most widely applicable
of all the covert conditioning techniques, can be used in all situations
in which the client is cooperative and can understand the instructions.

As mentioned above, the use of CPR is not limited to maladaptive
avoidance behaviors. CPR has been applied to the modification of a
wide range of behaviors, including test anxiety (Kearney, 1984; Kostka
& Galassi, 1974), heroin addiction (Wisocki, 1973b), homosexuality
(Denholtz, 1973), eye contact (Krop, Messinger, & Reiner, 1973),
attitudes toward the mentally retarded (Cautela et al., 1971), self-
injurious behavior (Cautela & Baron, 1973), estimation of circle size
(Wish, Cautela, & Steffen, 1970), and pain (Cautela, 1977c; Stevens,
1982). The bibliography section of this book contains a complete
listing of all published reports to date of CPR in a variety of
applications.

CPR has been successfully adapted to audiotape recordings (Kearney, 1984; Kearney, 1976). This can be helpful experimentally to control for therapist variables and clinically to help clients structure their CPR homework sessions.

The usefulness of relaxation training in CPR is sometimes questioned. Although it is not a required part of CPR, it has been argued that relaxation training can sometimes improve image clarity (Lang, 1977). Kearney (1976) showed that, in a situation where CPR and systematic desensitization were equally effective, subjects who received both CPR and relaxation training showed greater improvement than subjects who received any of the other treatments. It was not clear, however, whether this was due to improved imagery, a placebo effect of two additional treatment sessions, or some other unidentified factor.

Evaluation. CPR is one of the two most widely researched and utilized covert conditioning procedures (the other being covert sensitization). Anecdotal reports (Cautela, 1977c; Flannery, 1972a; Wisocki, 1970) and experimental studies have supported the efficacy of CPR.

Many of the experiments conducted on CPR involved maladaptive avoidance behaviors similar to those used in systematic desensitization studies (Flannery, 1972b; Guidry & Randolph, 1974; Wisocki, 1971). Studies which have compared systematic desensitization and CPR have found both procedures to be similarly effective (Kearney, 1976; Kostka & Galassi, 1974; Marshall, Boutillier, & Minnes, 1974).

A comparison of systematic desensitization and CPR reveals that:

1. Both were developed from well-established (but different) learning theories with impressive empirical bases. Desensitization is based on reciprocal inhibition (Wolpe, 1958), a form of classical conditioning. While CPR does have reciprocal inhibition components when dealing with anxiety responses, it is primarily an operant procedure.
2. Both procedures rely primarily on imagination.
3. Desensitization requires training in relaxation, whereas CPR requires the identification of positive reinforcers.
4. Desensitization requires the careful construction of an anxiety hierarchy, whereas the stimuli presented in CPR are arranged in a logical or temporal sequence.
5. In desensitization, only the anxiety stimulus is presented in imagination. In CPR, the client is instructed to imagine both

the anxiety stimulus and a comfortable feeling in response to that stimulus.

6. In desensitization, relaxation is used to reciprocally inhibit anxiety. Through repeated pairings with stimuli that increasingly resemble the fear stimulus, relaxation gradually becomes a conditioned response to those stimuli. In CPR, relaxation may be used as a new adaptive response to anxiety-provoking stimuli, but one that is operantly conditioned through the presentation of a positive reinforcer immediately following the relaxation response.

7. In CPR there is a possibility of reinforcer satiation.

8. Both procedures seem to be effective means of modifying maladaptive avoidance behavior, but CPR can also be used to modify maladaptive approach behavior.

9. While desensitization reduces the anxiety response associated with a given behavior, it does not directly increase that behavior. Positive reinforcement not only reduces the aversiveness of a given stimulus (Melvin & Brown, 1964) but directly increases the frequency with which an incompatible behavior is emitted.

10. CPR is learned relatively easily, is simple to apply, and seems more adaptable than desensitization as a self-control procedure.

11. Although the evidence is meager, it seems to indicate that CPR does not require as many treatment sessions as desensitization to obtain comparable results (Kearney, 1976).

12. Both techniques have been successfully used with psychotic subjects (Steffen, 1971; Zeisset, 1968).

One of the earliest empirical studies of CPR was conducted by Marshall et al. (1974). Snake-phobic subjects participating in this experiment were placed in one of six groups: a standardized version of systematic desensitization called experimental desensitization (ED), CPR, covert negative reinforcement (CNR), noncontingent CPR, placebo control, and no treatment. Marshall et al. found that experimental desensitization and CPR were equally effective and, together with CNR, which was not as effective in modifying approach behavior, were superior to the control conditions. The authors concluded that "CPR appears to be an equal alternative to ED and may be more economical of time, whereas CNR may only be useful when the other two procedures are not appropriate" (p. 469).

In an experiment primarily intended to test the learning paradigm of CPR, Ladouceur (1974) treated rat-phobic college students with either CPR or a reversed CPR condition. A no-treatment control group was also included. Although Ladouceur found no significant difference between CPR treatments, both conditions were superior to no treatment.

Bajtelsmit and Gershman (1976) found standard CPR to be effective in treating test anxiety. Several other variations of CPR were found to be effective as well.

Hurley (1976) also found CPR and a number of variations thereof to be superior to an attention placebo condition in treating an anxiety response, in this case, fear of snakes. As in the above studies, the variations were intended to investigate the effective components of CPR. Both behavioral and self-report measures were included and all treatment groups showed significant improvement as compared to the control group on both the behavioral and self-report measures.

The conclusions and implications of the above four experiments with regard to the theoretical basis of CPR will be discussed in detail in a later section of this book.

Blanchard and Draper (1973) published a well controlled case study in which they used CPR to treat a rodent phobia. When CPR was introduced, the subject showed improvement on all behavioral, self-report, and physiological measures. The next treatment stage involved the elimination of the reinforcing scene from the CPR procedure. During this stage the subject showed a relapse on the physiological measure and either relapse or no change on the various self-report measures. On the behavioral measure, however, the subject continued to improve at about the same rate as during the complete CPR stage. When the reinforcing scene was reinstated, the subject again showed improvement on all measures. This included the behavioral measure, on which the improvement rate increased over that recorded during the first CPR stage. Blanchard and Draper concluded that the reinforcement component was at least facilitative, if not necessary for improvement.

Rhodes (1978) conducted a series of three experiments to investigate the learning theory basis of CPR. The target behavior he chose was eye contact, and treatment groups included CPR, reversed CPR (R-CPR, reinforcing scene first), a CPR group (W-CPR) in which a weak reinforcing scene was used, and a noncontingent CPR (N-CPR) group which replaced W-CPR in the second and third experiments. Experiments two and three differentiated subjects on the basis of level of anxiety. Based on the various combinations of results, Rhodes concluded that an operant explanation more fully accounted for the results than a counterconditioning explanation.

Two more recent experiments using different experimental designs (Bennett & Cautela, 1981) examined the effectiveness of reciprocal inhibition and the operant components of CPR in modifying subjects' responses to pain. In both instances the CPR strategy proved to be more effective. Although anxiety, which can be lessened through the use of reciprocal inhibition, may influence perception of pain, several other factors are also involved in the pain response. Since CPR was more effective, it can be argued that either it is more effective than reciprocal inhibition in treating anxiety or it also successfully treated other components of the pain response.

In summary, the seven reports reviewed in this section include both group and single-subject design experiments. They represent a sample of published reports showing how CPR has been used to modify maladaptive avoidance behaviors, experimental behavior (eye contact), and the pain response. The Marshall et al. (1974) study provides evidence of the similar effectiveness of CPR and systematic desensitization while the Rhodes (1978) experiment provides support for the operant conceptualization of CPR.

Covert Negative Reinforcement

Covert negative reinforcement (CNR) (Cautela, 1970a) is another covert conditioning procedure which can be used to increase the rate of a target behavior. Like CPR, CNR can be applied to both maladaptive approach and avoidance behaviors. CNR is designed to increase the probability of a response by instructing a client to imagine an aversive event and to terminate that event by imagining the response to be increased. Originally, CNR was developed because certain clients, especially some of those who were labeled depressed (i.e., had a low reinforcement level) could not successfully imagine pleasant scenes.

Along with specifying the target behavior and completing the other preliminary steps common to all covert conditioning procedures, the therapist and client compose a number of scenes in which the client engages in the target behavior. As in CPR, the desired emotional response is included, and the scenes are varied to correspond to the actual situations which the client might encounter.

The therapist and client must also identify a number of stimuli which the client finds aversive and write scenes in which the client escapes from the noxious stimuli. The Fear Survey Schedule (Wolpe & Lang, 1964), Aversive Scene Survey Schedule, and Covert Conditioning Survey Schedule (Cautela, 1977a) have all proven to be useful in identifying noxious stimuli to use in CNR. In addition, the therapist might ask questions such as "What is the most frightening scene or experience you can imagine?" and "Tell me something you're afraid of that may not be on the questionnaires I gave you." The following properties should be looked for in an aversive stimulus:

1. The client states that the stimulus (e.g., being criticized) is extremely unpleasant (e.g., fearful, disgusting).
2. The client is able to imagine a scene of the stimulus clearly.
3. An image of the stimulus elicits emotional responses similar to those elicited by its overt counterpart.
4. The client is able to terminate the image immediately at the request of the therapist with little or no residual discomfort. This is necessary to avoid the association between the aversive stimulus and the response to be increased; otherwise, a decrease in the probability of the response may occur.

The therapist begins the actual application of CNR by instructing the client to imagine an aversive scene. The client is asked to signal the therapist, by means of the raised index finger, when the image is clear. The therapist then says "shift," which is the signal for the client to terminate the aversive scene and replace it with a scene of the behavior to be increased. For example, an individual with a fear of flying might imagine a drowning scene and then immediately switch to a scene of boarding an airplane. The probability of boarding a plane should increase, since this response removed the individual from the drowning situation.

The client must be careful to totally eliminate the aversive scene before switching to the target behavior scene in order to avoid associating the target behavior with the aversive stimuli. If, after a number of trials there is continued overlap, a new aversive stimulus is tried. If the difficulty continues, the client's behavior must be closely monitored to determine what effects the treatment is having. It may be possible to continue using CNR anyway. The use of noxious scenes involving nausea, however, should be avoided since the feelings of nausea are unlikely to end quickly when the client is instructed to shift scenes. The therapist must also guard against using scenes which are so aversive that they disrupt the client to such a degree that cooperation with the treatment instructions becomes too difficult.

Just as the reinforcing scenes used in CPR sometimes lose their effectiveness with overuse, some clients using CNR have reported that the aversive properties of the aversive stimuli in CNR weaken after a number of trials. This can be a beneficial side effect of CNR if the aversive scene involves a phobic stimulus the client would also like to overcome. This result may be due to satiation, the client's control of the aversive stimulus (Vernon, 1969), or the client's learning to make a new adaptive response when the aversive stimulus occurs.

Both the aversive scenes and target behavior scenes are varied during practice and, as in the case of CPR, it is important for the client to practice this procedure between sessions without the aid of the therapist. Audiotape recordings have been particularly useful for this purpose. If the client's homework requires the practice of 20 trials each day, a recording of 5 trials might be played four times during the course of the day.

Some clients report a preference for CNR to covert sensitization because of the aversion relief component. That is, the story has a happy, pleasant ending when the client successfully avoids or escapes the aversive stimulus. Although the therapist may feel that covert sensitization is a more powerful technique, this should be balanced against the likelihood of the client's cooperating with treatment and carrying out homework assignments. In other words, when the therapist tries to match the client with the most appropriate procedure, one of the client characteristics that must be considered is the face validity of that procedure to the client.

Learning Theory Basis. CNR is the covert counterpart of overt negative reinforcement. Although overt operant conditioning includes two forms of negative reinforcement, that is, escape conditioning and avoidance conditioning, to date only escape conditioning has been employed covertly. In escape conditioning, the performance of the target behavior brings about the termination of an aversive stimulus.

There are three points concerning negative reinforcement which should be emphasized:

1. The response rate of the target behavior is related to the intensity of the aversive stimulus. Up to a point, the more aversive a stimulus is, the greater the rate of responding. Extremely aversive stimuli can disrupt the organism to the extent that the escape behavior does not occur (Reynolds, 1968).

2. The closer the response to be increased follows the cessation of the aversive stimulus, the stronger will be the conditioning (Dinsmoor, 1968).
3. Once an escape response has been established, the intensity of the aversive stimulus may be reduced below the level originally needed to condition the response and still maintain that response (Reynolds, 1968).

Example. In preparation for using CNR, the client may be instructed as follows:

> In a minute, I'm going to ask you to close your eyes. I will then ask you to imagine the scene in which you [a description of the particular noxious scene chosen for use]. When the scene is clear and you feel upset, raise your right index finger. I will then say the word, "response." Then, immediately shift to the scene in which you [a description of the response to be increased]. As soon as that scene is clear, again signal with your right index finger. (Cautela, 1970a, pp. 274–275)

A scene constructed for a client with a fear of dogs might be as follows:

> Imagine you are trying to study for your final exams. These exams are very important, since a large portion of your grades depends on them. As you begin studying, your neighbor turns on a very loud, obnoxious lawn mower. The more you try to concentrate on your studying, the more difficult it becomes and the more upset and frustrated you feel.

When the client signals that the scene is clear and he/she is experiencing aversive frustration, the therapist says, "Shift," whereupon the client immediately ends the aversive scene and shifts to the prearranged target scene such as, "Your best friend and his dog, who had been playing in the distance, begin to approach you."

Applications. CNR can be used to treat both maladaptive approach and avoidance behaviors. It has been applied clinically to such diverse behaviors as tantrums, social anxiety, alcoholism, fear of breezes, and agoraphobia. CNR is particularly useful with clients for whom positive reinforcers cannot be identified or who have difficulty obtaining clear imagery of reinforcing stimuli. Many clients who encounter imagery problems when attempting CPR find CNR easier to use. Some have reported that it is easier for them to imagine unpleasant events, since they have so much firsthand experience with them in their daily lives. CNR is, therefore, more appropriate than CPR in working with clients said to be depressed because of the difficulty in obtaining enough reinforcing scenes.

Evaluation. The first published experimental investigation of CNR was conducted by Cautela and Wisocki (1969a). They demonstrated CNR to be significantly superior to a no-treatment control group in modifying attitudes toward the elderly.

A later study, by Ascher and Cautela (1972), found CNR to be superior to both noncontingent and no-treatment control groups in modifying estimation of circle size. They conducted a two-stage investigation of CNR. During the first stage, the subjects in one group imagined an idiosyncratic noxious scene followed by a neutral stimulus, the spoken word "bell," and the imagined ringing of a bell. Thirty trials were conducted. A second group imagined both scenes, but in a noncontingent manner. A third group received no imagery training. If negative reinforcement was, in fact, operating, the neutral stimulus—bell—should have acquired reinforcing properties vis-à-vis the subjects in the CNR group, but not in the other groups. Ascher and Cautela tested this hypothesis in the second stage of the study by using the word "bell" as a positive reinforcer in an attempt to modify subjects' estimation of circle size. Results showed that only those subjects who had originally been in the CNR group were influenced, with regard to their circle size estimation, by the bell, thereby confirming the CNR hypothesis.

In a large experiment involving six different groups, Marshall et al. (1974) found CNR to be less effective than modified forms of CPR and systematic desensitization in changing approach behavior to a snake, but equally effective in reducing subjective reports of anxiety. CNR was superior to placebo and no-treatment controls in both areas.

Other researchers who have found CNR to be effective include Shatus (1974) in reducing disruptive behavior, Nigel (1976) in increasing tooth brushing and flossing behavior, and Zemore, Ramsay, and Zemore (1978), who found CNR to be superior to no treatment in treating fear of snakes. On the other hand, Poetter (1978) did not find a significant difference between the effectiveness of CNR and a control group in modifying attending behavior.

Although relatively little research has been completed on CNR, the three studies included here illustrate the application of CNR to maladaptive avoidance behavior, attitudes, and an experimental behavior (circle size estimation). The Marshall et al. (1974) report suggests that while CNR is more effective than placebo treatment, it may be less powerful than either CPR or systematic desensitization. Ascher and Cautela (1972) provided evidence of the operant basis of CNR.

Covert Modeling

Covert modeling (CM) (Cautela, 1971b) is based on its overt equivalent, variously referred to as observational learning, modeling, and social learning (Bandura, 1969). CM involves the learning of new behaviors or the altering of existing behaviors by imagining scenes of others' interacting with the environment. CM can be used with behavior problems either alone or combined with other procedures.

In systematic desensitization and covert reinforcement, it is required that individuals imagine *themselves* actually performing the new behavior. Sometimes clients report difficulties imagining themselves involved in particular activities. Other clients may find it too anxiety provoking to imagine themselves approaching the aversive stimulus. Problems such as these led to the development of CM. A young woman who "just can't imagine herself" participating in a class discussion might, instead, imagine a person who looks like herself making statements similar to those she would like to make. In the scene, the statements are well received by the other participants. This scene might also be used as the first step of a shaping procedure. A four-step process would include the following:

1. Imagining others performing the target behavior.
2. If the client is able to imagine herself performing the behavior, a second step could be a scene in which the client observes herself performing the behavior.
3. The third step would be to have the client covertly experience performing the behavior, as in CPR.
4. The client performs the behavior in vivo.

Not all clients are able to easily proceed through this four-step process, but it is not always necessary. In many cases, accomplishing just one or two of the steps brings about satisfactory results. Although with additional time and effort most clients can, probably, be taught to master all four steps, the therapist must not be sidetracked and lose sight of the primary therapeutic goal, that is, to help the client learn to control the target behavior.

We have already mentioned that in using the covert conditioning procedures described earlier, the client is instructed to try to experience himself/herself actually in the scene. In CM, however, the client observes the model (usually others, but sometimes himself/herself) involved in the scene. In this way, the client, as observer, does not actively participate in the scene. The client's experience is more like watching a movie.

When using CM, the therapist first describes the scene and then asks the client if the image of the scene was clear, what feelings the client has about the scene (pleasant, unpleasant, or neutral), and whether or not the therapist described the scene at a comfortable pace. According to the client's answers, the therapist modifies the next presentation of the scene. Then the client presents the scene to himself/herself. The scene is repeated four more times by the therapist and four more times by the client. The client is told to practice the scenes alone at least 10 times each day.

As should be done in all covert procedures, the client is cautioned not to go through the scenes in a perfunctory manner, but to imagine every scene as clearly and carefully as possible. As with other covert procedures, the scenes may be varied.

In constructing scenes for CM, a number of variables should be considered. Perhaps the single most important factor is the immediate consequence of the model's behavior. The consequences play an important role in determining whether the behavior, once acquired, is likely to be performed.

After treatment has been begun with CM, the client is sometimes used as the model in an alternated-scene fashion. This procedure shapes the client to the use of covert conditioning procedures, such as CPR or covert sensitization, in conjunction with CM.

In using CM to teach relatively complex behaviors, it is sometimes helpful to employ a hierarchical or successive approximation approach. For example, a man working on assertiveness training may begin with a scene of a simple refusal of a telephone solicitation and, over a series of sessions, work his way up to some of the intricacies of going to small claims court.

Learning Theory Basis. As mentioned earlier, Bandura conceptualizes overt modeling as a two-step process involving contiguity and mediation. The mediation process includes symbolic verbal or imagery coding of the model's behavior (Bandura, 1971a). Other explanations, however, including an operant explanation, are possible. From an operant perspective, modeling can be thought of as an operant learned in infancy and maintained on an intermittent reinforcement schedule thereafter. The inability to identify frequently occurring reinforcement does not mean that no reinforcement is taking place. At most, it means that no reinforcement took place on the occasions of observation. A very thin reinforcement schedule may be controlling the behavior. The observed learning operations (positive reinforcement, extinction, etc.) will have similar effects on the observer. For example, if the model is positively reinforced, the observer will be more likely to perform the modeled behavior.

Modeling episodes have been effectively presented through several media. In addition to "live" models, movies, tapes, records, slides, and so forth, have all been successfully used in modeling. Since the use of imagery in other covert conditioning procedures indicates effectiveness, then a logical extension of modeling procedures is to present modeling episodes via instruction in imagination. CM is such an application.

Example. Before actually beginning CM with a client, the rationale of the procedure is discussed and any questions the client might ask are answered. A typical example of a rationale presentation is as follows:

A number of experiments have proven that just by watching other people say or do things, the behavior of the person watching is influenced, for example, the formation of language in infants is influenced a great deal by observing how older people use speech. Another example is an interesting experiment in which one group of children saw aggressive behavior being rewarded in a movie. Another group of children saw the same behavior being ignored. Still another group of children saw the behavior being punished. Immediately afterwards, the children were observed in play, and the amount of aggressive behavior was noted. The children who watched aggression being rewarded showed the greatest amount of aggression among the three groups. The children who saw aggression being punished showed the least amount of aggressive behavior, and the children who saw the aggressive behavior being ignored were somewhere in between the two groups in terms of amount of aggression. Similar procedures (these are called modeling procedures) have been used to decrease fears and to teach new habits.

The client is then given the following instructions:

What I am going to do is to vary this modeling procedure somewhat by having you observe certain scenes in imagination rather than have you directly observe a movie or actual interaction among people. I am going to use scenes that I think will help you change the behavior we agreed needs changing. In a minute, I'll ask you to close your eyes, and try to vividly imagine, as clearly as possible, that you are observing a certain situation. Try to use all the senses needed for the particular situation, e.g., try to actually hear a voice or see a person very clearly. After I describe the scene, I will ask you some questions concerning your feelings about the scene and how clearly you imagined it. (Cautela, 1971b, pp. 2–3)

The following scene was used with a college professor who felt tense and angry at his class while teaching:

> I want you to imagine that you are watching a professor go towards his classroom feeling calm and comfortable. He walks into the class, smiles, and looks enthusiastic. The students look kind of bored, but after the professor starts lecturing in an enthusiastic manner, the students start to look interested and appear at ease and friendly. (Cautela, 1971b, p. 5)

Applications.   CM is theoretically applicable in dealing with any behavior problem. It is particularly applicable with clients who have difficulty experiencing themselves in the various scenes attempted. General areas in which CM has been especially useful are social skills training and maladaptive avoidance behaviors. Although the evidence is quite limited, a few unpublished anecdotal reports suggest that CM has also been effective with athletes in modifying the rate and topography of motor behaviors.

CM is particularly useful with young children. It is generally easier for children to observe images of others than of themselves. Many children are quite used to being reinforced for observing others on television and in the movies. Since it is easier for children to observe their heroes functioning as mastery models, treatment with children is usually begun with CM and, if appropriate, other covert conditioning procedures are added later. This is particularly true in dealing with scenes of anxiety-evoking events. Visualizing oneself in an anxiety situation seems to elicit greater distress in children than adults.

Examples of the wide range of behaviors to which CM has been applied include fear of rats (Cautela, Flannery, & Hanley, 1974), assertiveness (Rosenthal & Reese, 1976), alcoholism (Hay, Hay, & Nelson, 1977), test anxiety (Bistline, Jaremko, & Sobleman, 1980), obsessive–compulsive behavior (Hay et al., 1977), agoraphobia (Flannery, 1972a), obesity (Devine, 1978), cigarette smoking (Nesse & Nelson, 1977), cross-gender motor behavior (Hay, Barlow, & Hay, 1981), and social skills training (Kazdin, 1982).

Evaluation.   Cautela et al. (1974) compared the effects of CM, overt modeling, and an attention placebo treatment in reducing fear of laboratory rats. Both modeling groups were superior to the control group on all six measures employed. The two modeling groups were equal on five measures with the overt modeling group being superior to CM on one measure.

In an assertion training program, Nietzel, Martorano, and Melnick (1977) compared two types of scenes. They found that CM was more effective if, in the modeled scenes, the model encountered initial resistance to his/her assertive response, but persisted in defending his/ her rights until the rights were recognized. The group that was trained with these "reply" scenes showed significantly greater improvement on post-test measures than no treatment, placebo control, or a CM group in which the model's assertive behavior resulted in immediate compliance. Although a four-month follow-up revealed that the differences had not persisted, the initial findings are worthy of future research and should be kept in mind when constructing CM scenes for clinical use.

Another study which also targeted assertive behavior, by Rosenthal and Reese (1976), found CM to be as effective as overt modeling. A third treatment group in which subjects had individually tailored scene hierarchies was no more effective than a standardized hierarchical group.

Kazdin (1973, 1974a, 1974b, 1974c, 1974d, 1975, 1976b, 1980, 1982) has conducted a series of CM studies in which he has investigated both the overall effectiveness of CM and several of the parameters involved. In addition to demonstrating the overall effectiveness of CM, Kazdin found several areas in which variables involved in modeling scenes have similar effects, whether the scenes are presented overtly or covertly. These findings have both theoretical and direct clinical implications for the use of CM.

Two studies by Kazdin (1974d, 1975) showed that scenes which included consequences reinforcing to the model were more effective than those which included only the behavior in increasing assertive behavior. These results were consistent with earlier findings by Bandura (1970, 1971b) with regard to overt modeling.

Kazdin (1973) demonstrated that treatment with CM was more effective if a coping model was used than if a mastery model was used. A coping model is a model who displays some anxiety which is overcome, resulting in a successful coping with the target behavior. Meichenbaum (1971) had already found that this was the case with overt modeling.

In a later study (1974a), Kazdin both replicated the earlier results regarding coping models and found that the similarity of the model to the observer improved effectiveness. This similarity was in terms of age and sex. Again, this had already been determined by Bandura, Ross, and Ross (1963) and Bandura (1971b) with regard to overt modeling.

Kazdin (1974a, 1975, 1976b) has also shown that it is more effective to vary the model used in CM scenes than to continue using the same model over and over. Bandura and Menlove (1968) found that watching more than one model deal with a feared object was more effective than a single model. An additional relevant finding by Kazdin (1974c) was that there was no significant difference between imagining oneself as a model and imagining a different person as a model.

Lowe (1978) conducted an interesting study comparing three types of models. In two of the treatment groups the subjects visualized scenes of themselves as models. In the first group, the model was the real self as perceived by the subject and, in the second group, the model was the ideal self as the model would like to be. The third group used an ideal person, someone other than the subject, as the model. All three treatments were significantly more effective than a control treatment, and both ideal model treatments showed greater improvement than the real self group.

In a study designed to investigate the effects of various factors in the treatment of test anxiety, Bistline et al. (1980) compared CM with a cognitive restructuring approach. A third group, which combined elements of both treatments, as well as a no-treatment group was included. After initially imagining a test-relevant scene, the CM subjects went on to imagine effectively coping with the situation. This was followed by a relevant covert reinforcer. The cognitive restructuring subjects began with the same scene but followed it with the correction and replacement of a negative self-statement. The combination treatment group received the cognitive restructuring sequence followed by a relevant covert reinforcer. Although all three treatments were effective, the CM treatment was significantly more effective than cognitive restructuring on one measure and showed greater, but not significant, change in two others. The combination of the treatments did not improve their effectiveness. The authors interpreted these results to indicate that the covert rehearsal and built-in CPR are the active ingredients in cognitive restructuring when it is effective. They suggest that a program relying on the intentional inclusion of these factors, as in CM, should be more effective overall than a program which may unintentionally include them, such as cognitive restructuring.

Hay et al. (1981) used CM to modify motor behavior. The client was a 10-year-old boy with gender-identity confusion. Many of his motor behaviors were considered to be rigidly feminine in topography and became the target behaviors of treatment. The behaviors selected were walking, standing, sitting, gesturing, and book-carrying. CM was the only treatment used, applied sequentially in a multiple-base-line design, to teach alternative masculine motor behavior. Each of the client's motor behaviors responded to CM as it was applied. A six-month follow-up revealed that behavior change was maintained.

In this section we have discussed 14 reports of the use of CM. One was a single-subject design study while the rest were group experiments. While most of the applications reviewed involved assertive behavior, CM was also used with maladaptive avoidance behaviors and a case of gender-identity confusion. In all of these studies CM was found to be effective. Of particular interest are the Kazdin (1974d, 1975) reports which showed that including appropriate consequences in imagery increased the effectiveness of CM, and the Bistline et al. (1980) experiment which found CM to be superior to cognitive behavior therapy in treating test anxiety.

3

Covert Conditioning Procedures, Part II

Covert Conditioning Procedures to Decrease Response Probability

Covert Extinction

Covert extinction (CE) (Cautela, 1971a) is a covert conditioning procedure used to decrease the rate of target behaviors. In CE the client imagines performing the target behavior, but does not imagine receiving the reinforcement maintaining that behavior. A simple example would be instructing an obese client to covertly experience eating tasteless ice cream. If taste is the reinforcing quality of the ice cream, withholding the taste withholds the reinforcer and, therefore, extinction occurs. CE is particularly useful in treating consummatory behaviors, but is also effective in treating maladaptive avoidance behaviors maintained by reinforcement.

The preliminary steps of behavior analysis, rationale, imagery training, and so forth remain the same in using CE as with the other covert conditioning procedures. When the use of CE is contemplated, the identification of maintaining consequences must be accomplished by the behavior analysis. As is the case in trying to use overt extinction, withholding the wrong reinforcer will not result in extinction.* Also, the same behavior may be maintained by more than one reinforcer on different reinforcement schedules. Our clinical experience indicates that sometimes stuttering can be an operant. There is some experimental evidence to support this assumption. The operant of stuttering can be maintained by either the positive attention of others or the uneasiness caused others.

The following is an example of a rationale that might be given to a client who stutters:

> Your behavior (e.g., stuttering) occurs because it is maintained by the environment. Whenever you perform that behavior, it is reinforced (or rewarded) by other people or in some other way. There are many studies in the field of learning that show that, if the reinforcing situation is prevented from occurring, the behavior that is influenced by reinforcement decreases in frequency (i.e., is weakened, is less apt to occur, or is even eliminated). We are going to have you imagine you are performing the behavior (stuttering) and then have you imagine that you are not being reinforced or rewarded. Do you understand? All right, now sit back and relax. Try to imagine the scene I am going to describe. Try to imagine that you are really there. Try not to imagine that you are simply seeing what I describe; try to use your other senses as well. If, in the scene, you are sitting in a chair, try to imagine that you can feel the chair against your body. If you are at a party, try to imagine that you can hear people talking and glasses tinkling. Now remember, the main point is you are actually there, experiencing everything. (Cautela, 1971a, p. 193)

Following the rationale presented above, the client would be instructed to experience a CE scene involving the target behavior. The essence of the instructions would simply be, "When you stutter, no one notices it."

Since, in CE, our goal is to withhold the reinforcing consequences, there is no consequent scene for the client to switch to during the treatment trials. As in covert sensitization, the complete experience is included in the evolution of a single scene during each trial.

Once the client understands the rationale and has achieved an adequate level of imagery, the therapist describes the CE scene 10 times while the client imagines the scenes. This is followed by 10 additional trials in which the client practices without the therapist. During this session, the client signals the therapist with a raised index finger at the end of each trial. Clients are usually assigned 10 CE trials

---

*Withdrawing a reinforcer which is not maintaining the target behavior might still result in a reduction in the rate of that behavior through the operation of response cost.

per day as their homework assignment, thus bringing the weekly total
to 90 trials.

In applying CE, some variations should be included in the scenes
from time to time to assist with generalization. For example, the client
might imagine eating several different tasteless snacks in a number of
different settings. A client may have to practice as many as 10 to 15
trials before being able to imagine eating food such as pizza without
any taste. It is easy to see how naturally occurring CE may be
responsible for instances of the phenomenon which is sometimes
referred to as change in a person's expectations.

Learning Theory Basis.   Although the term *extinction* is used to
describe important operations within both the classical and operant
paradigms, CE is considered to be the covert analogue of operant
extinction. In operant extinction, discontinuation of the reinforcing
stimulus leads to a decrease in the rate of the target behavior.

Spontaneous recovery is a problem that plagues all therapeutic
approaches. In using CE, as in overt extinction, a greater number of
trials reduces the likelihood of spontaneous recovery (Lawson, 1960,
p. 250; Pavlov, 1927, p. 58). Continuing extinction trials after the
response appears to be eliminated can further decrease the likelihood
of spontaneous recovery. While massed practice may speed up initial
extinction (Pavlov, 1927, p. 53; Rohrer, 1947, 1949), distributed
practice should be built into treatment programs (through homework
practice) in order to lessen further the probability of spontaneous
recovery.

Since there seems to be a direct relationship between the effort
involved in performing the target behavior and the rate of extinction
(Capehart, Viney, & Hulicka, 1958; Solomon, 1948), we suggest
having the client expend (covertly) as much effort as possible in
performing the target behavior. Potential problems in using extinction
should also be kept in mind. These include a temporary increase in the
target behavior (known as the extinction burst) and possible overt
aggression toward those who are perceived as covertly withholding
reinforcement from the client. This phenomenon is referred to as
extinction-produced aggression.

In discussing CE with the client, before beginning treatment, the
client should be informed about the potential difficulties. Also, while
laboratory applications of extinction result in a gradual, constant
decrease in the rate of the target behavior, applications in the natural
environment may result in a less regular decrease because of the
intermittent reinforcement which may occur there. This problem also

makes it more likely that the behavior will be reinstated by the natural environment after it is first eliminated.

Example. The following is an example of a CE scene used by a young woman who wanted to stop smoking. She reported that she particularly enjoyed smoking after a good meal.

> I want you to imagine you are in your favorite restaurant. You can hear the noise of talking and dishes tinkling. You have just finished a nice meal and you reach into your purse and take out the pack. You take one out and start to light up. You raise it to your mouth. As you light your cigarette you don't notice any smoke rising from it. Now I want you to imagine that you are taking a puff on the cigarette, but you don't taste anything—nothing at all. There is no taste. No taste of smoke. You don't feel anything in your mouth, no paper and no sensation of smoke. You don't even have the sensation of inhaling. There is nothing there. You exhale. You can neither taste, see, nor smell the smoke. Now remember, it is very important that you imagine that you are really smoking a cigarette and that it has no taste. You experience no sensation at all. It doesn't taste like cardboard; it doesn't taste like dirt. It has no taste.

Applications. The decision to use CE involves a number of considerations. In situations where overt extinction seems to be appropriate but people in the client's environment are unable or unwilling to withhold reinforcement, CE may be ideal. On the other hand, the therapist must be careful not to create a situation in which the client's behavior is maintained or even made more resistant to extinction through a more efficient reinforcement schedule. In other words, by providing a number of nonreinforced trials to go along with what may have been a continuous reinforcement schedule, the client's behavior may be reinforced on a relatively powerful intermittent schedule. Increased homework involving CE may overcome the effect of external reinforcement. In situations where the overt environment has been satisfactorily changed to prevent reinforcement of the target behavior, CE may be used to provide additional extinction trials, thereby facilitating the course of treatment.

An earlier paper (Cautela, 1971a) described a variety of situations in which CE was successfully applied. These included disruptive classroom behavior, phobias, psychosomatic complaints, obesity, and self-injurious behavior. Götestam and Melin (1974) reported the successful use of CE with four cases of amphetamine addiction.

Evaluation. In the Götestam and Melin (1974) report mentioned above, the four subjects had taken amphetamines intravenously for periods ranging from six months to seven years. Treatment was initiated by staff members, but gradually taken over by the clients. All four clients apparently went AWOL before treatment was completed and took amphetamines before returning to the program. Three reported that they were unable to experience the "rush" which had previously resulted from the drug. The fourth required a double dose to experience her rush. All four soon returned to and continued treatment. A nine-month follow-up revealed that three of the four subjects were still drug free.

The increased dosage taken by one client during the AWOL period is potential cause for concern. A second client is reported to have taken three consecutive injections with no rush, but it is unclear whether or not this was an increase. These two situations demonstrate not only the power of CE, but also the extinction burst and the possible dangers of incomplete treatment where a life-threatening behavior is involved.

Ascher and Cautela (1974) conducted a controlled study in which reinforcement and nonreinforcement conditions were crossed with three kinds of instructions (CE instructions, overt extinction instructions, no instructions). The experimental task required subjects to select representative words from a group of four words. The dependent variable was the number of trials the subjects worked at this task when told it was up to them to decide when they wanted to stop. Results showed no significant differences between overt and covert extinction groups, but both groups were significantly different from the no-instructions groups. These results suggested that CE was effective in facilitating extinction.

The two reports described above demonstrate the effective use of CE with both clinically relevant (amphetamine addiction) and experimental (word selection) behaviors. The Ascher and Cautela (1974) experiment also lends support to the similarity of CE and overt operant extinction.

Covert Sensitization

Covert sensitization (Cautela, 1966) was the first of the covert conditioning procedures to be developed. This covert technique is used to decrease the frequency of maladaptive approach behaviors. The term *sensitization* was chosen "because the purpose of the procedure is to build up an avoidance response to the undesirable stimulus" (Cautela, 1967, p. 459). In covert sensitization scenes, the target behavior is immediately followed by an imagined aversive consequence. Rather than using two scenes, as is generally the case with CPR, covert sensitization usually employs one scene which involves approaching the target response while experiencing aversive consequences.

Earlier forms of external aversive control, such as chemicals and electric shock, were commonly used in the treatment of alcoholism and sexual disorders during the 1950s and 1960s. Practical and ethical considerations, however, led to a decrease in their popularity. In many cases, with willing and cooperative clients, covert sensitization is an effective and humane alternative. According to Miller (1982), "The most recent addition to the aversion therapies [covert sensitization] is a promising one that requires neither drug nor shock and can be administered in out-patient therapy" (p. 16).

As in overt punishment, it is important that the consequences be aversive enough to lead to avoidance behavior. The imagined consequences are designed with the cooperation of the client. Vomiting scenes, however, have been employed most frequently because of their generally aversive components. Usually, the aversive component is introduced before the imagined maladaptive behavior is completed. This is done to disrupt earlier links in the behavioral chain. An example would be approaching, in imagination, a donut shop. As the client gets closer, a vivid description of an impending vomiting episode is given, which culminates in a messy, embarrassing, and extremely unpleasant scene before any donuts are actually eaten. The client turns to leave and immediately begins to feel better. On some occasions, covert sensitization is presented when the first act of the maladaptive behavior is performed.

The purpose of suggesting that the client starts to feel better as soon as the rejection of the appetitive object begins is to provide aversion relief. An avoidance response eventually replaces the approach behavior. This takes the form of a decreased desire or urge on the part of the client toward the maladaptive behavior. The stimuli, once associated with the evocation of the nauseous response, thus become discriminative stimuli for avoidance behavior.

Alternating with the aversive scenes are self-control scenes in which the client rejects the maladaptive behavior before actually engaging in it, thereby avoiding the aversive stimulus. This procedure is practiced with the therapist several times. Then the client is assigned the homework of practicing alone. The client is told to go through the procedure 10 to 20 times, twice each day. In addition, the client is instructed in the use of the self-control technique of in vivo use of covert sensitization such as imagining having just vomited whenever a temptation arises. For example, a woman with a weight problem might be eating out with friends. Although she did not order dessert, everyone else does and, when it is brought, she begins to experience an urge to order dessert too. Looking at a particularly tempting piece of cake, the client immediately visualizes maggots crawling all over the cake. If necessary, this scene can be extended as needed, emphasizing the nauseous feeling and including a vomiting episode.

The presentation of the aversive stimulus should begin on a continuous schedule and then be shifted to an intermittent schedule when the target behavior is strongly suppressed. Although the stimulus must not be noxious enough to disrupt the organism to the extent that it inhibits learning, it certainly must be of a severe enough degree to accomplish its purpose. Comfortably reviewing a scene is not sufficient; the client must be involved to the point where either a degree of physiological discomfort or at least a feeling of fear or disgust is actually experienced. Accordingly, scenes may have to be changed from time to time to avoid satiation. In the occasional case where the client is unable to experience nausea, alternate aversive stimuli, such as maggots or snakes, are usually effective.

In using covert sensitization, it is important that the target behavior be completely eliminated. Reducing the frequency is not sufficient to avoid relapse. Once the overt behavior is eliminated, treatment should be continued on both the client's strong and weak urges to engage in the target behavior. Treatment that does not eliminate both the overt behavior and strong urges is incomplete and relapse is likely. In treating some behaviors, such as smoking, it is helpful to continue treatment beyond the elimination of weak urges until the client reports the elimination of dreams about smoking.

It is also important to monitor the client's response to the noxious scene closely. Although some habituation is expected, continued overexposure may lead to an implosion or flooding effect. In implosion and flooding the client is exposed, usually in imagination, to the anxiety-eliciting stimulus for prolonged periods of time. It is hoped that the prolonged exposure will result in a decrease of the fear response. Although these procedures are often effective, the underlying mechanism responsible for their effectiveness is still uncertain (cf. Wolpe, 1982, pp. 236–247). If an aversive scene loses its effectiveness, it is, of course, time to employ a new aversive scene.

Learning Theory Basis. In the publication of the first paper on covert sensitization (Cautela, 1966), the operant basis of covert conditioning was not yet formulated. Although originally thought of as a counterconditioning procedure, covert sensitization was soon reconceptualized as the covert counterpart of punishment (Cautela, 1967). For a time it may not have been clear which theoretical basis was being proposed.

Since the presentation of an aversive stimulus decreases the frequency of the behavior which it follows, covert sensitization is an appropriate analogue for punishment. Additionally, covert sensitization shows some respondent features involving the conditioned emotional response. According to a classical conditioning conceptualization, the image of the inappropriate stimulus (e.g., alcohol) is the conditioned stimulus, and imagery involving aversive behavior such as getting nauseous and vomiting is the unconditioned stimulus. The aversive reaction when the conditional stimulus is encountered is the conditional response.

Dougher (1984) proposes that covert sensitization appears to operate by reducing the effectiveness of stimuli as reinforcers for relevant operants. That is, covert sensitization reduces the reinforcement value of the undesirable stimulus.

Practically speaking, it is difficult, if not impossible, to have a punishment trial without an accompanying negative reinforcement trial. When the aversive stimulus used to punish a given behavior is ended, this arrangement can also lead to negatively reinforcing whatever behavior immediately preceded the cessation of the aversive stimulus. Therefore the therapist must be careful that only appropriate behaviors directly lead to the termination of aversive stimuli in covert sensitization or CNR scenes.

In a discussion of the by-products of aversive control, Hutchinson (1977) has reviewed many of the studies in this area. Catania (1979) includes a section on the side effects of punishment, and Sulzer and Mayer (1972) discuss the disadvantages of the use of punishment. The earlier section of this book, which reviewed operant conditioning, listed several guidelines to consider when using punishment. Those guidelines also apply to the use of covert sensitization. An individual considering the use of punishment or other aversive procedures should be familiar with the material contained in these sources.

Whether counterconditioning, operant conditioning, or some other explanation accounts for the greatest portion of the effectiveness of covert sensitization is an important theoretical and experimental question. Experimenters must be aware of this when planning experimental applications of covert sensitization. What might appear to be only slight differences in the procedure used may have large effects.

It seems likely that a number of factors can operate in covert sensitization. Clinical applications, therefore, should be planned to take advantage of punishment, negative reinforcement, counter-conditioning, and expectancy factors, to the optimum benefit of the client.

Example. The following is an example of a covert sensitization scene which might be used to help treat a case of obesity. At this point, the client has already been instructed to relax and to close his/her eyes in order help with image clarity. Notice that the pie is never actually eaten; earlier links in the behavioral chain are punished. In addition to breaking the chain at a theoretically weaker link, we are also avoiding the probably reinforcing effect of the taste and consumption of the pie, which might thus counteract our aversive stimuli. Also note the escape conditioning component of the scene.

> I want you to imagine you've just had your main meal and you are about to eat your dessert, which is apple pie. As you are about to reach for the fork, you get a funny feeling in the pit of your stomach. You start to feel queasy, nauseous, and sick all over. As you touch the fork, you can feel food particles inching up into your throat. You're just about to vomit. As you put the fork into the pie, the food comes up into your mouth. You try to keep your mouth closed because you are afraid that you'll spit the food out all over the place. You bring the piece of pie to your mouth. As you're about to open your mouth, you puke; you vomit all over your hands, the fork, over the pie. It goes all over the table, over other people's food. Your eyes are watering. Snots, mucus are all over your mouth and nose. Your hands feel sticky. There is an awful smell. As you look at this mess you just can't help but vomit again and again until just watery stuff is coming out. Everybody is looking at you with a shocked expression. You turn away from the food and immediately start to feel better. You run out of the room and, as you run out, you feel better and better. You wash and clean yourself up and it feels wonderful. (Cautela, 1972)

Scenes such as the one above are alternated with avoidance self-control scenes in which the client rejects the appetitive object before it is consumed or the aversive stimulus is presented. For example:

> You are watching TV, and you decide to get a piece of apple pie. As soon as you decide to get the pie you begin to get this funny, sick feeling in the pit of your stomach. You say to yourself, "The hell with it, I'm not going to eat the pie!" As soon as you decide not to eat the pie you feel fine and proud that you resisted temptation.

Application. Covert sensitization has been used primarily in the treatment of maladaptive approach behaviors. Some of the applications of covert sensitization include alcohol abuse (Ashem & Donner,

1968), drug abuse (Wisocki, 1973b), sexual disorders (Barlow, Leitenberg, & Agras, 1969), obesity (Janda & Rimm, 1972), smoking (Cautela, 1970c), and self-injurious behavior (Cautela & Baron, 1973).

The Fear Survey Schedule (Wolpe & Lang, 1964), Aversive Scene Survey Schedule, and Covert Conditioning Survey Schedule (Cautela, 1977a) are useful in identifying noxious stimuli to use in covert sensitization.

In performing a behavior analysis in situations where the chief complaint involves an appetitive behavior, the therapist must be cautious not to overlook factors in addition to the consummatory pleasure which may be maintaining the maladaptive behavior. For example, a woman being treated for obesity may also have a fear of men. Maintaining her obese appearance helps her avoid social situations which would cause her a great deal of anxiety. Simply applying covert sensitization to the client's eating behavior would probably not be adequate treatment. If CPR were being considered as part of the treatment plan, "reinforcing" scenes in which the client imagines herself as thin and attractive are not usually powerful enough. Theoretically, in such a situation, the above-mentioned scene could actually function as a punisher and have the opposite effect of that intended.

In most situations which involve the removal of a behavior from a client's repertoire, such as the example cited above, the client must also be taught appropriate behaviors to fill in the gap in the behavioral repertoire. It is usually more effective to begin work on the new adaptive behaviors before removing the maladaptive behavior. Clients are much more at ease and willing to give up bad habits once they have alternative, effective ways in their repertoires of dealing with their environment.

In reviewing the rationale for covert sensitization with clients, it is explained that they are unable to stop indulging in excess (in whatever area the problem may lie) because it is a strongly learned bad habit from which they derive a good deal of pleasure. Therefore, in order to eliminate the bad habit, the pleasurable object should be associated with an unpleasant stimulus.

The results of covert sensitization are quite specific. In the treatment of alcoholics, for example, sensitizing a client to whiskey will have no effect on his drinking wine or beer. Each of these situations must be treated individually. Accordingly, it is possible to teach a client with an eating problem to eat just one steak and avoid a second one.

Treatment should not be discontinued as soon as the client stops engaging in the target behavior. It is important that overlearning take place in order to lessen the likelihood of spontaneous recovery and relapse. Treatment should continue for at least six sessions after the behavior first appears to be under control (Cautela, 1970c). During this time, emphasis should be placed on eliminating both the strong and weak urges to perform the target behavior.

Evaluation. There are six reasons why we suggest covert sensitization be considered as a treatment procedure when the therapeutic goal is to reduce the frequency of maladaptive approach behaviors. Five of these reasons were listed in an earlier paper by Cautela and Wall (1980, p. 160):

> ... (1) the rationale for the procedure appears easiest for the client to understand and accept, (2) covert sensitization is simpler in application than the other procedures, (3) clients usually have fewer problems in designating aversive stimuli that can be used, as compared with the items needed for covert response cost, (4) covert sensitization appears to work more rapidly than covert extinction, and (5) covert sensitization requires less scene elaboration and involves the client more directly than covert modeling.

A sixth reason is the self-control potential of covert sensitization in the form of in vivo applications and the construction, by the client, of scenes as needed in day-to-day activity.

Many of the earliest studies of covert sensitization applied it to alcohol and sexual disorders. In a series of cases, Anant (1967a) reported outstanding success in treating 26 alcoholics. Of the 26 participants, 25 completed treatment. Fifteen subjects were treated in four groups, while the remaining 11 were seen individually. Anant reported 100 percent abstinence over periods of time ranging from 8 to 15 months. Anant's application of covert sensitization was somewhat different than that described above in that he allowed his subjects to consume alcohol in imagination.

Ashem and Donner (1968) held the opinion that the use of drugs and electric shock were both effective treatments for alcoholism, but only as long as the subject stayed in the laboratory. Once the subject returned to the natural environment, the subject frequently reverted to former behavior. Impressed by the reports of the use of covert sensitization by Cautela (1967), Gold and Neufeld (1965), and Anant (1967a, 1967b), Ashem and Donner set up a controlled experiment to test its effectiveness.

Twenty-three male volunteers who showed no abnormalities on IQ or personality tests were selected for six weeks of treatment. All were patients at the New Jersey Neuro-Psychiatric Institute in Princeton and no more than 45 years old. Also, all had unsuccessfully tried some other form of treatment (including AA) at some time in the past. The experimental design was as follows:

The basic design of the experiment consisted of three conditions:

1. Systematic Conditioning: Forward Classical Conditioning (FCC)
2. Pseudo-Conditioning: Backward Classical Conditioning (BCC)
3. No Contact (Control)

The dependent variable was abstinence from drinking 6 months following treatment as measured by a follow-up questionnaire. (Ashem & Donner, 1968, p. 8)

The subjects were matched in groups of three and assigned to one of the above three groups. The FCC group imagined the vomiting as soon as they took their first drink, the BCC group before alcohol was even mentioned. In the results, both the FCC and BCC groups were combined. A 6 month follow-up showed 40% (6) of those treated were no longer drinking. Considering the limited amount of treatment, these results are considered very promising. Ashem and Donner claim the effectiveness of covert sensitization results from the "induction of phobic-type responses to alcohol" (p. 11). They recommend that the subject not drink during the beginning stages of treatment. This is because the desire to drink is still great, and the new aversive response is still not strong enough to overcome it.

With regard to the apparent effectiveness of the BCC treatment, it seems likely that, since nausea was used as the noxious component, the subjects continued to experience residual nausea after the introduction of the alcohol scene. In this way, there was overlap and contiguity conditioning of the alcohol and nausea. It seems likely that forward classical conditioning was operating in both treatment conditions.

Barlow, et al. (1969) were not satisfied with the sophistication of the numerous studies being conducted on the treatment of maladaptive sexual behavior with aversive techniques (cf. Feldman, 1966). On the basis of the reports available at the time of their study, it was impossible to tell whether the successes reported were really the result of the conditioning technique used or of the uncontrolled variables involved. In order to help fill in this gap, they conducted the following study to test the importance of the noxious scene in covert sensitization. One subject was a pedophiliac, the other a bisexual. The treatment consisted of sensitizing them to a hierarchy of scenes the subjects had considered arousing. This was followed by the extinction of the newly acquired behavior and, finally, reacquisition. The subjects responded to each condition in the expected manner. Barlow et al. concluded that "these findings demonstrate that pairing a noxious scene with a sexually arousing scene is a crucial procedure in covert sensitization" (p. 600). The events of this experiment were reported for 31 days only, and no follow-up or report as to the lasting effect of the treatment was given.

In a later study, Barlow, Agras, Leitenberg, Callahan, and Moore (1972) tested the importance of the expectations of subjects receiving covert sensitization treatment. They presented four subjects being treated for sexual deviations with a rationale describing responses to phases of treatment contrary to past empirical findings. Using single-subject designs, the subjects were first presented with scenes of the sexual stimulus with no aversive consequences, after being told this condition would be helpful in eliminating their maladaptive responses. After baseline data were gathered, the aversive consequence was then added together with the warning that this phase of treatment would lead to a temporary increase in their sexual deviation. After six sessions, phases one and two were repeated. In the second covert sensitization phase, subjects were told that, perhaps, this was the best treatment for them after all. Results clearly showed that, contrary to instructions and expectations, subjects improved under both covert sensitization conditions, but not under the extinction-placebo condition. Physiological measures were used to determine subjects' responses. Subjects verbally reported that they thought that they were getting better during the extinction phase and, with one exception, worse during the first covert sensitization phase. These results support the operant basis of covert sensitization and demonstrate that subject expectations are not *the* crucial factor.

Brownell, Hayes, and Barlow (1977) published a report of five case studies in which covert sensitization was used to treat a variety of sexual deviations. Measurements included a card sort, record of urges (three subjects) and penile circumference (two subjects). All subjects responded positively to covert sensitization in all areas measured. A 6-month follow-up revealed that all subjects maintained their improvement. This is probably the result of eliminating urges to perform the deviant behavior and of training in desired sexual behavior.

Janda and Rimm (1972) applied covert sensitization to the treatment of obesity. Eighteen subjects were assigned to three groups: covert sensitization, attention-control, and no treatment. After six sessions, subjects in the covert sensitization group showed significantly greater improvement than subjects in either of the other groups. The effects of covert sensitization remained highly significant at a six-week follow-up.

In a study to test the effects of various types of pretreatment instructions on cigarette smoking, Emmelkamp and Walta (1978) compared covert sensitization with electrical aversion and a no-treatment control group. In addition to finding that therapeutic instructions were more effective than experimentally oriented instructions, they also found that covert sensitization resulted in a significant decrease in smoking behavior, whereas electrical aversion did not.

An important factor to consider is the permanence of treatment effects. When a treated client is returned to the same environment which originally shaped a maladaptive behavior and the client begins engaging in the maladaptive behavior again, it is sometimes said that the client has suffered a relapse, or the treatment failed. If one looks at this situation in terms of an A-B-A experimental design, however, the return of the earlier behavior or decrease in the new behavior would be expected and predicted unless the new behavior is quite firmly established.

This observation is not intended to diminish the importance of follow-up reports but rather to put them in a somewhat untraditional perspective. Certainly a procedure with relatively long-lasting effects has the advantage of allowing more time for either naturally occurring contingencies to gain control of the behavior or appropriate and practical modifications to be made in the environment.

Covert sensitization has been shown to have relatively long-term effects. Olson, Ganley, Devine, and Dorsey (1981) recently published a 4-year follow-up report on various treatment approaches used with hospitalized alcoholics. The 113 patients in the study were placed in one of four groups. These four groups were: (1) milieu therapy, (2) milieu therapy plus transactional analysis (TA), (3) behavioral (milieu plus covert sensitization and relaxation training), and (4) combined (milieu plus TA plus covert sensitization and relaxation training). The results showed significant or near significant* differences favoring treatments which included covert sensitization. This degree of difference continued for up to 1.5 years. At longer follow-up points, trends still favored the behavioral treatments, but not significantly.

---

*Although near significance is not specifically defined, a review of the data presented by Olson et al. (1981) suggests that the authors considered results in the $p=.07$ to $p=.10$ range to be near significant.

The eight reports reviewed in this section include case reports, single-subject design studies, and group experiments. Together they exemplify how covert sensitization has been demonstrated to be effective in the treatment of alcoholism, obesity, smoking, and sexual behaviors. The Olson et al. (1981) report is of particular interest because of the unusually long-term follow-up data.

Covert Reponse Cost

As mentioned earlier, response cost involves the loss of a reinforcer contingent upon the performance of an undesirable behavior. Covert response cost (CRC) (Cautela, 1976) involves the removal or deprivation, in imagination, of a reinforcing stimulus contingent upon the performance of a target behavior. The distinction between response cost and extinction is that the reinforcing stimulus removed in response cost is *not* the reinforcing stimulus which has been maintaining the target behavior. As with covert sensitization and CE, CRC is used to decrease the frequency of a given behavior. An example of CRC would be having an alcoholic client imagine entering a barroom and then switching to a scene in which the client has just lost his/her wallet right after cashing his/her paycheck.

There are a number of situations in which the use of CRC is appropriate. CRC is often used as a companion treatment to covert sensitization. CRC may be alternated with covert sensitization in order to reduce the number of covert sensitization trials and, thereby, to reduce the likelihood of habituation to the noxious scenes in covert sensitization. Covert response cost can also be used with clients who do not find covert sensitization aversive enough to have the desired effect. In addition, CRC is useful in treating clients with several behaviors to eliminate.

Some clients find the CRC consequences (e.g., losing a wallet, having one's car stolen) more realistic and easier to imagine than the noxious scenes used in covert sensitization, such as vomiting in public. Most clients have had direct or, at least, modeled experience with many of the aversive consequences commonly used in CRC. Having prior in vivo experience with such a loss may increase the ability of the thought of a similar loss to elicit a strong emotional response. Clinical experience suggests that the use of scenes in which the item is destroyed or stolen can sometimes be more powerful than overtly losing the item. When an item is lost, sometimes there is hope of finding it again.

In conducting behavioral analyses when considering the use of CRC, it is helpful to query clients about actual or observed losses they have experienced. The Covert Response Cost Survey Schedule (Cautela, 1977a, pp. 93–95) is a tool which may be employed in identifying appropriate consequences to use in CRC. In selecting a reinforcer to use in CRC, the use of a very powerful stimulus, such as the loss of a loved one, should not be used. Consequences such as this may be too disturbing for the client and therefore hinder treatment.

As in the other procedures, the scenes to be used in CRC are checked for clarity and aversiveness. Scenes are developed in a series of steps, alternating the target behavior with the aversive consequences. A single scene may, thereby, include eventually three or four trials at various links in the behavioral chain.

As with covert sensitization, the client is asked to imagine the aversive consequence before the completion of the target behavior and sometimes immediately after. In this way, the behavioral chain can be interrupted at several points.

After practicing CRC with the therapist, the client is asked to practice 10 trials at home each day. The client is further instructed to vary three or four aversive consequences so they will maintain their aversiveness and the trials will retain their effectiveness.

Learning Theory Basis. CRC is the covert analogue of overt response cost. Accordingly, the loss of a usually reinforcing stimulus (other than the reinforcer maintaining the target behavior) contingent upon the performance of a given behavior decreases the likelihood of the target behavior occurring again.

Since response cost is an aversive procedure, those employing it should be cautioned to watch for undesirable side effects such as resistance to treatment and aggression.

Example. Clients being prepared for CRC are told that experimental and clinical evidence show that loss of something of value usually results in the decrease of the behavior which preceded the loss.

> We have found that, in many instances, if we ask people to imagine they are being deprived of or lose something, after they imagine doing something undesirable such as smoking or even feeling anxious, they are less apt to perform the undesirable behavior. (Cautela, 1976, p. 399)

A scene sequence actually used with an alcoholic client is described below. The client has been in the habit of beginning to drink upon returning home from work on Friday nights.

> "As you walk into the house after work, you say to yourself, 'I think I'll start out with a belt.' " When he signals that the scene is clear, the therapist says "Shift." He then imagines that his new car is smashed against a tree. When

he signals that the image is clear, he is told to imagine that he is walking toward the liquor cabinet to pour himself a straight shot before his wife knows that he is home. "Shift." (Smashed car scene.) The next scene he is told to imagine is that he opens the bottle and raises it to his lips. "Shift." (Cautela, 1976, p. 401)

Applications. CRC has been used successfully with many maladaptive approach behaviors. Cautela (1976) reports a series of cases in which he has used CRC, including alcoholism, pedophilia, obesity, fear of driving through tunnels, and exhibitionism.

Evaluation. The anecdotal data reported by Cautela (1967) suggest that CRC is an effective and useful addition to the behavior therapist's armamentarium.

Weiner (1965) compared the effects of imagined response cost and actual cost on an overt button press task. He found that, although actual response cost was more effective than imagined response cost, both treatments successfully suppressed response as compared to a no-cost condition. Weiner concluded that this finding supported Wolpe's (1958) contention that the effects of imagining an aversive event are comparable to the effects produced by the actual occurrence of that event.

In a well controlled study using multiple baselines and reversal designs, Tondo, Lane, and Gill (1975) treated two overweight clients with CRC. Their results showed that not only was CRC effective in reducing eating behavior, but that the effects of CRC, like the effects of covert sensitization, were quite specific. That is, there was little generalization to foods other than those specifically targeted for treatment.

One of the apparent advantages of CRC as compared to overt response cost is that the client does not actually have to possess the reinforcer in order to lose it. For example, a client who does not own a car might imagine having it stolen. It may be, however, that the actual possession or nonpossession of the reinforcer could make a difference in the effectiveness of the procedure. This is one area which needs to be researched.

Another advantage of CRC is that the agent who removes the reinforcer, in imagination, does not have to be a person known to or identifiable by the client. Using CRC in this way should reduce the tendency of clients to build up resentment toward those administering aversive procedures.

A third advantage of CRC is its potential applicability for self-control use. Self-control applications of covert conditioning will be discussed in a later section.

Although not much research has been published on CRC to date, both of the studies discussed above were well designed and yielded favorable results. The Tondo et al. (1975) report demonstrated that the effects of CRC can be very specific. As with covert sensitization, there appears to be little generalization to stimuli related to the target stimuli. CRC is a procedure which warrants further research.

Self-Control Triad

A recently developed behavioral strategy which involves the use of CPR in combination with other behavioral techniques is called the self-control triad (SCT) (Cautela, 1983). The SCT includes thought stopping, relaxation, and CPR. After the client has learned the individual components of the SCT, the three elements are practiced in sequence. The client imagines the target scene and covertly yells "Stop!", quickly relaxes, and finally reinforces this new response with a pleasant scene. Like the other covert conditioning procedures, the SCT is practiced twice a day. Practice sessions usually consist of 10 trials with eyes open and 10 with eyes closed. A delay of at least 10 seconds between trials is recommended, and a different reinforcer should be used each session. Each morning a reinforcer should be chosen for "emergency" use in actual anxiety-related situations that day. Before going to bed each night, the client should review the day's events. If a situation occurred in which the client did not respond appropriately, it should then be imagined with an appropriate response and followed with a reinforcing schedule.

Learning Theory Basis. Counterconditioning, reciprocal inhibition, and positive reinforcement all appear to contribute to the effectiveness of the SCT. Analyzing the three components of the SCT, we find that thought stopping serves as a distraction. The relaxation and related deep breathing serve both as distractions and as responses antagonistic to the target behavior. The reinforcing scene acts as a further distraction, as an antagonistic response, and as a reinforcer for the use of the SCT.

Example. While the other six covert conditioning procedures were developed to be used primarily in neutral situations to help clients to learn to deal more effectively with situations they will face later, the SCT was developed primarily to give clients a quick and effective technique to use as a self-control device in troublesome situations.

The following example illustrates how the SCT was employed (along with CPR, systematic desensitization, and in vivo desensitization) to treat a case of agoraphobia. The client, a young man who had recently moved to a large metropolitan area to attend graduate school, was troubled with thoughts of high buildings toppling over on him and, when going someplace new, not being able to find his way back to his apartment. After an unproductive course of psychodynamic treatment at a major hospital, he decided to seek a behavior therapist. During behavior therapy the client was taught the SCT, practiced it both during therapy sessions and as a homework assignment, and was instructed to use it whenever the above or other troublesome thoughts occurred. Both progressive muscle relaxation and CPR had already been used, thereby enabling the client to learn the SCT quickly. The thought-stopping component was practiced first, followed by the addition of relaxation, and finally the reinforcing scene was included. The client was cautioned not to let the individual components overlap, and then reminded that in actual practice it would probably be necessary to repeat the SCT several times on each occasion it was needed. Since in vivo desensitization is frequently used in agoraphobia, the SCT is an ideal procedure for clients to have available during in vivo practice.

Since the SCT procedure has also been quite helpful in modifying pain behavior, the application of the SCT procedure to pain control will also be reviewed as an example.

The client is instructed to employ the SCT whenever he/she experiences pain. The procedure consists of saying "Stop" (thought stopping); then taking a deep breath, exhaling through the nose while relaxing the whole body; and finally imagining a pleasant experience. Thought stopping serves as a distraction. The relaxation and breathing serve both as a distraction and a response antagonistic to pain. The pleasant experience acts as a distraction and antagonistic response, and as a reinforcer to the use of the SCT when the individual is in pain. After being taught the procedure, the client is given the following instructions in written form:

The SCT can be a valuable self-control procedure for the rest of one's life. The procedure can be used to reduce discomfort or anxiety, as well as to gain control over such behaviors as overeating or smoking or pain. Practicing these procedures every day will also reduce a general tension level and will aid in coping with daily experiences.

1. Practice the triad of thought stopping, deep breathing and relaxing, and covert reinforcement two sessions per day.
2. Each session consists of doing 10 triads with eyes open and 10 triads with eyes closed.

3. There should be at least 10 seconds between triads when practicing.
4. There should be a different reinforcer imagined for each session. This is important to avoid satiation, which will reduce the effectiveness of the scene.
5. When you wake up each morning, choose a reinforcer that you are going to use for the day outside the practice sessions.
6. Practice imagining the reinforcer until it is clear and pleasant and can come to mind readily.
7. During the rest of the day, this reinforcer can be used in self-control triads when needed.
8. If at any time during the day you experience any discomfort or anxiety, immediately use the self-control triad.
9. If discomfort or anxiety persists, continue to use the self-control triad over and over until the anxiety is greatly diminished or eliminated.
10. The self-control triad can also be used as a self-control against temptations such as the desire to overeat wrong foods or drink alcoholic beverages, to take pills or other form of drugs, or to engage in sexual fantasies that are enjoyable but not appropriate.

The client is then told to employ the SCT whenever pain, nausea, dizziness, and so forth are experienced, until the symptoms subside.

Applications. The SCT is particularly applicable in anxiety-provoking situations to reduce stress and to increase the likelihood of responding appropriately. Although not labeled as such, the SCT was described in an earlier case report of the treatment of a case of arthritic pain (Cautela, 1977c). Other clinical applications have included the treatment of obesity, drinking, smoking behavior, and depression (Cautela, 1984).

Evaluation. The first controlled study of the SCT was conducted by Cleveland (1982). Fifty subjects, suffering from myofascial pain dysfunction syndrome (sometimes referred to as temporomandibular joint syndrome—TMJ) were assigned to one of five groups. The five groups were SCT, relaxation training, biofeedback, placebo (false biofeedback), and no treatment. Each subject received eight 30-minute treatment sessions. Dependent variables were scores on a variety of self-report questionnaires and by the EMG measurement of masseter muscle tension.

An analysis of post-test scores revealed that both the no-treatment and placebo groups had reported greater pain than any of the three treatment groups. In addition, the SCT group reported significantly less pain than the biofeedback group but not less than the relaxation group. There was no significant difference between the biofeedback and relaxation group. With regard to the physiological measure, all three treatment groups were significantly improved as compared to both the placebo and no-treatment groups. The placebo group was also significantly superior to no treatment.

The SCT appears to be a promising new behavior therapy device, combining three firmly established procedures and readily adaptable to self-control use. Much additional research, however, must be done to empirically determine its effectiveness.

4

Common Elements and Special Problems in Covert Conditioning

Common Elements in All Covert Conditioning Procedures

Much of the information presented in the last two chapters about the implementation of the individual covert conditioning procedures is applicable to the use of all of the procedures. It will be helpful to review some of these points and to mention several others which are pertinent in using covert conditioning.

Guidelines for Applying Covert Conditioning Procedures

Points that should be remembered when employing covert conditioning are listed below:

1. Prior to presenting a covert conditioning procedure to a client, the rationale for the covert conditioning approach should be clearly presented as well as the rationale for that particular procedure.

2. Clients must be able to assess the quality and clarity of their imagery, each component to be measured on a scale from 1 to 5 (1 = "not at all" and 5 = "very much"). Only the imagery that rates 4 or 5 is acceptable. Clients are also asked to rate their involvement in scenes on a 1-to-5 scale.

3. As a new scene is begun, the therapist should inquire as to the degree of clarity, enjoyment, and involvement.

4. The time of the interval between trials depends upon the covert conditioning technique being employed. In CPR, trials should be spaced approximately 30 seconds apart. However, in covert sensitization this 30-second interval is not necessary; in fact, it is advantageous to have a shorter interval between trials because one trial's aversive consequences can also affect the target scenes which follow on the next trial. Trials are usually presented about 5 seconds apart. However, the scene should not be so aversive that the client is unable to concentrate.

5. In a non-CM scene, the client must be able to perceive himself/herself performing the behavior and be able to imagine that he/she is really "there." The scene should be continually checked upon, using the 1-to-5 scale for clarity and quality.

6. The length of each scene depends upon how long it takes clients to feel involved in the scenes, for example, imagine it clearly and feel as though they're skiing or really feeling nauseous and miserable. When they experience the appropriate involvement, they are asked to signal by raising their right index finger.

7. If covert sensitization and CPR scenes are being alternated, approximately 1 minute should be allowed between each scene, because the aversive effects of covert sensitization may linger and overlap with the reinforcing scene. In the same way, it is undesirable to have the positive reinforcing scene overlap with an aversive scene presented later.

8. As many different reinforcers and aversive consequences as possible should be used to avoid satiation.

9. Sexual scenes as reinforcers are not ordinarily used because of possible ambivalence that the client may have regarding moral aspects or current anger toward the person who is the sexual partner in the scene. There is also the possibility that the scene may be too erotic, thus interfering with other scenes.

10. No scene that is so strongly aversive as to be disrupting should be used, for example, a mother being told to imagine that her child is dead.

11. Two types of scenes related to the target behavior can be differentiated:

    (a) Consequences involving nonrelevant scenes, for example, using skiing to reinforce getting on an airplane (if skiing has nothing to do with going on an airplane) and

(b) Consequences involving a scene that is related to the target behavior.
  (i) Relevant scenes in terms of sense modality. (Make sure senses utilized apply to senses involved with the target behavior.) A scene involving vomiting would apply to a target behavior of smoking or a scene of becoming blind would apply to a target behavior of voyeurism.
  (ii) The consequences of the response related to the target behavior, for example, someone who is afraid of flying but wants to fly to go skiing in Aspen, Colorado. The reinforcing scene could be skiing on the slopes at Aspen.

12. In general, aside from being a part of the SCT, relaxation does not have to be taught in employing covert conditioning unless the client is so anxious that it hinders concentration. It is not taught for covert sensitization unless the client is so anxious that it is necessary for cooperation in the procedure.

13. Scenes should involve every situation in which there are antecedents and/or discriminative stimuli for which the behavior is likely to occur at an undesirable rate. The more varied the imagery situations used are, the more likely it is that generalization will occur.

14. Homework scenes should not usually exceed 10 scenes of the same situation per day per any one technique. In fact, they should be varied as much as possible, for example, in treating alcoholism, the 10 assigned homework covert sensitization scenes could include 3 of a bar, 3 of a cocktail party, and 4 of drinking alone at home. Exceptions are made, however, for immediate problematic situations, for example, a smoker who usually smokes to excess while studying for an exam and who has an exam scheduled during the next few days. In this case, all of the covert conditioning scenes would involve studying for an exam.

15. Scenes should continue even after the target behavior has been attained (or eliminated) to make sure that strong and weak urges for the undesirable behavior disappear as well.

16. If a target behavior has been attained or eliminated to the desirable criterion through a schedule of continuous reinforcement, the procedures should, at first, be continued at the same schedule for overlearning; then a schedule of intermittent reinforcement should be employed; gradually the schedule should be thinned out as much as possible. Termination of treatment should not occur until this entire process has been carried out.

17. Before termination of treatment, the client should be well trained in doing a behavioral analysis and in using covert conditioning procedures as self-control for the prevention and modification of any undesirable behavior.

18. When treating children, CM is usually the procedure of choice. Whenever possible, CPR and CM are preferred over other methods with aversive components.

Relaxation Training

While relaxation training is generally recommended for use with covert conditioning procedures not employing an aversive stimulus, it is not necessary unless the client is so anxious that concentration is hindered. High levels of anxiety can interfere with concentration and image clarity. According to Lang (1977), reduction in arousal levels seems to improve imagery ability. Relaxation training, therefore, may help to overcome this difficulty.

Originally, relaxation training was routinely employed with covert sensitization (Cautela, 1966). Currently, however, relaxation is rarely used during the actual application of covert sensitization, CNR, or CRC, since the object of these procedures is to induce arousal by aversive stimulation. There is no evidence that relaxation training directly improves image clarity in covert sensitization. Moreover, Little and Curran (1978) have speculated that muscle relaxation may diminish the effectiveness of covert sensitization and suggest that clients be instructed to tense their muscles during scene visualizations, thereby increasing the aversiveness of the scenes. In cases where clients are so upset that they are having trouble cooperating, however, relaxation training may help by lessening interfering thoughts and images.

On the other hand, relaxation appears to facilitate clear imagery and involvement in the use of CPR, CM, and the SCT (Cautela, 1983). Kearney (1976) has shown that subjects trained in relaxation, prior to treatment with CPR, tend to show somewhat greater improvement than those treated with CPR without relaxation training. After a review of the seemingly contradictory literature, Kearney (1984) suggested that there may be an optimal range of autonomic arousal during which the most vivid imagery might occur.

A brief four-step procedure is often useful to help clients to relax at the beginning of imagery sessions. In this procedure the client is first instructed to assume a comfortable, relaxed position. In the second step, the client is told to take a deep breath and exhale while relaxing the whole body. The third step involves having the client identify the most relaxed body part and concentrate on the feeling there. The client then allows the relaxed state to flow into contiguous body parts and finally spread throughout the rest of his or her body.

The fourth step is similar to a hypnotic deepening technique. The client is instructed to imagine being alone in an elevator on the tenth floor of a building. Further instructions to look at the floor indicator lighting panel and to watch the floors go down as the therapist counts from 10 to 1 are then given. As the therapist counts, the client feels the elevator going down and experiences an ever deepening state of relaxation. These four steps take about five minutes in total and are often used before beginning a series of CPR or CM scenes.

Various forms of relaxation training are so widely used in our culture today that most clients seem to have some exposure as well as a positive attitude toward it. Introducing relaxation training fairly early in treatment can be useful in reducing reluctance and skepticism in new clients toward relatively unfamiliar and more difficult-to-understand procedures. This can be thought of as a shaping procedure in which the unsophisticated client is taken from the known and familiar to the relatively unknown and unfamiliar. This helps bridge the gap between what clients will accept and procedures which may be so foreign to skeptical clients that they cannot accept them at first.

Procedure Variations

Several adaptations and variations have been reported in the clinical and experimental use of covert conditioning. Some investigators have reported following overt behavior with covert consequences (Krop, Calhoun, & Verrier, 1971; Krop et al., 1973; Wish et al, 1970). This practice is consistent with the assumptions listed above and is also considered a form of covert conditioning. Other researchers (Marshall et al., 1974; Wisocki, 1971) have reported a three-step process in which a scene of an unpleasant situation (e.g., taking a test) is followed by an appropriate response (e.g., relaxation) which, in turn, is followed by a reinforcing scene (e.g., ice cream cone). This procedure would also be considered a variant of covert conditioning.

Procedure Combinations

One of the most important facts about the covert conditioning procedures in clinical practice is that a single covert conditioning procedure is rarely used alone. They are nearly always employed in conjunction with other covert conditioning techniques and often with other behavioral techniques. This point is illustrated by the use of relaxation training with most clients, taught as a procedure independent of covert conditioning.

Empirical studies, for the most part, are limited to the use of single procedures. These rigid experimental arrangements, of course, make it easier to answer apecific questions about the relative effectiveness and effective components of various procedures. Case studies, on the other hand, are more useful sources of information with regard to the clinical applications of therapeutic methods. The case reports cited below describe some of the ways covert conditioning procedures are used in combination.

Although it was not labeled as such at the time, the procedure of alternating punishment and escape or avoidance trials, described in the first covert sensitization article (Cautela, 1966), was essentially a combination of covert sensitization and CNR. Flannery (1972a) employed CPR and CM along with thought stopping and relaxation training to a case of agoraphobia. Wisocki (1970) used covert sensitization to eliminate a client's obsessive compulsive clothes-folding behavior. CPR was used to increase the rate of appropriate but incompatible clothes-handling behavior. Whether covert or overt procedures are used, when behaviors are elminated from a client's repertoire, new, appropriate behaviors should be established in their place.

One of the most unusual cases to which covert conditioning has been applied was reported by Cautela and Baron (1973). They treated a hospitalized college student, diagnosed as schizophrenic, for self-injurious behaviors, including eye poking and lip and tongue biting. The treatment used included relaxation training, thought stopping and desensitization to antecedent stimuli. The self-injurious behaviors were treated directly with covert sensitization and overt extinction. Appropriate behaviors were taught and strenthened through the use of behavioral rehearsal and CPR. Although predictions at the onset of the behavioral treatment were that the client would be dead within 3 months if the behavior continued, a 10-year follow-up revealed that the client had not engaged in self-injurious behavior during that time, had graduated from law school, and appeared well-adjusted.

There has been a great deal of recent research and clinical interest in the area of organic dysfunction. It is becoming increasingly apparent that there can be a large operant component to the pain experience (Fordyce, 1976a, 1976b). Components of pain can be shaped and maintained through interactions with the environment. Since the reaction of others can reinforce expressions of pain, extinction is theoretically the treatment of choice. Because of the extinction burst phenomena discussed earlier, however, this is a particularly difficult situation in which to use extinction. The probability of getting significant others in this client's environment to really totally ignore protestations of pain from a loved one, particularly when their protestations begin to increase, is not great. If CE is to be used, it should be used together with other procedures such as CPR and CM. CM could be used, for example, to teach clients more enjoyable ways of getting reinforcement from their environment. CPR could be used to have the client imagine being in situations which formerly occasioned pain behavior, but in which they are now behaving in alternate, non-pain-related ways, and being reinforced for these incompatible responses.

Perhaps the most formalized combination of procedures involving covert conditioning is the SCT (Cautela, 1983).

Individualized Treatment

Idiosyncratic covert conditioning scenes are developed for each individual client. Several experimental studies (e.g., Kearney, 1976; Marshall et al., 1974; Wisocki, 1973a) have used standardized scenes for all subjects, and this is certainly both justified and necessary for purposes of experimental control. Although even the use of automated and standardized treatment can be effective (Kearney, 1976; McGlynn, Reynolds, & Linder, 1971; Mealiea & Nawas, 1970), the target behaviors to which prepackaged programs are applied should probably be relatively uncomplicated. For example, the use of automated preprogrammed material for the treatment of test anxiety or public speaking phobia can be cost-effective when used by college and high school counseling centers. A live therapist must, of course, still conduct the behavior analysis, adapt parts of the program to the individual client, and monitor the program.

When choosing scenes to use as reinforcers, the therapist must be careful in dealing with reinforcers that once were, but no longer are, obtainable by the client. For example, a scene which involves a deceased loved one or having a paralyzed former football player imagine scenes of physical activity can sometimes be aversive. Obviously, the therapist must assess the situation closely when choosing scenes.

In individualizing treatment for the special needs of the client, problem areas that are of immediate concern are usually targeted first.

For example, a client with a drinking problem is likely to be treated using scenes of the barroom across the street before imagining being in a vineyard in France. An individual wishing to reduce homosexual urges should probably be sensitized first to a particular person that he/she is attracted to and works with on a daily basis. The client would then be sensitized to someone seen less frequently.

It is also important that the client does not modify the scene without discussing the modifications with the therapist. Some clients have a tendency to edit out, or weaken, the important part of scenes that involve unpleasant events or other aversive stimuli. It is probably best to caution the client against this when first explaining covert conditioning, and to monitor treatment periodically by having the client describe some of the scenes as they are imagined.

The length of scene presentation varies with the complexity of the scene and the number of sense modalities involved. Once the scene is clear and the client can experience the appropriate affective component, which usually takes about 5 to 15 seconds, the scene may be ended. In general, covert sensitization and CM scenes tend to take a bit longer than those emloyed in the other procedures. As scenes are repeated and the client becomes more familiar with them, they are usually completed more quickly than when first introduced.

The amount of time between scene presentations also varies with the procedure used. In order to decrease the possibility of simultaneous conditioning while using covert sensitization, the therapist should wait until the nausea from one trial subsides before beginning the next trial. With CPR, on the other hand, any simultaneous conditioning that might occur is likely to be advantageous to the treatment. Therefore, unless the application is in the context of an experiment, there is no need to try to avoid this possibility, and the CPR trials may be administered more quickly.

In working with clients who are particularly anxious, it is often helpful to break down the target behavior sequence into smaller segments. For example, if working with a client with a fear of flying in airplanes, it may be necessary to describe a series of scenes and activities leading up to and including the flight. The client may be reinforced for packing a suitcase, leaving the house, riding to the airport, and several of the other component steps. A less anxious client may not need to have the sequence broken down so finely.

Experiencing Scenes

In using covert conditioning (except for CM), it is important that the client does not just passively observe the scene described, but gets actively involved in it and experiences the events as if they were really happening. This is critical with regard to the emotional response which the stimuli should elicit. A supposedly noxious scene about which the client is quite blasé is not going to be very effective.

Clients should be told that they are not to imagine they are watching newsreel or film of themselves, but they are really in the scene. With some clients it is helpful to use the phrase, "You are experiencing . . . " rather than "Imagine that you. . . . " Others may require somewhat more instruction and practice in the effective use of imagery. As many sense modalities as possible should be involved, and becoming adept at this will take longer for some than others.

After clients become skilled at visualizing and experiencing various situations with their eyes closed, it can be helpful to have them practice with eyes opened. In this way, useful self-control procedures for in vivo use can be developed. For example, when a man with a weight problem dines out, he may find it helpful to visualize vomit on all the strawberry shortcake he sees being served to other diners.

Homework

In order to control for number of trials, homework assignments are often omitted from experimental applications of covert conditioning. Clinical applications however, nearly always include the use of homework assignments. Although specific homework assignments vary from case to case, the covert conditioning portion of homework usually consists of one or two sets of 10 trials per day.

There are several advantages to having clients practice covert conditioning between sessions. The most obvious advantage is that it increases the number of trials per week and, therefore, the amount of treatment each client receives. By spreading the trials out over a week's time, the benefits of distributed learning are incorporated into the treatment. The client has the opportunity to practice in several different locations and situations, thereby increasing the likelihood of generalization of the new behavior. The client's self-confidence is often improved as a result of these assignments, since many clients report that it gives them more of a sense of participation and control over their own lives. Finally, the use of homework can be a successive approximation toward teaching the client to use the covert conditioning procedures as self-control devices, both as treatment progresses and after formal therapy has ended.

The therapist must, of course, monitor the homework assignments at the regularly scheduled sessions. Monitoring should include asking whether or not the assignment was completed, assessing the effectiveness of the assignment, and providing assistance with difficulties that might have arisen.

Homework seems to be nearly universally aversive to children. In using covert conditioning with children, we have found it helpful to tape record homework assignments. Arrangements can be made with parents to allow their children to stay up an extra half-hour to listen to the tape and to complete the homework assignment.

In working with most children and with adults who did not like school, we do not label the client's assignments as homework. For example, depending on the particular situation, the assignment might be referred to as listening to the "fun tape," "relaxation tape," or "Dr. X's talk with you."

Self-Control

One of the advantages of behavior therapy is the emphasis on actively involving clients in their own treatment. The use of behavioral techniques as self-control devices is an example of client involvement. Self-control is the use of certain responses to control the rate, duration, and intensity of other responses (Cautela, 1969). The already discussed use of homework is a form of self-control.

In addition to the advantages of the use of homework assignments listed above, self-control uses of behavioral procedures have the additional advantages of being applicable in the natural environment. That is, the client can apply the procedures in the actual situations which originally led to and/or are maintaining the maladaptive behaviors under treatment. For example, a woman with a drinking problem may have to pass her favorite barroom on the way to and from work every day. As the client passes the bar without going in, she can enjoy a self-administered reinforcing scene.

The use of behavioral procedures on a day-to-day basis for immediate correction of maladaptive behaviors and practice of adaptive behavior requires clients to take a share of the responsibility for modifying their own behavior. Unless clients cooperate by practicing and actively reporting back to their therapists, the treatment is not likely to succeed.

In preparing a client for homework and self-control uses of covert conditioning, the therapist alternates the responsibility for conducting the scenes with the client. A client being treated for test anxiety with CPR may have a sequence of 10 scenes in chronological order to work on. First, the therapist describes scene one (T_1). Then, the client practices the same first scene alone $(C1_1)$. Next, the therapist does scenes one and two with the client ($T_{1\text{-}2}$). This alternation of scene delivery continues as follows: T_1; Cl_1; $T_{1\text{-}2}$; $Cl_{1\text{-}2}$; $T_{1\text{-}2\text{-}3}$; $Cl_{1\text{-}2\text{-}3}$; $T_{1\text{-}2\text{-}3\text{-}4}$; ... $Cl_{1\text{-}2\ldots9\text{-}10}$. When the client reports that the stimuli no longer elicit anxiety, the CPR is changed to an intermittent schedule.

Covert conditioning procedures are particularly adaptable to self-control use. Since no equipment or overt movement is required, they can be used in nearly every situation which may arise. Once the client learns the procedures, they can be available for immediate use as a sort of behavioral hygiene if new problems occur. The client may return to the therapist from time to time to review the progress being made and the procedures being used. Teaching the SCT and/or other self-control devices is one of the most important steps in preparing clients for the eventual termination of treatment.

Termination

The ideal criteria for termination are the following:

1. The inappropriate behavior, including urges, fantasy, and overt behavior, should be zero.
2. There should be a period of overlearning in which the covert conditioning procedures are employed after the zero criterion has been reached. Clinically, that means at least six more consecutive sessions of the application of the procedures in which zero frequency of the target behavior has been reported. That is, the criterion is seven sessions of zero frequency.
3. The client should be well acquainted with covert conditioning procedures so that he can use them the rest of his life for maintenance, booster sessions, or the modification of new problematic behavior.
4. The client should be convinced that no further therapeutic effort involving the therapist is needed.

Review Sessions

Occasionally booster sessions are needed to help clients maintain their treatment gains after termination. While using covert sensitization in treating sexual dysfunctions, Maletzky (1977) found that a program which included three monthly booster sessions followed by a booster session each third month for a 9-month period was useful in treating clients who were unable to make appropriate life-style changes. Clients who were able to make appropriate life-style changes did not, for the most part, need the booster sessions to maintain their treatment gains. Booster sessions in this study essentially consisted of additional "assisted" covert sensitization trials. Maletzky recommends that clients use tape recordings and home practice, on an as-needed basis, to guard against particularly troublesome situations they may face.

There is a need for occasional review sessions with certain clients, to review various self-control procedures they were taught. It is often the case that clients who are having trouble maintaining treatment gains either are no longer using the self-control procedures or are using them improperly. These review sessions should be considered more as "mini refresher courses" than just "booster" sessions. By including not only additional trials but also a more current behavioral analysis and a review of self-control procedures, there is greater likelihood of eventual client success independent of the therapist. In addition, as clients become more proficient at covert conditioning, their ability to use the procedures to change other emerging behaviors (a sort of behavioral hygiene without therapist intervention) increases. For example, before going to bed each night someone might review the day's event and select a "mistake" or a situation in which he/she would like to have behaved differently. Then the individual could conduct 5 to 10 covert conditioning trials in an attempt to modify future behavior in the desired direction.

Special Problems

Imagery

One of the most frequently reported problems in using imagery-based techniques is the difficulty in obtaining clear, vivid imagery. The use of the term *imagery* should not be thought of as limited to visual imagery alone, but includes all sense modalities. Since imagining is a behavior, it too is subject to the laws of learning and can, therefore, be modified.

The following are some of the steps a therapist may take to help improve a client's imagery ability.

1. When describing scenes, use great detail. Use familiar scenes at first.
2. Ask the client to look at an object, for example a plant, chair, person, and so forth. Then ask the client to close his/her eyes

and describe the object. Repeat this exercise until the details are reported accurately, including color, shape, size, and so on.

3. Repeat the exercise described above using a simple picture.
4. Repeat the exercise described above using a complex picture with many details.
5. Ask the client to listen to music. Then turn off the music and have the client try to hear the music without the actual music playing. This is sometimes easier to accomplish with closed eyes. Again repeat until the client reports hearing the melody or tune clearly.
6. Do the same as above with smelling certain odors and then imagining the odor.
7. Have the client practice tasting certain foods and then practice imagining the tastes.
8. Use movies or videotapes. Control the stop-action or slow-motion mode, repeating until the client can describe the sequence or pictures with clarity and detail.
9. Instruct the client to go to the actual places needed for scenes, such as the supermarket, airport, or elevator. The client should practice looking at the surroundings and hearing its sounds until the sights and sounds can be repeated in imagery.
10. Ask the client to listen to the voices of significant others on tape. Repeat until a good auditory image is achieved.
11. Use tactile stimulation such as sandpaper, silk, and ice cubes. Then ask the client to reproduce the sensations in imagery.
12. Instruct the client to attend to kinesthetic movements while walking, sitting down, lying down, or playing sports.
13. Start treatment with one sensory modality, for example, music and hearing. Then gradually add complexity by including other modalities. A beach scene might be described as follows: "Feel the warm sun. Smell the salt water. Hear the waves. . . . Hear seagulls. . . . Feel the sand underneath you. . . . Feel the warm breeze. See the sailboat on the horizon."
14. Ask the client particularly to attend to interesting and enjoyable experiences which occur, trying to savor them for later retrieval.
15. Use audio- or videotapes for clients who report imagery problems outside of the office. The therapist can record imagery instructions and include delays for visualization of scenes on the tape for later use by clients.

Although, as a general rule, we strive to improve image clarity, there are situations in which a certain lack of clarity may have advantages. For example, clients wishing to change their sexual orientation may experience greater generalization if the faces of persons in the scenes are undiscernable.

A second imagery problem is controllability. By controllability we mean the client's ability to control and maintain appropriate images. Controllability is extremely important because, unless the client is able to obtain appropriate imagery, there is little chance of therapeutic success. Kazdin (1977) stated that there is not a consistent correlation between image vividness and behavior change. He found that combined high levels of vividness and controllability were the most successful, whereas high vividness and low controllability correlated least well with behavior change.

Perhaps the most common control problem is difficulty in switching from target to pleasant scenes. Often pleasant scenes are begun only to end up with an unpleasant conclusion. One client who tried using a reinforcing scene of skiing down a hill usually ended up falling. CM and the flow-scene manner of scene presentation described by Kearney (1984) can be helpful with scene-switching difficulties. In using flow scenes the client simply employs consequences related to the target behavior which can naturally flow from the target behavior portion of the scene. For example, a young man with public speaking anxiety might rehearse a scene in which he successfully makes a class presentation and is then sincerely praised by the professor whose opinion he values highly.

Some of the other ways in which clients have been helped with control problems are listed below:

1. The client is assured that the fantasy totally belongs to him/her, and since he/she is the writer and director, he/she may change it however he/she likes. The client is then asked to repeat the scene, this time describing it out loud as it is experienced.
2. If the control problem continues, a shaping procedure is sometimes used. For example, the client using skiing scenes may imagine falling without getting hurt. In the next scene, the client may start to fall but regain balance before going down.
3. A third method requires clients to keep, for one week, a thorough log of events that lead to anxiety or depression. In this way, the client becomes more aware of these stimuli, can recognize the sequences as they begin, and can, therefore, correct the imagery at an earlier point in this sequence.

Client Involvement

Lack of client involvement in, or client commitment to, the use of covert conditioning can obviously be a very serious problem. This situation usually results from the client's not being convinced of the validity of the procedure being used. Occasionally, a client to whom covert conditioning lacks face validity may ask, "How can pretending do any good?"

Problems such as this often can be helped by reviewing the rationale for covert conditioning. The presentation of the rationale must, of course, be adapted to the sophistication and intellectual level of the individual client. Since the rationale presentation usually takes place early in the therapeutic process, the therapist may be more likely to misjudge the client and present an inappropriate rationale. Simply repeating a modified version of the rationale may be sufficient to obtain the client's enthusiastic cooperation.

Occasionally, in dealing with relatively sophisticated clients, a discussion of the nature of reality has proven helpful. Usually the client has complained that knowing he/she is just pretending and that the scenes are not real detracts from their effectiveness. The therapist might respond by agreeing that it is difficult, if not impossible, to know true reality. However, would not the client agree that dreams exist and that images do exist, too? Obviously, that which exists is real. There is no way to determine which of these realities is more valid, since there is no third criterion to measure them against. Therefore, the client should not pretend the events in the scene are happening, but rather experience the scenes as really occurring.

In some cases the client readily admits to preexisting inappropriate covert psychological behavior. For example, frequent thoughts of binge eating may precede actual violation of one's diet. It can be helpful to agree with the client's assessment and take it a few steps further, one step at a time, explaining how, for example, the client's faulty imagery can be used to advantage. If the client believes that maladaptive covert psychological behavior influences overt behavior in undesirable ways, it is often only one more step to accepting the idea that adaptive covert psychological behavior can influence overt behavior in adaptive ways.

From time to time parents report that their child, who may or may not be fully cooperative in the office, resists practicing homework assignments. Homework assignments given to children usually involve the use of audiotape recordings. Parents can usually obtain the needed cooperation by allowing the child to stay up an extra 30 minutes at night to listen to the tape. This procedure has also been effective with children who refuse to cooperate in the office.

Are There Limitations to the Use of Covert Conditioning?

It is difficult to determine in an a priori manner the limitations of covert conditioning, as long as the client is willing and able to cooperate. Clients who are reluctantly involved in treatment, such as institutionalized individuals, those participating in treatment in order to avoid an aversive consequence (e.g., incarceration, loss of driver's license, nagging by spouse) and some children are not generally as enthusiastic as most clients and are less likely to cooperate with treatment. Lack of cooperation in these cases often takes the form of the client's giving lip service to practicing the scenes with very few, if any, trials actually being practiced. Since there is still no way to directly monitor a client's covert processes, the therapist should spend extra time pointing out to these clients the advantages of changing their behavior. However, the therapist should not assume that all observations are correctly reported, particularly if there is no verifiable behavior change. It is probably wise to consider overt procedures at least as companions to covert procedures in working with clients such as these.

Clients with seemingly limited intellectual ability should not necessarily be dismissed out of hand from consideration of treatment with covert conditioning. Baron and Cautela (1983–1984) reported two case studies in which covert conditioning was successfully used with an 8-year-old mildly retarded boy and a 4-year-old autistic boy with near normal intelligence.

Groden and Cautela (1984) conducted a study in which covert conditioning was used with two students from a class for the trainably retarded. The first, a 15-year-old hydrocephalic boy, had been engaging in a number of disruptive behaviors for 2 years. These behaviors were emitting honking noises, wrist bending, and excessive rocking, which included head and stomach banging. CPR was applied to the various behaviors in a multiple baseline design. A demand control condition was implemented prior to CPR. As CPR was applied to each behavior, the rate of each decreased below baseline levels. The second subject was a 13-year-old girl with Down's syndrome. Head banging, nose picking, and tongue chewing, the target behaviors in this experiment, were reported to have been of very long duration. The design employed was similar to that used in the first experiment. This time, however, the technique chosen was CM. As in the first case, all three behaviors responded favorably to treatment. A 3-month follow-up revealed that the improvement was maintained.

In an earlier experiment, Groden (1982) used covert conditioning with a number of autistic adolescents. As in the Groden and Cautela study, CPR was modified by providing shorter, but more frequent, sessions, strongly emphasizing all sense modalities, and using simplified language to describe scenes and frequent questioning of the client as to the scene content. Although other procedures were also used, a multiple baseline design was employed, and CPR was shown to be effective in increasing the rate of verbal initiations with this population.

Another population which often requires special procedural adaptations is the elderly (Cautela, 1981a). In general, treatment progresses more slowly. Greater detail in describing scenes is usually necessary. Fewer trials can be completed within each session, and more overall trials are needed to bring about behavior change than with younger clients, thereby lengthening treatment. A related problem, when CPR is being considered, is the difficulty of identifying a sufficient number of reinforcers to use (Cautela, 1981a).

II

Applying Covert Conditioning to Specific Problems

5

Maladaptive Approach Behaviors

Throughout the earlier chapters, examples have been given of the wide range of behaviors to which covert conditioning procedures have been applied. Covert conditioning has been widely applied to behavioral problems such as maladaptive approach behaviors, organic dysfunctions, social skills deficits, and phobias. The next five chapters of this book will deal, in greater detail, with applications of covert conditioning in these areas.

Maladaptive approach behavior is a term used to describe patterns of behavior in which the individual approaches, or consumes, various stimuli. These behavioral patterns are maintained primarily by immediate positive reinforcement, whereas maladaptive avoidance behaviors, on the other hand, are maintained primarily by immediate negative reinforcement. Maladaptive approach behaviors can encompass some sexual dysfunctions (which are discussed elsewhere), excessive gambling, stealing, and consummatory behaviors such as overeating, pica, and substance abuses including the use of drugs, alcohol, nicotine, and other potentially addictive substances. This section covers the application of covert conditioning to problems involving the abuse of food, alcohol, drugs, and cigarettes.

Experimental Studies

Nearly all of the experimental studies which have employed covert conditioning techniques in the modification of maladaptive approach behaviors have involved food, alcohol, or nicotine consumption. Many of these studies have already been described in the sections on the various covert conditioning procedures. Usually covert sensitization has been compared with either no treatment or an attention-placebo condition. Occasionally experiments employing CNR (Baugh, 1977), CM (Bornstein & Devine, 1980; Wadden & Flaxman, 1981), and CPR (Brunn & Hedberg, 1974; Manno & Marston, 1972; Ramsey, 1978) in treating obesity and CM (Nesse & Nelson, 1977) in treating smoking have also been reported. The Baugh (1977), Manno and Marston (1972), and Ramsey (1978) studies included covert sensitization as well as the procedures mentioned above.

The results of these experiments (a more complete list of which can be found in Part IV, Bibliography) generally support the effectiveness of covert conditioning procedures in modifying consummatory behaviors (e.g., Ashem & Donner, 1968; Bellack, Glanz, & Simon, 1976; Brunn and Hedberg, 1974; Gerson & Lanyon, 1972; Nesse & Nelson, 1977; Olson et al., 1981; Snowden, 1978).

Case Studies

Case studies do not, by their very nature, lend empirical support to particular treatments. They are useful, however, as illustrations of procedures and because of their role in generating hypotheses for research.

In the late 1960s Anant published at least seven single- and multiple-case reports of the use of a verbal aversion technique with alcoholics (Anant, 1966a, 1966b, 1967a, 1967b, 1968a, 1968b, 1968c). Although Anant did not label it covert sensitization, his published descriptions of this procedure sound remarkably similar to descriptions of covert sensitization. Other applications of covert conditioning in this area have included hydrocarbon inhalation (Blanchard, Libet, & Young, 1973), smoking (Cautela, 1970c), obesity (DeBerry, 1981), amphetamine addiction (Götestam & Melin, 1974), barbituate addiction (Polakow, 1975), heroin addiction (Wisocki, 1973b, 1977), and LSD use (Flannery, 1972c).

In 1972, Flannery reported a case which involved a college-age female who frequently used marijuana, LSD, and Darvon. The client reported using these drugs to escape tensions caused by problems with her family and boyfriend. Behavioral rehearsal, thought stopping, coverant control therapy, and CM were all used to control different behaviors at various stages of the treatment. Treatment was not aimed directly at the drug abuse but rather toward anxiety reduction and improvement of social skills. This led to improvement of the client's interpersonal relationships and subsequent decreases in her drug use. Six months after the conclusion of treatment, both the client and her family reported good grades and successful completion of her course work. Depression and somatic complaints were no longer reported and communications with family members had improved. Although the client reported four instances of social drug use during this period, Flannery considered this amount of drug use to be consistent with the local norms. She had broken off the relationship with her former boyfriend (by then committed to a hospital) and was frequently dating others.

Thompson and Conrad (1977) used covert sensitization together with contingency contracting, systematic desensitization, assertiveness training, rational-emotive therapy, and thought stopping to treat an involuntarily committed male with a seven-year history of opium dependence. In this case, the covert sensitization was directed at the chain of behavior leading up to injection. Although one cannot always assume the cooperation of incarcerated clients in actually visualizing described scenes, the subject of this case appears to have been quite cooperative since the authors report he actually vomited following his third covert sensitization scene.* An 18-month follow-up revealed very limited drug use at 2 months and none during the subsequent 16 months. It should be pointed out that the drug use at 2 months was limited to tablets taken orally.

A report by Wisocki (1973b) of successfully using covert conditioning to treat a heroin addict is particularly interesting in a number of ways. First, the only procedure used, other than covert conditioning, was thought stopping. Second, Wisocki doubted the treatment would be successful in an office setting and made this quite clear to the client, thus reducing both client and therapist expectations. Third, the client had previously failed in several other drug treatment programs, including Synanon and methadone main-

---

* Elkins (1976) has also reported several cases and Wilson and Tracey (1976) a single case of actual vomiting following covert sensitization of alcohol consumption. Perhaps, rather than nausea, other aversive stimuli such as insects, fire, or imagined electric shock would be less "dangerous" and more effective to use with clients who have such extensive experience with vomiting that it comes easily to them and may no longer be a particularly aversive experience. Although to date we have never had the experience of having a client actually vomit during treatment with covert sensitization, this issue does present an interesting research question. Is treatment more effective if the client actually vomits during covert sensitization, does it make no difference, or, as suggested above, might it for certain groups of "easy vomiters" be less effective?

tenance. Fourth, the client expressed his willingness to cooperate fully with treatment, as he had with the earlier treatment programs.

Initially, CPR was used to strengthen drug refusal. Next, thought stopping was added to interfere with reinforcing thoughts about heroin. Finally covert sensitization was applied to scenes of attempted heroin use. Instead of vomiting scenes, which are often employed in CS, Wisocki alternated among scenes of insect swarms, contracting leprosy, and wallowing in sewage. Treatment was limited to 12 sessions, since the client was very adept at self-control applications of covert conditioning. Eighteen months after treatment, the client remained heroin free.

Covert sensitization was used in conjunction with electrical aversion, relaxation training, and systematic desensitization by O'Brien, Raynes, and Patch (1972) to successfully treat two heroin addicts. According to the authors, the "use of verbal imagery as a USC permitted a substantial reduction in the number of shock deliveries" (p. 79).

An interesting case reported by Tepfer and Levine (1977) suggests both the potential power of covert sensitization and the use of related natural consequences in constructing the aversive components of the scenes. The client, a 58-year-old male, had a 32-year history of heavy alcohol abuse. During a 7-week treatment program, the therapist began by treating the client's preexisting alcohol-related health concerns and developed scenes of liver and stomach deterioration and other related physical complications. Social reinforcement was minimal in that the client's wife refused to compliment him for his changes in behavior and his reduced domestic quarreling. Nevertheless, a 78-week follow-up revealed that the client was still free from alcohol use.

DeBerry (1981) used covert sensitization in the context of a Basic ID program (Lazarus, 1973) for treating a 298-pound woman for obesity. Covert sensitization was applied sequentially to particularly troublesome foods and food groups in a multiple baseline-like approach. The woman had lost 103 pounds at the time of a 2-year follow-up. DeBerry points out that the effects of covert sensitization were highly specific. Although beer drinking was targeted, with the effects generalizing to other alcoholic beverages, there were no changes in other areas until fried foods were targeted. According to DeBerry (1981):

> The fact that other baseline measures showed no change further reinforces the power and specificity of covert sensitization. Covert sensitization appears to be very powerful and specific in its effect and seems indicated in treating eating responses of a highly specific nature. (pp. 17–18)

In a brief 1973 case report, Maletzky described the use of valeric acid to strengthen the effect of covert sensitization in assisting a client to overcome her chocolate-eating behavior. Valeric acid is a particularly foul-smelling substance. Maletzky further describes this procedure, which he calls "assisted" covert sensitization, in additional reports listed in the Bibliography. Maletzky's report on its application to drug abuse (1974) is particularly relevant to the present topic.

Hay et al. (1977 used a variation of CM to treat a longstanding drinking problem. The variation was that the model used in the scenes was the client himself. The client was taught to use CM as a self-control device during troublesome situations.

A typical scene employed by the authors is described below:

> Imagine yourself walking in town and running into a group of your old drinking buddies. They have already been drinking heavily and ask you to join them. They are drinking White Lightning. They look happy and you are alone. In the past you would have taken a drink and probably have become drunk. Now, cope with the situation. Imagine yourself feeling the "urge" to drink but refusing and slowly turning and walking down the street. (Hay et al., 1977, p. 71)

An 11-month follow-up revealed one 3-day drinking binge at about 3 months.

Although CM as originally developed (Cautela, 1971b) involved having the client observe another individual as the model, sometimes after observing another model clients have been instructed to observe themselves as the model. This is especially useful when shaping clients to imagine that they are actually performing the behavior, rather than observing a model.

Recommendations

Before starting out on a program of using covert conditioning to modify a client's maladaptive approach behavior, it is usually helpful to ask the client to try to decrease the behavior without direct therapist intervention. The behavior and situations they report as still being troublesome then become likely targets of covert conditioning.

Covert sensitization is clearly the most frequently used covert conditioning procedure with consummatory and other maladaptive approach behaviors. Both experimental and clinical reports testify to this fact. In some instances CE has also been effective with these kinds of problems. It should be emphasized, however, that in the elimination of these unwarranted behaviors, other appropriate incompatible behaviors must be established and strengthened.

Maladaptive approach behaviors are generally more difficult to treat than avoidance behaviors, probably because giving up reinforcement puts the organism into extinction, which results in aggression. Also, in many maladaptive approach behaviors the number of reinforcements is often large. In the case of cigarette smoking, for example, suppose an individual averages one package per day for 10 years. That is 20 cigarettes times 365 days times 10 years, or 73,000 cigarettes. Assuming, conservatively, that only one puff per cigarette is reinforcing, that still is a strong reinforcement history to overcome.

Reinforcement for engaging in maladaptive approach behavior is usually positive, but sometimes negative as well. Positive reinforcement may come from the taste (e.g., food, drink, cigarettes), physiological reaction (e.g., drug high), and social approval of peers (usually more important when individuals are first beginning to use potentially addictive substances). Negative reinforcement can come into play when the consuming of the substance reciprocally inhibits the anxiety which the individual may have been experiencing prior to ingestion.

Intermittent reinforcement schedules strengthen behavior. Occasional trials which do not result in the sought-after high, reduced anxiety, or other desired effects may only serve to more firmly establish the maladaptive behavior. Both antecedents and consequences must be neutralized in treating maladaptive approach behaviors. In treating antecedent conditions such as anxiety, CPR, CM, the SCT, thought stopping, relaxation training, and systematic desensitization have all proven particularly useful. Covert sensitization and CE are helpful in eliminating the maladaptive response by changing the consequences, and CPR, CM, behavioral rehearsal, assertiveness training, and contingency contracting all can be employed in establishing the new, adaptive behavior.

When performing the behavior analysis of a maladaptive approach behavior, a chain of behaviors leading up to and culminating in the consumption of the substance of concern can usually be identified. Through pairing with the final link—the consumption—the next to last link becomes a conditioned reinforcer, which then reinforces the preceding link. In this way, all links become conditioned reinforcers and serve a dual function as the reinforcer of the preceding link and also as the discriminative stimulus for the following link.

A series of links in a hypothetical chain for a "compulsive eater"—which could, of course, easily be broken down into finer steps—follows below. The recommended covert conditioning procedure for treating each link is included in parenthesis.

1. The individual notices a stack of bills that are nearly due (CPR—to reduce anxiety).
2. The individual becomes anxious (CPR).
3. The anxious individual walks into the kitchen (covert sensitization—to reduce the probability of this behavior),
4. goes over to a cabinet (Co. Sens.),
5. opens the door (Co. Sens.),
6. reaches for (Co. Sens.), and
7. takes out a box of cookies (Co. Sens.).
8. The individual opens the package (Co. Sens.),
9. reaches in (Co. Sens.),
10. takes out a handful of cookies (Co. Sens.), and
11. starts placing them in his mouth (Co. Sens.).
12. He chews quickly and (Co. Sens.)
13. swallows (Co. Sens.).

For a short time there is a reduction of anxiety (negative reinforcement) and perhaps the consumption of the cookie is positively reinforcing in itself.

Once a behavioral chain is set underway, it can be compared to a snowball running downhill, gathering momentum as it goes on. The events that occur toward the end of the chain are closer to the final reinforcer and are, therefore, more strongly reinforced and firmly established than earlier links in the chain. Those events closer to the beginning are more removed from the unconditioned reinforcer and probably are relatively new components of the chain and have received less reinforcement.

A chain is obviously more easily broken at its weaker links. Occasionally a segment of one chain may link with another established chain, thus bringing about a situation with, at least temporarily, the weakest link somewhere in the middle of the new, longer chain. Usually, however, the weakest links are at the beginning of the chain and should be targeted for disruption by covert sensitization.

Several points for interruption of the maladaptive approach sequences should be included in treatment. These interruptions should take place prior to the actual consumption of the abused substance. In the case of the cookie eater described above, the sequence might be disrupted at various points using different procedures. For example, CPR could be used to reduce the anxiety related to unpaid bills. Covert sensitization could be applied to the sequence from opening the kitchen cabinet through chewing the cookies. CE might normally be considered for use with the taste of the cookies, but some individuals with eating disorders do not attend very closely to the taste of the food they are eating. Other stimuli such as sensation involved in swallowing, for example, may also serve as reinforcers of the eating disorder. CE must therefore eliminate all consequent stimuli, not just the taste. In many cases reinforcement may result from reduced anxiety. In these cases, CE might not be particularly useful.

On the other hand, CNR would be useful to alternate with the covert sensitization trials. The client could be instructed to imagine rejecting the cookies and immediately experience relief from the anxiety and aversive scene, thereby being negatively reinforced for avoiding or escaping the cookies. CPR or CM might be used in conjunction with the above procedures to increase the likelihood of more appropriate behavior, such as paying one's bills on time. Finally, the client could be instructed to use thought stopping and the SCT to reduce the subsequent guilt and anxiety on occasions when the cookies actually are consumed.

In experimental studies in which covert conditioning is used for the modification of maladaptive approach behaviors, the number of trials is understandably predetermined for purposes of experimental control. The amount of treatment experimental subjects receive is almost always less than clients receive in clinical settings. The number of trials required clinically is substantially higher than the number of trials reported in experimental studies. In group factoral studies, a statistically significant trend is usually adequate for success. Clinical applications, however, require not only the elimination of the overt behavior, but also additional trials after the behavior appears to be eliminated to provide overlearning to help protect the client against relapse. These additional trials, which may last approximately four to eight sessions, should be directed at the elimination of both strong and weak urges to engage in the unwanted behavior as well as at the behavior itself. With regard to drug abuse, for example, clinical experience suggests that at least 200 to 300 covert sensitization trials are required to eliminate urges toward drug-related stimuli.

Covert sensitization is specific in its effect. Someone with a general alcohol problem, for example, may have to be sensitized independently to beer, wine, and hard liquor. When working with a client with an eating problem, individual food groups should be targeted, not just the act of eating. Specific troublesome situations, such as eating between meals, second helpings, and midnight snacks, must also be targeted. Clients who have difficulty limiting themselves to a caloric count of, for example, 1000 calories per day are often instructed to use covert sensitization on whatever foods take them over the desired total.

An additional consideration when dealing with drug abuse is the phenomenon of state-specific learning. Learning that takes place while under the influence of one drug may not transfer to other drugs or to the nondrugged state. Therefore, treatment may have to be conducted before, during, and after drug withdrawal if possible.

While the influence of consequences on behavior has been emphasized, the importance of antecedent conditions and stimulus control is, unfortunately, often overlooked. In dealing with anxiety-related behaviors, relaxation training can be particularly useful in weakening the control of certain environmental stimuli. If it is known in advance that an anxiety-provoking situation is approaching, the client can be taught to relax before, during, and after exposure to situations that in the past have led to excessive eating, drinking, smoking, or drug use. Thought stopping or the SCT can be used to control covert responses which may be precursors to maladaptive approach behaviors. Occasionally it may be helpful and necessary to employ CPR to desensitize the client to the situation and to the tensions arising from not consuming.

The importance of teaching new behaviors to replace those eliminated cannot be overemphasized. Eliminating a behavior that has served to reduce a client's anxiety without replacing it with more appropriate means of handling the anxiety is incomplete treatment. It leaves the client in a situation where the environment will randomly select some other response or response chain to condition to the anxiety-provoking stimuli. In terms of temporal sequence, it is usually more effective to have new behaviors in place and receiving reinforcement before eliminating old behaviors. This is not always practical, however, particularly in cases of excessive drug or alcohol abuse in which covert sensitization may have to be employed immediately to begin getting the maladaptive behavior under control. In cases like this, it may be possible to target both an inappropriate behavior for deceleration and an appropriate incompatible behavior for acceleration at the same time. By alternating CPR and covert sensitization trials, both could be treated simultaneously.

Covert conditioning is usually used in conjunction with other behavioral procedures, such as relaxation training, systematic desensitization, contingency management, and thought stopping. Treatment should continue until the overt behavior and strong and weak urges have been eliminated. More adaptive behaviors must also be taught to the client to replace those eliminated.

Case Example

A 35-year-old woman gave as her presenting complaint the eating of two dozen bagels a day, besides her regular meals. The client was quite obese. She was 5'1" and weighed 250 pounds. She felt that if she could just stop eating bagels, she would lose weight, since she also ate three regular meals every day. CE was employed to reduce her urges to eat bagels. She was presented with the following rationale:

> Whatever the original reasons or present reasons you eat bagels, we know that, at the present time, you have severe cravings for bagels and that you enjoy the taste, the sensation of swallowing, and the feeling of fullness you get when you eat the bagels. There is a technique I can teach you to help you lose your craving for bagels. Of course, if you lose your craving, you will be able to control whether you eat them or not. Now, close your eyes and relax. Now, I want you to imagine that you are taking a bite out of a bagel and you start chewing it, but you don't taste anything—nothing at all. There is no taste. You only have sensations of biting through something. When you swallow, you don't notice the sensation of swallowing. There is nothing there and your stomach doesn't feel full. Now, remember, it is very important that you imagine that you are really eating a bagel and that it has no taste. It doesn't taste like cardboard; it doesn't taste like dirt. It has no taste.

Ten scenes were necessary before she could really start to imagine that she was eating bagels and that they had no taste. The scene involved eating different kinds of bagels in different situations. The scenes were all taped, and she was asked to play the tape twice a day. At the next session, she reported excitedly that her craving had decreased and that she was down to a dozen bagels a day. The following week she reported averaging five bagels a day, and she was continuing her practice sessions faithfully.

On the fourth week she reported she had completely lost the urge to eat bagels. It is important to note that she did not substitute other foods for the bagels nor did she feel in any way deprived. She felt highly reinforced by being able to control her "will power."

She was seen for 6 more weeks in order to continue CE and relaxation training. She was also taught CPR with feeling comfortable when she had an empty stomach. At the time of discharge, she had lost 55 pounds. A 6-month follow-up indicated that she was still no longer eating bagels and weighed 150 pounds. She was continuing to lose weight very slowly.

6

Sexual Dysfunction

The ethics of attempting to change particular sexual behaviors, especially with regard to sexual preference, has sometimes been questioned. From both an ethical and a practical point of view, it is our contention that the decision of whether or not to change an individual's sexual orientation must be made by the client rather than by society at large or subgroups of that culture. The practical dimension is simply that unlike many overt behavior modification procedures, covert conditioning requires the client's cooperation. In support of this point, Alford, Wedding, and Jones (1983) conducted a single-subject design study involving sexual responses in which the subject demonstrated the ability to employ competing imagery to fully block the intended effect of covert sensitization.

Also to this point, in a 1980 study Maletzky (1980b) found a variation of covert sensitization, which he referred to as "assisted" covert sensitization, to be as effective in treating exhibitionistic and pedophilic behavior of involuntary subjects as in treating self-referred subjects. Maletzky described involuntary, court-referred subjects as "The patient entered therapy under coercion from a legal source" (p. 308). A careful reading of this report, however, suggests that although the clients did not begin treatment fully of their own accord, they were cooperative with treatment once underway. Therefore, even if there were no ethical factors to be considered, covert conditioning could not likely be used to change a client's behavior against his/her wishes since it is the client who actually performs the covert conditioning. The therapist is simply the instructor or guide. For the purposes of this chapter then, we will consider any sexual behavior dysfunctional if the client has expressed a desire to change that behavior.

Aversive Conditioning of Sexual Behavior

Since the advent of behavior therapy, various techniques falling under the broad heading of aversion therapy have been used in attempts to modify maladaptive approach behavior, that is, the " . . . approach to undesirable but pleasurable activities" (Cautela, 1966, p. 33). In the early years of behavior therapy, classical conditioning was the primary approach used in dealing with sexual deviations. In the late 1950s and early 1960s, the use of chemicals, usually apomorphine (Freund, 1960; James, 1962), was experimented with quite extensively by therapists and researchers. The application of chemicals, however, has caused many problems. Among them is the fact that the use of chemicals may lead to increased aggressiveness on the part of the client toward the therapist. It is impossible to time the noxious stimulus for the best opportunity to pair it with the behavior to be modified. It is considered dehumanizing by many. It may have unpleasant and/or lasting side effects. It is not a desirable or practical self-control stimulus.

As the use of chemical aversion became less popular, the use of electric shock became more widespread (Clark, 1965; MacCulloch, Feldman, & Pinschoff, 1965; McGuire & Vallance, 1964; Solyom & Miller, 1965; Thorpe, Schmidt, & Castell, 1964). Electric (or Faradic) shock had many advantages over the use of chemicals. It was much more easily controlled and measured with regard to both timing and intensity. It could also be used as a partial reinforcer, it provided better opportunities for the substitution of alternative responses, and it was not messy. Electric shock also had limitations, however. The necessity of additional equipment, charges of dehumanization, aggressiveness by the client, ill feelings toward the therapist, and lack of client control were among these.

Since there were many difficulties with overt aversive stimuli, Gold and Neufeld (1965) began working with an aversive technique which required neither the use of chemicals nor the application of electric shock. Working with a 16-year-old male homosexual, they constructed a hierarchy of the major anxiety-provoking situations in his life. After desensitizing him to these situations through the use of systematic desensitization, they began their direct attack on the overt homosexual behavior. After relaxing the client,

> . . . an emotive image was suggested of the patient in a situation of danger. He was encouraged to visualize himself in a toilet alongside a most unprepossessing old man. It was suggested that he would not under any circumstances solicit such a person. When the patient agreed to this suggestion (by signal), he was rewarded with the words "well done." The

images of the man whom he rejected in this way was slowly changed to a more attractive form, but at the same time surrounded by prohibitions, such as the image of a policeman standing nearby. With this technique the patient quickly learned to reject an otherwise acceptable and attractive young man, even in the absence of prohibitions. (p. 203)

In the final stage of their treatment, Gold and Neufeld presented the subject with a discriminative learning task—the choice of a young man or a young woman. The choice of the woman was originally associated with positive cues and the choice of the man with negative cues. As these cues were gradually faded out, the subject continued to choose the female stimuli. A one-year follow-up reported the cessation of homosexual behavior and the presence of normal heterosexual activity.

Kolvin (1967), " . . . due to a reluctance to use physical methods with adolescents . . . " (p. 245), searched for a technique which would achieve the same ends, but without the use of physical means. His result, which he labeled " 'Aversive Imagery Therapy' essentially consists of the evocation, in the imagination, of the specific erotogenic or compulsive stimulus and the immediate disruption of it by the evocation of a noxious aversive stimulus" (p. 245).

Empirical Evidence and Case Reports

As we shall see in the case studies described below, the general pattern in employing covert conditioning to modify sexual behavior is to use CPR and CM to teach and strengthen new behaviors and to use covert sensitization and the SCT to eliminate behaviors inconsistent with the client's goals.

McConaghy, Armstrong, and Blaszczynski (1981) compared covert sensitization with electrical aversion for treating compulsive homosexuality. Divided into two groups of 10 subjects each, participants were treated with either electrical aversion or covert sensitization. The behavior targeted was compulsive homosexual urges. Results of a one-year follow-up showed covert sensitization to be as effective as electrical aversion. The authors concluded that covert sensitization should therefore be considered the treatment of choice.

Because of the nature of sexual problems, it is almost impossible to conduct experiments involving large groups of subjects receiving various treatments. Therefore nearly all of the published reports of the use of covert conditioning to treat sexual dysfunctions have been case studies and single-subject design experiments. A review of the literature shows that uses of covert conditioning in treating sexual dysfunction usually involved covert sensitization applied to various behavioral patterns, including homosexuality (Hayes, Brownell, & Barlow, 1983; Maletzky & George, 1973), pedophilia (Hayes et al., 1983; Levin, Barry, Gambaro, Wolfinsohn, & Smith, 1977; Maletzky, 1980b), gender-identity confusion (Barlow, Reynolds, & Agras, 1973), incestuous behavior (Harbert, Barlow, Hersen, & Austin, 1974), clothes fetish (Glick, 1972), fire fetish (Lande, 1980), promiscuity (Anant, 1968d), exhibitionism (Alford, Webster, & Sanders, 1980; Hayes et al., 1983; Hughes, 1977; Maletzky, 1980a), obscene phone calling (Alford et al., 1980), transvestite fantasy (Gershman, 1970), and sadistic sexual fantasies (Hayes, Brownell, & Barlow, 1978). In additional applications, CPR has been used to assist in encouraging heterosexual behavior (Kendrick & McCullough, 1972), and Hay et al., (1981) used CM to treat gender-identity confusion (see section on CM in Chapter 2).

Through the use of the Reinforcement Survey Schedule (RSS) (Cautela & Kastenbaum, 1967), Kendrick and McCullough (1972) found that a homosexual client judged homosexual fantasies to be extremely vivid and reinforcing. Since the client wished to change his sexual orientation, the authors employed the Premack Principle in applying CPR. That is, the high-probability homosexual images were visualized immediately after the less frequent and less reinforcing heterosexual images. Over a 6-week period, the ratio of heterosexual to homosexual images was gradually increased to 5:1. Covert sensitization was then applied to homosexual urges and fantasies while nonsexual reinforcers identified through the RSS replaced the homosexual images to continue strengthening the heterosexual images and urges. At a 3-month follow-up session the client reported that his homosexual urges were greatly diminished and his heterosexual behavior continued to increase.

Burdick (1972) successfully used covert sensitization to treat six cases of exhibitionism. Treatment ranged from 10 to 26 sessions, and at the time of the follow-up contacts, which ranged from 2 to 6 months after treatment, all of the clients had refrained from exposing themselves. Burdick reports that it was evident that the reinforcers maintaining the exhibitionistic behavior in most cases were the orgasms the clients experienced while either overtly or covertly exposing themselves. Burdick also identified three situations in which the exhibitionistic behavior/orgasm reinforcer took place: (1) masturbating while overtly exposing oneself, (2) masturbating while covertly (fantasizing about) exposing oneself, and (3) having intercourse while covertly exposing oneself.

Evidence of the specificity of covert sensitization effects was found by Brownell and Barlow (1976) while treating a male exhibitionist who also frequently attempted to engage in sexual behavior with his stepdaughter. Although after treatment the stepdaughter no longer elicited sexual arousal in the client, he still maintained a strong desire to interact with her in a nonsexual manner.

Hayes et al., (1978) reported a "self-administered covert sensitization" (SACS) program in which the client was taught to use covert sensitization primarily as a self-control device when the therapist was not directly and immediately accessible for assistance. SACS was used to sequentially treat exhibitionistic arousal and sadistic rape arousal. Similar to Burdick's (1972) clients mentioned above, this individual seems to have strengthened his dysfunctional fantasies by pairing them with masturbation while he was imprisoned for armed robbery. The aversive components of the covert sensitization scenes used were related natural consequences such as being caught, arrested, and divorced by his wife, rather than the more traditional aversive scenes such as vomiting, insects, fire, or feces. This client was considered to be already quite heterosexually skillful, so the authors found the use of SACS to control the dysfunctional fantasies sufficient treatment for him.

In a series of more recent cases, the same authors (Hayes et al., 1983) treated four additional clients with assorted sexual dysfunctions. This time, however, the authors found it necessary to provide the clients with 11 one-hour comprehensive social skills training sessions prior to beginning 8 covert sensitization sessions. The social skills training was successful in reducing the remaining inappropriate arousal. Interestingly, all four subjects showed further improvement in social skills following the covert conditioning stage of treatment. The authors commented that:

> It may be that covert sensitization allows subjects to show heterosexual skills which were suppressed by competing behaviors (private statements about the deviant tendencies, resultant anxiety and so on). Since this effect was shown even in subjects with little apparent remaining deviant arousal, if supported such an interpretation would imply that covert sensitization has value beyond the suppression of sexual arousal *per se*. (p. 391)

Although many authors comment that the effects of covert sensitization are quite specific (e.g., Brownell & Barlow, 1976, above), Alford et al. (1980) reported a case in which there appeared to be some generalization. The client was to be treated first for obscene phone calling and then for exhibitionism using both therapist-administered covert sensitization and the SACS procedure described by Hayes et al. (1978), which was mentioned above. During the obscene phone calling stage, the client reported a decrease in exhibitionistic urges. The authors speculated that this may have resulted from common elements of both behavioral patterns.

> Both entail sudden unsolicited attempts to gain the attention of strangers to exhibit either verbally or behaviorally sexually oriented expressions and one's sexual arousal. Both involve sexual gratification for the perpetrator without physical contact with the victim, but with desired and provoked fear, aversion, or "shock" responses by the victim. (p. 23)

One could also posit that since the client, a former college student and successful businessman, was already employing the SACS procedures on obscene phone calling, unknown to the therapist he might have begun applying it to exhibitionistic behavior as well.

When covert sensitization is used clinically, it is often helpful to alternate covert sensitization trials with scenes in which the client avoids or escapes from the aversive situation by performing an adaptive behavior incompatible with the maladaptive behavior. For example, an individual imagining him-/herself about to make an obscene phone call while becoming nauseous turns and leaves the phone booth and immediately feels better. Although this procedure is sometimes referred to as covert aversion relief, it is essentially CNR presented in a flow-scene manner.

Bellack (1974) treated a homosexual man using a variation of this procedure. After three sessions of covert sensitization, Bellack added the CNR-aversion relief component. A 3- to 6-minute homosexual–vomiting scene was followed by a 3- to 6-minute heterosexual relief scene. A 4-month follow-up found the client heterosexually adjusted.

A report by Hughes (1977) describes the use of escape and avoidance components with covert sensitization in treating exhibitionism. In the escape scenes the therapist instructed the client to imagine extreme nausea while in the act of exposing himself. The nausea was escaped when the client, in imagination, fled the situation. The avoidance trials were conducted by having the client begin to get nauseous at earlier points in the chain leading to exposure. The extreme nausea was avoided when the client disrupted the chain and experienced relief. Although the client had been exposing himself four or five times a month for 5 years, only 22 scenes, over five therapy sessions, were apparently sufficient. When contacted 3 years later, the client reported that he had not exhibited himself since the termination of treatment. Although the therapist suggested that the client do home-work scenes, he declined fearing the imagery "would focus his attention on the undesired thoughts" (Hughes, 1977, p. 178).

Typically, self-control applications of covert conditioning have focused on lessening anxiety or counteracting urges to engage in maladaptive behavior. As shown by Denholtz (1973), however, covert conditioning can also be used in a self-control manner to strengthen appropriate behavior. In addition to teaching homosexual clients to use self-control covert sensitization to control day-to-day homosexual urges, Denholtz instructs clients to notice positive responses to women which occur in daily life and to consequate those responses with reinforcing imagery, thereby adapting CPR to self-control use.

Probably the best-known variation of covert sensitization is "assisted" covert sensitization (Maletzky, 1973). In this procedure the therapist's description of a nauseous scene is accompanied by holding an open bottle of valeric acid under the client's nose. Although "assisted" covert sensitization has been used with other approach behaviors (e.g., eating disorders), most of the reports in the literature describe applications to sexual dysfunctions. Sexual dysfunctions treated with "assisted" covert sensitization include homosexuality (Maletzky, 1973; Maletzky & George, 1973), exhibitionism (Maletzky, 1974), and pedophilic behavior (Levin et al., 1977; Maletzky, 1980a). Follow-up reports are quite good, although booster sessions have been found helpful with those clients who do not undergo a larger life-style change (Maletzky, 1977).

The following case illustrates one way in which covert conditioning has been used together with other procedures in treating sexual dysfunction. Rehm and Rozensky (1974) used covert sensitization as one part of a multiple treatment approach to treat a homosexual client. The authors first employed an informational counseling strategy to clear up many of the misconceptions the client had about homosexuality. This was followed by the use of systematic de-sensitization with the client's heterosexual anxiety. The client was asked to keep records of heterosexual and homosexual contacts between sessions. Reporting homosexual contacts was aversive to him and may have helped reduce their frequency (or at least the reporting of their frequency). Covert sensitization was simultaneously used to reduce overt homosexual behavior. The authors also employed Faradic shock in conjunction with both male and female slides and homo-sexual imagery scenes. Orgasmic reconditioning (Marquis, 1970) was then introduced to change his masturbatory fantasies from male to female. Finally, assertiveness training and role-playing were used to reestablish appropriate heterosexual behavior.

The first known successful change of gender identity of a trans-sexual was reported by Barlow et al., (1973). In a complex treatment program, which involved a great many behavioral treatment procedures, the authors sequentially modified several of the client's gender stereotypical motor, social, and speech behaviors. This was followed by changing sexual fantasies and sexual arousal patterns from homosexual to heterosexual, again requiring the use of multiple procedures including covert sensitization.

Recommendations

Many of the recommendations made with regard to consummatory behaviors are also pertinent to maladaptive sexual approach behaviors. Two of the most important recommendations are, first, to establish a repertoire of appropriate behavior to replace the behaviors to be eliminated and, second, to weaken the target behavioral sequence at early links in the chain as well as nearer the end. It is also helpful to remember that one of the reinforcers involved in many sexual dysfunctions (orgasm) is often very powerful.

When performing the behavior analysis of sexual dysfunctions, it is particularly important to attend to specific details of inappropriate sexual stimuli. For example, does the client prefer sexual partners who are obese or thin, short or tall, young or old, intellectual or frivolous, athletic or sedentary, assertive or compliant, willing or unwilling? After the troublesome sexual stimuli are identified,

> One essentially builds up a hierarchy of the desirable sexual objects and the avoidable contacts of likely sexual stimulation. Covert sensitization is applied to all items in the hierarchy, with the most desirable sexual objects being treated first. (Cautela, 1967, p. 468)

Clinical applications of covert conditioning to the treatment of sexual dysfunctions should be continued until overt behaviors and the strong and weak urges are eliminated. Clients can also be taught the SCT and other self-control procedures to help them through temptations they face in daily life.

The general pattern of most treatment programs for sexual dysfunctions is to begin strengthening appropriate behaviors before eliminating inappropriate behaviors. The development of appropriate behaviors is often the most difficult aspect of this approach and varies considerably depending on the client's current behavioral repertoire. Techniques such as CPR and systematic desensitization can be helpful in overcoming anxiety related to approaching appropriate sexual partners. CPR can be employed to strengthen attraction to the appropriate sexual stimuli. Behavioral rehearsal, modeling, CM, CPR, and assertiveness training are useful in teaching appropriate social skills for heterosexual situations. Assertiveness training can also make it easier for some clients to refuse approaches by former homosexual partners. Clients who have received a great deal of reinforcement from a subculture centered around sexual behavior patterns can require a lot of supportive counseling and assistance in finding ways of replacing those external sources of reinforcement and social networks.

In working with homosexual clients, the use of male and female co-therapists has been effective (Cautela & Wisocki, 1969b). The therapist of the same sex works with the client to reduce sexual attraction to persons of the same sex and to develop appropriate assertive behaviors, while the opposite-sex therapist helps the client to reduce anxiety related to the presence of persons of the opposite sex and to acquire appropriate social skills with and attraction to the opposite sex. An advantage of this approach is that the same-sex therapist is the recipient of any ill feelings related to the use of aversive procedures, whereas the opposite-sex therapist is associated with reduced anxiety. Each co-therapist must be careful not to get involved in discussing with the client the aspect of the problem being treated by the other co-therapist, other than to verbally reinforce appropriate statements made by the client.

An opposite-sex co-therapist in the same age range as persons with whom the client hopes to be interacting is particularly useful since it would seem likely that such a person would be more familiar with appropriate heterosexual social practices such as dating behavior than a person of another generation and would be more effective in behavioral rehearsal scenes. Clients with whom the co-therapist approach has been employed have reacted quite positively to it, in terms of both effectiveness and their stated satisfaction.

The general procedure recommended in treating sexual dysfunction includes four steps:

1. Raise the client's general level of reinforcement. This serves to counteract the reduction in general level of reinforcement which might otherwise result from modifying previously reinforcing sexual behavior in the early stages of a treatment program.
2. Provide the client with alternative sexual behaviors. It is not sufficient to simply eliminate undesirable sexual behaviors. The

client must also develop a new repertoire of appropriate sexual and related social behaviors to maximize the chances of treatment success. CPR and CM are frequently used for this purpose.

3. Use CPR and/or other nonaversive techniques to begin weakening the target behavior. CPR can, for example, be applied by having the client imagine a situation which in the past might have occasioned the performance of the inappropriate behavior, but now in the scene the client chooses not to engage in the target behavior.

4. Continue to weaken the undesirable target behavior. Covert sensitization can be used on the actual behaviors performed, fantasizing about engaging in those behaviors (nondirected covert self-modeling), and urges to perform the target behaviors. Covert sensitization can be taught to the client to use as a self-control device in in vivo situations too. The SCT can also be taught to use on urges or other antecedent behaviors leading up to the target behaviors.

Case Example

The following case is presented because of its complexity and because it required many interventions which illustrate how covert conditioning can be employed with sexual problems. An additional factor in choosing it for inclusion is that unlike the other cases presented in this chapter, which deal with the deceleration of inappropriate sexual approach behaviors, this case demonstrates the application of covert conditioning to increasing sexual behavior by treating a deficit in sexual arousal. The case is presented by the therapist involved, J.R. Cautela.

A 34-year-old woman complained that her husband was no longer interested in her sexually. She felt that this was an indication that their marriage was deteriorating and that her body had become physically unattractive to her husband. A discussion with her husband revealed that, indeed, he no longer found her physically attractive in any way, but he did feel strongly sexually attracted to other women. He agreed that if he were sexually attracted to his wife, he would feel the marriage was much more compatible, since she had many desirable qualities. When asked if he would like to be "turned on" to his wife, he said yes but he didn't think it was possible. He was asked if it were possible, would he want to try to be attracted to her. After a few moments, he responded, "Well, no, I don't know whether I want to change or not."

I suggested we delay the decision while we worked on other areas of his marriage and, if compatability was achieved in other areas, we would discuss the issue again.

After further marital therapy, the couple began to be very reinforcing to each other. In many areas they were able to communicate with each other and they both wanted to spend the rest of their lives with each other.

The husband still did not find his wife physically attractive, but now he wanted to cooperate in an effort to have her become more physically attractive to him. First, we tried to determine what there was about his wife's appearance or behavior that tended to make her physically unattractive to him. We then discussed possible ways to either have her change her behavior, if she were willing, or desensitize him to the aversive stimuli. For example, he perceived that she had a slight mustache but was hesitant to tell her about it because he was afraid that she would become hurt or enraged. After the three of us discussed this issue, she agreed to remove the facial hair and thought it was appropriate to do so. Also, she often snored loud enough to wake her husband during the night. That would enrage him. He would push her hard to get her on her side, then she would get angry and they would have an argument. We decided to desensitize him against her snoring by employing CPR.

An additional factor was that the husband was convinced that, no matter how well he performed, he would never be able to satisfy his wife sexually. In a three-way discussion, he was assured that at no time along the treatment process would she make demands beyond his current ability to perform sexually. Removing the above barriers did not automatically lead to sexual desire for his wife, but they did eliminate obstacles to his cooperation. Therefore the following procedures were introduced next:

1. Since he frequently masturbated while fantasizing having sex with other women, he was asked to imagine engaging in various touching and sexual behaviors with his wife just before orgasm (orgasmic reconditioning).
2. He was asked to scan his wife sexually as much as possible. For example, he was to deliberately look at her breasts and say to himself, "Wouldn't it be nice to have them in my mouth. It would feel good." When she bent over, he was asked to imagine that he was lying up against her back while they were both naked.

3. CPR was used to increase sexual fantasy involving his wife and to reinforce the effect of fantasy. For example:

> You and your wife are on vacation. You both are lying down on a beautiful beach. There is no one else around. Your wife has a skimpy bathing suit on. You look at her and say, "She has a nice body" (reinforcement). You reach over and start stroking her back. She groans with pleasure (reinforcement).

The fantasy was continued along until he was having intercourse with her on the beach, really enjoying it. He continued to be reinforced during various parts of the sexual fantasy. The scenes were put on tape and he was asked to play them every day. A number of other sexual fantasies that he rated as possibly enjoyable were also employed in CPR. Again he was asked to listen to the tape of these fantasies on a daily basis and all five fantasies were used.

Meanwhile, during this period, the couple was asked not to engage in any sexual behavior (paradoxical intention?). When the husband said he was really ready, really felt "turned on," sensate focus was employed. This involved the following regimen:

1. The couple was first instructed to lie side by side naked for half an hour while relaxing themselves (three sessions).
2. After they were able to do this successfully, they were to touch each other lightly all over their bodies except for their genitals, while giving each other feedback.
3. After they completed step 2 successfully, they were asked to add touching of the genitals lightly without any further sexual behavior for three sessions.
4. This step involved the other steps, including relaxing. By this time, they were able to stimulate each other in any way they desired for three sessions, but they were not to have intercourse. After they accomplished this regimen, they continued the last step and, if they both wanted to have sexual behavior, they were "allowed" to do so but they understood it was not required of either one of them.

During the sensate focus period, we discussed the results of the Sexual Behavior Survey Schedule (Cautela, 1977a) that was briefly administered. Covert conditioning was also used to eliminate anxiety with certain sexual behaviors if they both agreed it was appropriate for each other. The wife did not enjoy oral sex and found it to be highly distasteful, but she agreed to be desensitized to it and CPR was employed to possibly help it become more enjoyable.

At the end of the sensate focus period, three sessions after they began unlimited sexual touching, they had intercourse. They both found it quite enjoyable and then, for a period of 2 months, sex was quite frequent—between four and five times a week. Gradually by the end of 6 months, sexual performance leveled off to two or three times a week. They now felt they were sexually compatible and were quite happy about the marital situation.

7

Organic Dysfunction

Behavioral Medicine: Emergence of a Theory

In recent years, there has been a rapid development and increasing interest in the field of behavioral medicine. There is now an Academy of Behavioral Medicine within the National Academy of Science, and a Behavioral Medicine Interest Group within the Association for Advancement of Behavior Therapy. There is also a division of Health Psychology (Division 38) within the American Psychological Association. In addition, a Society of Behavioral Medicine has been formed; there are an increasing number of papers concerning behavioral medicine presented at conventions involving the helping professions; and there are a number of journals related to behavioral medicine receiving more and more submissions for publication.

For this emerging field, a definition of the discipline is still being sought. The Yale Conference on Behavioral Medicine (Schwartz & Weiss, 1977) proposed the following definition:

> Behavioral Medicine is the interdisciplinary field concerned with the development and integration of behavioral and biomedical scientific knowledge and techniques relevant to the understanding of health and illness, and the application of this knowledge and techniques to prevention, diagnosis, treatment and rehabilitation.

Behavioral medicine can be defined as "the application of behavioral principles to the prevention, assessment, and treatment of organic dysfunction."

In the last 20 years, while the covert conditioning model has been under development, covert conditioning procedures have been applied to produce changes in various organic dysfunctions. These dysfunctions were presented as either the major complaint (problems often referred to as "psychosomatic") or as an accompanying problem to the presenting complaint.

While empirical studies in behavioral medicine indicate much promise, there is a dearth of theoretical speculation and lack of a comprehensive theory to integrate the various approaches and resulting data. At this stage, the development of a theoretical model can have heuristic value. Some of the efforts of investigators to alter behaviors traditionally thought of as "purely organic" (e.g., seizures with known lesions in the cortex) have been met with skepticism, resistance, and even hostility. A theoretical model provides a context in which such attempts appear reasonable and logical. Derivations from the model can provide a source for the development of testable hypotheses.

Of particular importance to such a model is the *universal influence of consequences assumption* stated earlier. There is already some evidence indicating that operant conditioning can influence neural activity, cardiac rate, skin temperature, and pain (Cohen, 1967; Miller, 1935; Mostofsky, 1976; Schwartz & Higgins, 1971). Indeed, Weiss has commented that when you are reinforcing or establishing contingencies to behavior, you may be affecting the brain catecholamines (Seligman & Weiss, 1980, p. 483).

It is important to emphasize that an organic illness, such as arthritis, involves a disturbance in all three classes of behavior, for example, saying to oneself, "I feel like a cripple" (on a covert psychological level), the inflammation of the joints (on a physiological level), and the limitation of mobility, such as walking (on an overt behavioral level). An example concerns pain. An individual who has cancer complains of pain. He or she is reinforced by sympathy, or negatively reinforced by avoiding an aversive situation. Three classes of behavior are simultaneously reinforced: the verbal behavior of complaining, the covert behavior of thoughts of despair, and the sensation of pain and proliferation of cancer cells (if they are occurring at the time of the reinforcement). Another example: If an individual has an epileptic seizure (even with known organic etiology), and this is followed by reinforcement (that is, hugs, words of sympathy, avoidance of a particular situation), one would expect the following events to occur: The frequency of seizure behavior would increase; the nervous system activity present during the seizure is more apt to be repeated; and whatever covert processes are going on immediately prior to, and during, the seizure would increase in probability of occurrence. There is some evidence that seizures can be influenced by antecedents and consequences (Cautela & Flannery, 1973; Forster, 1966; Lubar & Bahler, 1976). In an unpublished case, a variety of covert conditioning procedures were employed with a 6-year-old hospitalized girl who had akinetic seizures with demonstrated brain pathology. After a 3-month period of baseline behavioral analysis and staff training, treatment was started. CPR was used to reduce the effects of antecedent conditions, such as requests and refusals. Overt extinction and CE were also employed on the seizure behavior. The staff was asked to ignore the child when she fell to the floor, as long as there was no medical or observable damage (she wore a helmet). Since the staff found it difficult to cooperate with extinction, the girl was trained in CE. She was asked to imagine pleasant scenes after not having a seizure in different situations (CPR). Seizures were markedly reduced during treatment.

Covert conditioning can be a useful procedure in severe cases of movement paralysis, such as amyotropic lateral sclerosis (ALS). The imagery procedures can be useful to treat levels of reinforcement, compliance, and fear reduction. One such case has already been treated. Even though the client could only signal with his eyes or finger, CPR was used to desensitize him to fear of going off a room respirator to a portable respirator.

If the assumption is valid that consequences, such as reinforcement, punishment, and extinction, influence *all* ongoing behavior of the organism simultaneously, there are far-reaching implications as to the influence of responses of significant others who are present when maladaptive behaviors occur in any of the three classes of behavior. A problem arises for the therapist when medically ill individuals are in one way or another expressing their symptomatology, that is, when and how do you respond to the behavior to indicate sympathetic support or to obtain more information? A suggested procedure is to listen attentively and sympathetically when the client expresses the symptoms one or two times, and then ignore the complaints expressed and continue the therapy session. While trying to ignore the behavior as much as possible, of course, any change in symptomatology is explored further. One must be careful, though, not to reinforce increased changes in symtomatology, while at the same time being alert for symptom change.

The Concept of Psychosomatic Medicine

Historically, the term *psychosomatic* has had three different meanings:

1. Body and mind (psychological factors) interact and influence each other.
2. The mind (psychological factors) can influence bodily factors (involving both the somatic and autonomic nervous systems).
3. The mind (psychological factors) can influence the autonomic nervous system to produce diseases (as distinguished from conversion reactions).

A study of the journals concerning psychosomatic illness and compilation of a list of illnesses considered psychosomatic indicate that the third definition appears to be the current operational one. However one defines "psychosomatic," there appears to be no a priori way to judge whether an illness is psychosomatic or not. Historically, labeling a disorder as psychosomatic appears to occur in the following manner:

1. A therapist notices that while a patient is improving psychologically, there is concomitantly an improvement in a particular organic dysfunction.
2. The assumption is then made that perhaps the organic dysfunction is influenced by psychological factors.
3. The therapist is then sensitized to observe the effects of psychological factors on that particular illness.
4. The therapist then notices that as the psychological condition varies, there is a similar variation in the organic illness.
5. The therapist sets out to treat the organic illness by manipulating psychological factors. In a number of instances, the attempts are successful.
6. The therapist publishes the observations and other therapists report similar anecdotal observations.
7. Controlled experiments are performed to test the assumption.

Unfortunately, the last step has not been rigorously pursued for investigation of illnesses termed "psychosomatic." According to the covert conditioning model, every illness has both psychological and physiological components interacting. Therefore, all illnesses require both behavioral and medical analysis and behavioral and medical treatment.

Applications of the Covert Conditioning Model to Organic Illness

Many of the applications of covert conditioning presented elsewhere in this book could easily have been included in this chapter. For example, substance abuse, obesity, stress/anxiety management, treatment of dental fears, and some sexual dysfunctions are commonly considered appropriate topics for the field of behavioral medicine. However, the amount of information available in several of these areas warrants their inclusion as separate chapters. The present arrangement should also make it easier for readers to locate topics of particular interest.

While behavioral medicine includes aspects of health care such as increasing compliance by the patient and helping the patient and family cope with illness, this chapter will focus on direct attempts to modify organic dysfunctions. Attempts to modify organic dysfunctions directly have a history in hypnosis (Kroger, 1963; Kroger & Fezler, 1976). More recently, biofeedback investigators have attempted to deal directly with such illnesses as migraine headaches (Epstein & Abel, 1977), stomach acidity (Welgan, 1974), and Raynaud's disease (Blanchard & Epstein, 1977). In the covert conditioning approach, organic illness is viewed in a manner similar to psychological disorders. The behavioral analysis proceeds in the same manner for organic illness as previously explained concerning psychological disorders (Cautela & Upper, 1976). Over 20 Organic Dysfunction Survey schedules are available to help with the behavior analysis (Cautela, 1981c). The organic dysfunction is operationally defined and attempts are then made to describe antecedents and consequences. For example, if the target behavior is asthmatic attacks, then the asthmatic attack is carefully described and records are kept concerning the frequency, duration, and intensity of the attacks. During the same period, environmental and psychological consequences (what occurs after the attack) are recorded. Behavioral analysis may reveal that entering fearful situations is likely to be followed by an asthmatic attack. Anger toward significant others may also precipitate an attack. The consequences observed may involve expressions of sympathy and love from significant others and avoidance of particular situations, such as going to work or school. In these situations therapy may include teaching the patient how to relax immediately when an asthmatic attack is beginning. In some cases, clients have been able to abort an asthmatic attack by making a relaxation response. The patient can be desensitized to the fearful situations that precede the attack and taught assertive behavior to decrease anger and increase feelings of mastery. Loved ones are encouraged to show attention and love when the client is not having an asthmatic attack, and ignore him or her as much as medically possible immediately before, during, and after the attack. CPR can be used to teach the client to approach situations that are avoided by the attack.

The pain response (Cautela, 1977c) is receiving a lot of attention, as evidenced by journal articles and the increasing number of clinics specializing in chronic pain. Our approach to the modification of pain behavior is to consider it a response that has antecedent and consequence components. One covert conditioning procedure often used to treat pain is the SCT.

Case Reports and Experimental Findings

Pain management has been an area of focus of a number of investigators (Craig & Best, 1977; Fordyce, 1973, 1976a, 1976b; Weisenberg, 1977). Scott and Leonard (1978) found that the effectiveness of the use of cognitive strategies could be increased by following the cognitive strategies with CPR scenes. A typical strategy used was imagining that the cold water one's hand was immersed in was refreshing. Subjects trained with CPR demonstrated a significantly higher pain threshold, when instructed to remove their hand from a container of ice water as soon as they experienced what they considered pain. Four additional experiments will illustrate the application of covert conditioning to pain control.

In the first study, Bennett and Cautela (1981) examined the relative contributions of reciprocal inhibition (RI) and covert conditioning to alter the pain response. One group of subjects imagined a cognitive strategy scene (adapted from the Scott and Leonard cognitive strategy scenes mentioned above) to reduce pain, followed by imagining an individually selected pleasant scene (CPR procedure). Another group imagined a pleasant scene followed by a cognitive strategy scene (RI procedure). A third group was employed in single-case experiments using CPR and RI to ask the same question. The overall results demonstrated the greater efficacy of the CPR procedure in modifying the pain response, thus lending support to an operant interpretation of CPR.

A second study, by Cleveland (1982), on Myofascial Pain Dysfunction syndrome (MPD), was designed to compare four distinct treatment modalities with a no-treatment control group for their relative effectiveness in alleviating reported pain and masseter muscle tension in MPD patients. Pain was measured by the McGill-Melzack Pain Questionnaire (Melzack, 1975) and the Visual Analogue Scale (Scott & Huskisson, 1976). Bioelectrical measures of masseter muscle tension were taken with a Cyborg J-33 electromyograph (Cyborg, 1979). The independent treatment variables were EMG biofeedback, relaxation training, covert conditioning, a mock biofeedback placebo, and a no-treatment control. In general, the results indicate that covert conditioning and biofeedback were effective for the reduction of reported pain and masseter muscle tension in cases of MPD syndrome. These results were maintained at a three-week follow-up. In addition, the covert conditioning group reported less pain than all other groups at the time of the follow-up.

The third study, carried out by McAndrew (1981), compared covert and overt conditioning in modifying pain behavior. In the first stage of the experiment, the author attempted to empirically validate reinforcers in the following manner. Four groups of 20 subjects received either covert reinforcement, covert punishment (covert sensitization), overt reinforcement, or overt punishment (response cost) contingent upon responding with certain numbers to instructions to emit numbers from 0 to 100. Although both overt and covert procedures proved to be effective, subjects exposed to overt consequences demonstrated greater changes. Fewer than 18 percent of the subjects could explain the contingency.

Eight groups of 10 subjects participated in the second stage, which employed the previously validated reinforcers in attempts to modify pain behavior. The first condition was CPR, in which the subjects imagined submerging a hand in ice water, followed by a reinforcing scene. The second condition provided subjects with external reinforcement for imagined water immersion. In the third condition, subjects performed the target behavior in vivo, followed by a covert reinforcer. The fourth condition consisted of overt immersion followed by overt reinforcement. Subjects in group five were asked to imagine first a reinforcing scene, then imagine increased pain tolerance, while subjects in the sixth group simply imagined increased pain tolerance. The seventh condition was an attempt to distract subjects by requiring them to count backwards, and subjects in the last group were simply asked to relax.

Results showed that while covert rehearsal of the target behavior was equivalent to overt rehearsal, covert reinforcement was more effective than overt reinforcement. In vivo exposure to the ice water, followed by covert reinforcement, was the most successful of all the treatments employed. The distraction, which obviously takes place while engaging in covert conditioning, may have been a factor contributing to the greater effectiveness of covert conditioning than overt conditioning in this experiment.

Stevens (1982) conducted the fourth study of the usefulness of covert conditioning in modifying pain behavior. As in the McAndrew (1981) study reported above, a cold-pressor pain task was used as the pain stimulus. In addition to CPR and an expectancy control group, subjects were also assigned to two additional imagery conditions. The author found that all conditions were effective in increasing pain tolerance and decreasing self-reported pain. While all groups showed significantly greater variance in pain tolerance at post-test than pre-test, only the CPR group shared greater post-treatment variance on the subjective pain rating.

In an anecdotal report of the uses of covert conditioning in pain management, Cautela (1977c) described treating a 37-year-old woman for pain related to her psoriatic arthritis condition. Pain was generalized throughout her body, with knees, toes, and wrists particularly severe. She had already undergone 5 years of psychotherapy for depression without apparent relief and was currently taking several medications. Relaxation training, the SCT, and CPR were used together with instructions to the client and her family. The CPR scenes involved having the client imagine herself in what, up until then, were painful situations (e.g., walking, unscrewing lids), but without pain. The client reported that after 3 weeks she no longer experienced pain in her knees and feet. Daily scene presentation was continued for an additional 3 weeks, and treatment as a whole continued beyond that. Eight months later, gains had been maintained and the use of some medications had been ended.

Wasserman (1978) used CPR to treat a 12-year-old boy with frequent complaints of stomach cramps and diarrhea related to school attendance. The legitimacy of the cramps was medically confirmed. The boy received 2 years of treatment in an outpatient clinic, relaxation training, and rational-emotive therapy before CPR was attempted. In order to decrease complaints and increase school attendance, Wasserman employed a variation of CPR in which the related reinforcing consequence flowed from the performance of the target behavior, thus avoiding the necessity of switching scenes. In these scenes, the boy imagined arriving at class still feeling comfortable and receiving a great deal of praise from significant others. After five CPR treatment sessions, complaints ceased. A six-month follow-up revealed no further complaints.

Speculation and Recommendations

In a previous article, Cautela (1977b) speculated that stress can exacerbate the development of cancer as well as hinder treatment effects. Our approach to cancer is to try to remove as much stress as possible, increase treatment compliance, reduce aversive symptoms, such as vomiting, nausea, and pain, and try to improve the quality of life by having the patient engage in more reinforcing activities. Since publication of that article, there seems to be a growing acceptance that stress can be a factor in the development and treatment of cancer.

One of the problems with organic illnesses, such as cancer and high blood pressure, is that it is very difficult to do a behavioral analysis in a traditional sense, since the increase in cancer proliferation and changes in blood pressure are not directly observable on an ongoing basis (thus, antecedents and consequences have to be inferred). This makes treatment less precise and less effective.

Many of us have witnessed that sometimes psychotropic drugs produce a paradoxical effect, rather than producing the intended effect (Kornetsky, 1976, p. 13). In the example of using drugs to decrease violent behavior, but violent behavior increases, it is possible that the patient imagines he is hitting and being violent, in spite of getting the drugs, and imagines the desired results, such as avoidance by others (CNR) or satisfaction in beating the system (CPR).

Cautela and Baron (1973) treated a case of severe self-injurious behavior in which many drugs had previously been administered in attempting to reduce the client's eye poking and lip biting. In spite of almost hypnotic doses of various drugs, self-injurious behavior had increased in frequency and severity. When the authors became involved in the case, they explored the nature of the client's imagery concerning self-injurious behavior. The client revealed that he would constantly imagine that he had the urge to poke or bite himself. Then he imagined the self-injurious behavior and the relief he would feel while engaging in the behavior. He also imagined the effect it would have on the staff in the institution. Covert conditioning was used to eliminate the maladaptive behavior. A hypothesis derived from the covert conditioning model would suggest that sometimes the paradoxical effects of a drug may be due to imagery that is antagonistic to the intended drug effect.

In the treatment of organic dysfunction, the importance of involvement by physicians is crucial. Clients should be under a physician's care, and communications between the physician and behavior therapist must take place and should be of an ongoing nature. The use of covert conditioning in treating organic dysfunction should, in no way, be thought of as a substitute for, or replacement of, medical treatment, but rather as a psychological intervention which can be useful in dealing with psychological aspects of the dysfunction.

Much has been written about operant components of pain. Earlier, studies were reviewed in which at least the pain stimuli, if not the pain perception/response, were objectively quantified. Case examples were given of how CPR and the SCT appear to have been helpful in modifying pain perception. Two other covert conditioning procedures which seem particularly well suited to the treatment of operant pain are CE and CM.

Although exceptionally cooperative clients might be required, CE might be employed to try to speed up the extinction process by providing additional learning trials while the client's family and medical staff attempt to overtly extinguish the pain responses. For example, the client would simply be instructed to imagine making inappropriate pain-related statements which are ignored by significant others. A potential use for CM would be in cases where the clients have received so much reinforcement from family members for physical complaints that they cannot imagine not receiving attention from loved ones for complaining.

The natural concern for the well-being of an ill family member is quite understandable. Unfortunately, well-meaning concern also has the possibility of reinforcing a greater rate of complaining and pain perception. Family members in these situations are often particularly susceptible to manipulation by the client, who in turn can be shaped into being a more effective manipulator, perhaps particularly adept at the use of hypochondriacal verbalizations, as time goes on. Even if the client recovers from a current ailment, there is the potential of the generalizing of complaining and manipulative behavior to other areas. An interesting analysis of manipulative verbal behavior is included elsewhere, in a paper on maladaptive verbal behavior (Glenn, 1983).

Client compliance with components of treatment plans, such as medication regimens and diet and/or exercise programs, is another problem to which covert conditioning can be applied. A behavior analysis of the situation may reveal that the client is receiving a great deal of attention for not complying and/or may be receiving reinforcement for behaving in a sickly manner. The client may fear that by getting well this reinforcement will be lost. While theoretically any of the covert conditioning procedures could be used in this area, CPR and CM appear to have the most straightforward application potentials. For example, we have successfully used CPR to improve client compliance to physician-prescribed medication schedules and both CPR and CM to increase adherence to exercise programs.

Case Example

The client was a 27-year-old schoolteacher who had six to eight asthma attacks per week. Although he had received drug therapy, he felt that it was not having any effect on the asthma. He was then seen for behavior therapy on a weekly basis for 6 months. A behavioral analysis, which included the use of the Asthma Survey Schedule (Cautela, 1981c), revealed the following antecedent conditions to asthmatic behavior: Just before or during a PTA meeting, socializing in the teachers' room, family social situations, and his wife leaving him alone with two children while she either did errands or went out with her friends. He also sometimes avoided the antecendent situations. One consequence identified was that when he was going through his attack, his wife would hug him and hold him in her lap and stroke his head.

He was taught progressive muscle relaxation to reduce the general level of arousal and instructed how to use the SCT when he felt an attack was about to occur. He sometimes noticed that he would start to feel slight chest pain and a funny feeling in the pit of his stomach before an attack. He was asked to use the SCT whenever he thought an attack was coming. CPR was used for fear of criticism by parents at PTA meetings. CPR was also used to reduce social anxiety in the teachers' room. He was desensitized to fear of saying something foolish or inappropriate. In the family social interaction, he was quite often belittled by his brother-in-law and mother- and father-in-law. He was taught assertive training, especially targeted at PTA parents and his in-laws.

It was also clear that he needed desensitization toward authority figures. His wife was asked to ignore his frequent complaints about being sick and to ignore him completely when he had an attack, while paying more attention to him at other times. CE was also applied to his complaining behavior by having him complain and imagine she was ignoring his complaint. She was asked to cooperate with raising his level of reinforcement by asking her to compliment him more and go out with him to recreational activities.

CE was used in the following manner. He was asked to imagine he was having an attack but his wife was ignoring him by reading the paper or walking without him.

At the end of 2 months' treatment, the asthmatic attacks, as self-recorded, started to decrease to four per week. At the end of 3 months, it was down to one to three times per week. At 6 months, they stopped completely. At this time, he consulted with a physician and the drugs were gradually withdrawn. Results were maintained at a 1-year follow-up without the use of drugs.

8

Social Skills

During the last decade social skills training has become one of the most widely encountered topics in the behavioral literature. In addition to the appearance of several professional and self-help books in this area, an individual journal issue (*Behavioral Counseling Quarterly*, 1981, Vol. 1, No. 4) has been devoted to social skills training. Although there is some variation in programs, many include the four steps of Structured Learning Theory (Goldstein, Sprafkin, & Gershaw, 1976): modeling, role playing, social reinforcement, and transfer training. Covert conditioning can be helpful with each of these steps.

Experimental Findings

Most of the research on the use of covert conditioning in social skills training has employed CM, and a great deal of this research has been conducted by Alan Kazdin and his colleagues (Hersen, Kazdin, Bellack, & Turner, 1979; Kazdin, 1974d, 1975, 1976a, 1976b, 1980, 1982; Kazdin & Mascitelli, 1982). Kazdin's 1975 experiment included both self-reports and behavioral role-playing tests as dependent variables. The independent variables were variations of CM which involved one or more models and reinforced versus nonreinforced models. A nonassertive-model control group was included in which subjects imagined the same general scenes as subjects in the CM groups, except that the model exhibited no assertive response to the situation portrayed and no consequences followed the models' performance. Results showed that while the multiple-models condition was more effective than the single-model condition and the reinforced-model condition was more effective than the no-reinforcement condition (which is consistent with and lends additional support to the operant explanation of covert conditioning), all four groups showed significantly greater improvement than the control group. In addition to a post-test of role-play situations of the same behavior used during the pre-test assessment, subjects were also presented with a series of novel situations on which they also performed well, thus demonstrating some degree of generalization of treatment effects. A similar study published the following year yielded similar results (Kazdin, 1976b).

While conducting this study, Kazdin observed that several subjects elaborated on and enhanced their scenes beyond the standardized scene descriptions provided to them. In a later study, Kazdin (1979) found that when subjects were instructed to elaborate and change the scene, while keeping the model assertive, treatment was more effective than CM without the additional scene elaboration.

Kazdin also found that having subjects verbally describe and summarize the contents and events included in scene visualizations after the imagery trials were completed enhanced the effects of CM. In more recent experiments, Kazdin has also found that CM can be as effective as overt modeling in developing assertive behavior (Kazdin, 1980) and that using both covert and overt modeling together is more effective than using either procedure alone for developing assertive behavior (Kazdin, 1982).

Attempting to evaluate the importance of overt practice in social skills training, Kazdin and Mascitelli (1982) compared CM, CM plus overt rehearsal, CM plus overt homework practice (*not* homework of CM scenes), CM plus overt rehearsal plus overt homework practice, and a waiting-list control condition. With good generalization and maintenance at eight months, as measured by both self-report and behavioral tests, their results showed: (1) CM alone was significantly superior to the waiting list condition in five of six measures. (2) On five of six measures, there was no significant difference between CM and any treatment that did not include *both* overt rehearsal *and* homework practice. (3) On the sixth measure the CM plus overt rehearsal condition was superior to CM alone. While in the opinion of the authors the effectiveness of treatment was improved when practice was included, it appears that in most cases both overt rehearsal and overt homework practice had to be added to CM to improve the effectiveness of treatment.

Rosenthal and Reese (1976) conducted a comparison of overt and covert modeling on assertive behavior. The CM subjects were divided into two groups: those who imagined standardized scenes and those with individually tailored programs. Subjects in the former CM group imagined someone else as the model, while those in the individualized group served as their own models. The three treatments were equally effective on self-report and behavioral tests, but subjects in the individually tailored CM group reported that they thought their treatment was more helpful to them than did subjects in the standardized CM group.

Kazdin (1974d) found that although CM was significantly superior to placebo imagery in teaching social skills, CM scenes in which assertive behavior was followed by favorable consequences for the model was more effective than CM without imagined consequences. Nietzel et al. (1977) took this a step further and compared two variations of scene content in applying CM to assertiveness training. One group of subjects visualized the model making an appropriate assertive response in a given social context, which was followed by immediate compliance. The second group of subjects visualized the same social context, but this group visualized the model's initial assertive response being met with noncompliance, whereupon the model replied with a second assertive response which did result in compliance. A placebo group which visualized the social context only and a no-treatment control group were included. Results showed that the treatment in which subjects overcome an initial noncompliance was more effective than any of the other conditions and led to greater generalization to novel situations.

Zielinski and Williams (1979) found both CM and behavioral rehearsal to be equally effective in bringing about significant improvement on 10 of 13 measures of assertive skills. Subjects reported to the authors both before and after treatment that they had greater expectations of improvement from behavioral rehearsal than CM. However, Watson (1977) applied several variations of CM to the teaching of job interview skills. While subjects in the standard CM group did better on written tests, subjects who visualized themselves as models performed better on behavioral tests. Adding a covert reinforcement component after visualization of the CM scene appeared to distract subjects rather than have a facilitative effect.

Although most of the research studies conducted on covert conditioning with social skills problems have employed CM, Stevens (1974) found CPR and a CM-like procedure equally effective and equally superior to a placebo treatment in teaching "friendly" assertive behavior. After conducting a study in which psychiatric patients were used as subjects, DeLancey (1979) reported that CPR was effective in increasing self-reports of assertiveness when combined with a social skills training program to increase subject feelings of social skillfulness.

In addition to overt social behaviors as such, covert conditioning has been used to enhance social self-esteem. Marshall and Christie (1982) found both CPR and a condition in which the pleasant scene preceded the target scene superior to a condition in which no pleasant scene was visualized at all. In a second study, Marshall, Christie, Lanthier, and Cruchley (1982) found CPR and overt reinforcers equally effective and both superior to a control condition, again in modifying social self-esteem. The authors also found that desirable, infrequent events and frequent natural events served as the best reinforcers.

The use of covert conditioning in social skills training has not been limited to what are generally considered to be normal populations. In addition to the DeLancey (1979) study cited above, Hersen et al. (1979) conducted a CM experiment using psychotic, neurotic, and character-disordered psychiatric patients as subjects. The result of this experiment showed that CM was as effective as live modeling and both procedures were superior to no treatment in teaching assertiveness skills to these subjects. Although the addition of rehearsal to both treatments did not improve overall assertive behavior, subjects in the CM plus rehearsal group did show some improvement on two measures.

As part of a five-step program, Michael Lowe (1978) used CM to train depressed subjects in social skills. The intervention began with the videotaping of subjects in a staged situation. After receiving verbal feedback about their performance, subjects employed CM to observe appropriate behaviors performed by a model. Finally, subjects were videotaped in the staged situation again, first with the same individual and next with someone new. While improvement was made with the same individual, there was little generalization to the situation with the new person.

Lewis (1979) treated a schizoid personality using CPR within a hypnoperant framework to teach dating skills and related social behaviors. Groden (1982) used CPR to increase social interactions within a group of autistic adolescents. Covert sensitization was included by Hayes et al. (1983) as part of an attempt to include heterosocial-skills training in the treatment of sexual deviants.

A case study reported by Wisocki (1976) described how both CPR and CNR were integrated with several other behavioral procedures (e.g., systematic desensitization, thought stopping, behavioral rehearsal, verbal reinforcement, and contingency contracting) to help a client overcome fear of social rejection. The behavior analysis revealed that although the client was a doctoral level physicist, her social skills were such that her fears were well founded. During 17 months of behavior therapy, Wisocki worked with the client on skills to increase her personal physical attractiveness, improve her interpersonal social skills and improve her job satisfaction. CPR was specifically used to increase the frequency of positive self-statements and to shape more assertive job-related verbal behavior. CNR was employed by having the client switch from extremely aversive scenes of social rejection to very pleasant scenes of appropriate and effective social behavior. Wisocki also employed a procedure she named "covert reinforcer sampling" to help her client explore potentially reinforcing new social activities.

Summary and Recommendations

In summary, research findings have shown that covert conditioning, particularly CM, is an effective procedure to assist in teaching social skills to normal, neurotic, and psychotic populations. When using CM to teach social skills, it may be advantageous to employ a variety of models in different scenes in which the model first meets resistance but perseveres, succeeds, and is finally reinforced for the new, appropriate behavior. It may also be helpful to allow the client to elaborate on the scene, as long as no crucial element is deleted, and to ask the client to verbally summarize scenes after their conclusion. CM can be as effective as overt modeling (Kazdin, 1980), but using both CM and overt modeling together is more effective than using either one alone (Kazdin, 1982). The only known comparison of CM with CPR in teaching assertiveness skills found both procedures to be equally effective (Stevens, 1974).

As more behavioral problems are recognized as involving social skills deficits, the use of covert conditioning to teach alternative behaviors is likely to increase. While most of the research on using covert conditioning to teach social skills has centered on the covert modeling of assertive behavior, there are other ways in which covert conditioning can be useful. For example, once the appropriate social skills have been acquired through either CM or some other means, performance of those skills may still be a problem. Social anxieties may have to be treated, either by CM again or by CPR. The SCT can be employed to assist clients in a wide variety of social situations in the natural environment, such as when faced with personal criticism, a situation in which an assertive response is appropriate, or a specific social anxiety. (Chapter 9 of this book, which deals with the use of covert conditioning in the treatment of phobias, includes examples of reducing anxiety in some social situations.)

Case Example

Assertive behavior includes:

1. Giving compliments.
2. Being able to accept compliments.
3. Originating conversation.
4. Speaking up when an injustice is done.

It is important to emphasize that assertiveness training should be employed with clients who are considered aggressive or inappropriately assertive as well as with clients who need more assertion.

The following case illustrates a client who needed assertive training in all the above areas. The client was a 65-year-old married woman, in good physical health, attractive, always neatly dressed, and possessing a pleasant smile. Her presenting complaint was that she was anxious and depressed and felt that her family did not appreciate her and that everyone took advantage of her.

A year before the first interview, the client had found the stress of working as a secretary in a physician's office so great that she dreaded going to work and started to resent the physician and the receptionist. Even though she had worked in this office for 20 years, she decided that the stress was so great that she had to quit. After quitting her job, she did not try to get employment again because she was afraid she could not handle the stress of any job.

When the therapist discussed her house and children with her, she became quite agitated and angry. She complained that although he was kind to her, her husband was also quite domineering. Her two married sons and single daughter did not live at home. They were affectionate and loving, but when they visited her they expected to be waited on and did not help in either preparing meals or cleaning up afterwards. In fact, she said, she felt like a robot. Her family would all sit down at the table and then would continually ask her, in a not too polite way, to get more food or drink, get extra napkins, and so forth. She felt like a yo-yo, getting up and down. She never was able to sit through a full meal without getting up and down 5 to 10 times. The situation was so extreme that, if somebody at one end of the table wanted something at her end, she would have to get up, go around, and bring it to the other end of the table. This meal situation typified the manner in which they expected her to wait on them. Not only did she feel that they were unreasonable in their demands and lack of cooperation, but she said they indicated to her that this was her role and obligation and they showed no appreciation.

The client was administered the Assertive Behavior Survey Schedule (Cautela, 1977a). The Assertive Behavior Survey Schedule and interview indicated that she was not only unassertive to her family but that she was unassertive in almost all situations. At work, the situation became unbearable because, throughout the years, the physician, receptionist, and some patients would take advantage of her or continue treating her unfairly, but she never spoke up. Even when she resigned, she was not able to tell the physician, whom she had known for 20 years, the real reason for her quitting (because she felt she was being treated unfairly and they did not appreciate her enough at work).

It was explained to her that what she apparently had done over the years was to train the people at work and the people at home to order her around without consideration because she reinforced those behaviors by readily complying and never complaining. When asked why she did not assert herself at home or in a work situation, she replied that it was her duty and obligation, as an Italian wife and mother, to render everything to the family without complaining. This was because she felt that if she did not fulfill the role of being an Italian mother—always being available for service—she would be rejected by the family because she would not be a good mother. She said that at first she did not complain or speak up at work because she was afraid of being fired and that after awhile they expected the same compliant behavior she originally showed on the job. Even though after a few years she felt safe from being fired, she was afraid that if she asserted herself, people would be offended, yell at her, or think that she wasn't nice anymore.

In situations where she had to deal with people outside of the home or work, she was also quite reluctant to speak up. For example, at a department store she once waited 15 minutes for a salesperson to complete a personal call before she walked away in disgust. At no time in this period did she try to get the attention of the salesperson or ask to get waited on. She was often sold items in stores because she could not say "no" to a sales clerk. Her husband complained that she bought practically everything sold at the door or over the telephone.

It was also apparent that whenever anyone complimented her she almost always issued a disclaimer. For example, if anyone complimented her on her cooking, she would always say it was easy, premade, or nothing. If they complimented her on her clothing, she would say how inexpensive the dress was or how long she had had it. She said she had trouble complimenting others because she thought they would think she was "buttering them up." Her circle of friends was very limited, involving almost exclusively family members. While she admitted that she was well liked by people who knew her, she said she would never, at any function such as a wedding or church event, go up to anybody and introduce herself. In fact, even if there were some acquaintances at these events, she would not go up to them to strike up a conversation.

While the behavior analysis was being carried out, it was frequently pointed out to her that she needed assertiveness training, and that when she learned to assert herself she would be less anxious and depressed and have confidence in herself. Whenever the therapist suggested the possibility of assertiveness training, she said she did not want to become pushy or aggressive. The therapist would constantly assure her that that was not what was meant by assertive training.

After the initial behavior analysis was complete, the therapist gave her the following rationale concerning the need for assertive training:

It is clear to me that one of your main problems is that you don't speak up enough when injustice is done to you. Now, when people know you are not going to speak up, they tend to take advantage of you. This leads to resentment on your part and you feel inadequate and helpless in their presence. You also feel inadequate and inferior because you cannot face them and speak up; that is, you don't have any respect for yourself. Of course, if other people know they can step all over you, they won't respect you, even your own family. Your family may love you, but I doubt if they really respect you. From a practical point of view, if you don't assert yourself most of the time, you won't get what you want. Until you learn to be assertive in all situations, in a diplomatic way, which I will teach you, you will stay anxious and depressed and feel you are not appreciated and that people don't really understand you. Also, if someone pays you a compliment and you let them know that you are unworthy of the compliment, you are not only conveying that you are unworthy but you are also criticizing their judgment. You are putting them down. This decreases the likelihood that they are going to please you again. For example, if someone tells you that you are wearing a nice outfit and you tell them it is a cheap outfit you got at a discount, they are going to feel put down. Now when you compliment anyone, if you are sincere, most people will feel good about it and they won't feel you are buttering them up. Incidentally, if you are concerned about being liked, it is important that you compliment or reinforce other people as much as possible as long as you are sincere. You should look for characteristics to compliment in any individual, even your husband and children. It is clear that you should develop more friends. You are too dependent on the family approval interaction for your social life. There are many people similar to you who would like to make new friends. I will try to help you to be less anxious in approaching and talking to other people.

Treatment included teaching the client relaxation based on imagery. A tape was made and she was asked to play the tape twice each day. The tape included suggestions that she was a worthwhile person deserving of respect and love and that she had the right and obligation to speak up when an injustice was done to her.

Behavior rehearsals were done, including role reversals concerning situations where assertive training was needed. For every behavioral rehearsal session, a CM scene was presented in which she saw another woman her own age engaging in assertive behavior in the same situation rehearsed overtly. For example, we rehearsed a scene in which her husband was sitting in the lounge chair with a newspaper two or three feet away from him on a coffee table. Even though she was at the other side of the room, he asked her to get the paper. She would reply, "No, you get it. You are closer to it than I am." We then did a CM scene where she saw a husband sitting in a chair asking for the newspaper and the wife saying, "No, you get it yourself." The behavior rehearsal and CM modeling scenes not only reduced the anxiety about being assertive, but also gave her information on how to be properly assertive. CPR was also used on being able to speak up when an injustice was done and on the other three assertive behaviors. For example:

> You are in a department store at a jewelry counter. The salesperson starts to wait on someone who came after you, and you say, "Pardon me. It is my turn." When you say that you feel calm and relaxed (reinforcement).
>
> Another example: You are sitting down having supper with your family in your home. Your daughter says, "Ma, would you get some more cheese for the spaghetti." You look at her and smile and say, 'It would be nice if you got it.' She looks a little surprised and so does everyone else. This makes you feel good. They are going to learn to appreciate that your time and activity are valuable (reinforcement).
>
> Another example: You are at a relative's wedding. You bought a new dress. You walk into the reception and your cousin says, "Marie, you look terrific. That is a great dress." You smile and say thank you. It really makes you feel good and comfortable (reinforcement).
>
> Another example: After the First Communion of your grandson, you go to the reception in the basement of the church where they are serving coffee, juice, and pastry. A woman is sitting across from you and you feel that the way she has her hair cut is quite stunning. You say to the woman, "Pardon

me. I couldn't help staring. I love the way your hair is done." As you are saying it, there is a feeling of being friendly and nice. She radiates and says, thank you (reinforcement).

After the second session of behavior rehearsal, CM, and some CPR, she was asked to be assertive in every situation possible. She was asked to speak up in every situation in which there was an injustice. She was also asked to compliment everyone as much as possible and instructed to say thank you whenever anyone paid her a compliment, whether she believed it or not.

After some scenes in initiating conversation with people, she was asked to try it at a wedding she was going to attend in the near future. She was asked to keep a record of every time she was properly assertive and every time she should have been assertive but was not. She also kept records of giving and receiving compliments and participating in conversations. The records served as feedback to construct new scenes and situations not covered previously or to do more scenes on similar situations. The records also provided opportunities for the therapist to deliver reinforcement. The client was quite cooperative in playing the tapes, sometimes up to 2 hours a day. All the behavioral rehearsals were taped. She kept excellent records. As she started to become assertive, she realized catastrophes did not happen and she often got what she wanted. She also noticed that her family began to appear to be regarding her in a new way. They would hesitate before they made any requests that appeared at all unreasonable. In fact, they were asking her how they could help and, many times, if someone would ask her for something, other relatives would say, "No, you stay. I will get it."

Her husband at first felt that her therapist was turning her into "one of those feminists." Soon, however, he began to appreciate her and encouraged her assertive behavior after a few sessions with the therapist. He observed that she had become less anxious, was more sure of herself, slept better, and was much happier. In fact, the client said, "My husband said you made a new woman out of me. He likes what he sees. He asked me to give you this present" (a 2-liter bottle of Chivas Regal).

After 6 months of treatment, she was able to be assertive in all four areas and feel very good about herself, was not depressed, and developed new friends by volunteering to work at a hospital and attending classes (such as how to play bridge). One of the characteristics of learning assertive behavior (if it is done carefully and properly), is that there very rarely is a relapse because the client gets reinforced almost immediately after starting to learn to be assertive.

What must be guarded against is the occasional possibility that assertive behavior will be followed by yelling or rejection by the person who is doing the injustice. The client was told that the important thing is that she speak up immediately when the other person does not understand that the injustice was their fault. Scenes were done to desensitize her against the possibility that someone would react negatively when she asserted herself.

Two years later, the client brought in one of her friends for assertive training and reported that she was still as happy as ever.

9

Phobic Behavior

A Behavioral Approach to Phobic Behavior

The term *phobia* is used to describe situations in which an individual's response to a stimulus includes disproportionate levels of fear. The presence of fear is usually inferred from observations of avoidance behavior, physiological measures, and self-reports. The phobic reaction can be a response to a stimulus that most people do not consider fearful (e.g., flowers, wind, pigeons), stimuli that make many people feel uncomfortable (e.g., rats, snakes, heights, public speaking situations), or a dysfunctional or incapacitating fear reaction to stimuli that most people do find anxiety provoking (e.g., nuclear war, sharks, being evaluated by others, dead bodies).

Over the years, many theories of phobia development have been set forth. From a behavioral perspective, it is apparent that fear responses can be learned in several ways. John B. Watson's famous experiment in which he developed a fear response in little Albert by pairing the presentation of a furry object with a loud noise (Watson & Rayner, 1920) demonstrated one way in which fear responses, or phobias, can be learned. After the original classical conditioning trial, generalization commonly takes place and soon other stimuli, with some similar qualities, elicit responses similar to those elecited by the original CS.

Modeling is a second way in which fear responses can develop. Children often learn avoidance, and other fear-related behaviors, by observing these behaviors being performed by parents and older siblings. When the child then imitates the model's fear-related behaviors, he or she frequently receives large doses of sympathy,

consolation, and positive reinforcement from others, thus strengthening the fear responses and demonstrating what is sometimes called the
"modeling and coddling" theory of phobia development.

A third way in which fears can develop is through nondirected
covert conditioning. A young preschool girl might, for example, be told
that Ms. Smith, the kindergarten teacher, is a "real monster."
Without any further information, and without ever seeing Ms. Smith,
the child starts visualizing scenes of a monster who lives in the school
building and as time goes on embellishes and elaborates upon this
scene, including images of all sorts of aversive things being done to
children by Ms. Smith. After tens, or even hundreds, of trials of this or
similar scenes, the girl reaches school age and is expected to start
school in Ms. Smith's class. To everyone's surprise, the child appears
to be in a state of panic on the first day of school. When the child
exhibits the fear-related behaviors, she does not do so in an environmental vacuum. Others react in various ways to her behavior. For
example, she may be immediately removed from Ms. Smith's
classroom, or possibly even the school building, thereby relieving the
anxiety and, of course, negatively reinforcing the behaviors which
preceded the reduction of anxiety, for example, overt physiological
motor avoidance or flight response, verbal expressions of horror,
extreme muscle tension, covert physiological responses of the sympathetic nervous system, and covert psychological behaviors, such as
aversive imagery and negative subvocal statements involving Ms.
Smith and/or the school. Well-meaning and sympathetic adults
observing the child's behavior, as would be expected, then try to
comfort and console the child. Another common adult reaction is to
try to distract the child or "get her mind off the matter," perhaps by
attempting to engage the child in a usually pleasurable activity, such
as playing a game or telling a story. All of these well-intended
reactions by adults, or even other children, often backfire by positively
reinforcing the child's behavior, thereby leading to more severe and/or
difficult to modify phobic responses in the future.

Once a phobia develops, regardless of whether nondirected covert
sensitization, CNR, CM, or any other covert conditioning is involved,
nondirected covert sensitization can operate to maintain the phobic
behavior, even in the absence of overt exposure to the fear stimulus.
This nondirected covert sensitization may take the form of "reliving"
or covertly rehearsing a particularly traumatic or aversive incident or
even embellishing the images involving the fear stimulus. This may be
done to the extent that the images are considerably more aversive than
any overt incidents involving the fear stimulus which the client has

either experienced or observed. It follows then that even if it seems that an obvious traumatic event brought about the phobia, covert events as well as overt events must be considered when conducting the behavior analysis.

Several other plausible scenarios for the development of phobias, consistent with learning theory principles, could also be presented. All of them probably explain the reasons for the development of some phobias, operating either alone or together with other sequences of events. The point is that most dysfunctional fear responses are learned.

Systematic desensitization has been called "probably the most tested, retested and experimented-with therapeutic technique in the history of psychology" (Kearney, 1976, p. 3), and "the first psychotherapeutic procedure in history to withstand rigorous evaluation" (Paul, 1969, p. 116). The vast majority of the work with systematic desensitization has involved the treatment of fear responses. Covert conditioning, particularly CPR, is also well-suited for the treatment of fear responses and is often less complicated to employ than systematic desensitization; furthermore, its effectiveness, which appears to be similar to that of systematic desensitization, is supported by an ever-increasing number of empirical studies. We will now take a brief look at some of that evidence.

Experimental Findings

Most of the experimental applications of covert conditioning procedures to fear responses have involved the use of either CPR or CM. These applications have included CPR to treat test anxiety (Finger & Galassi, 1977; Guidry & Randolph, 1974; Kearney, 1984; Kostka & Galassi, 1974; Wisocki, 1973a), rodent phobia (Flannery, 1972b; Kearney, 1976; Ladouceur, 1974), snake phobia (Sanders & Hammer, 1979), and public speaking anxiety (Park, 1979). In addition, Marshall et al. (1974) tested the effectiveness of both CPR and CNR in treating snake phobia. CM has been tested in modifying test anxiety (Bistline et al., 1980; Gallagher & Arkowitz, 1978; Harris & Johnson, 1980, 1983), rodent phobia (Cautela et al., 1974), fear of spiders (Denny, Sullivan, & Thiry, 1977), fear of snakes (Kazdin, 1973, 1974b, 1974c; Tearnan, Lahey, Thompson, & Hammer, 1982; Thase & Moss, 1976), and dental fears (Chertock & Bornstein, 1979).

In the Wisocki (1973a) study, CPR was found to be superior to a no-treatment control condition in treating test anxiety, but not in increasing test scores as such. Guidry and Randolph (1974) essentially replicated the Wisocki study, adding a placebo-control group. CPR was again shown to be superior to no treatment on all measures of anxiety reduction and superior to the placebo condition (visualization of reinforcing scenes without the fear stimuli) on two of the three self-report measures employed.

Kostka and Galassi (1974) compared CPR with systematic desensitization in treating test anxiety. After 8 to 10 group treatment sessions, both treatments were equally effective and superior to the control condition.

In an experiment designed to compare the relative effectiveness of standard CPR and CPR employing reinforcing scenes related to the target behavior in content and format, Kearney (1984) found both CPR treatments to be more effective than either no treatment or a control condition in which subjects visualized the same basic test-related target scenes without the reinforcing component. While both CPR treatments were generally similar in effectiveness, there were tendencies for subjects in the standard CPR condition to show greater, but not significantly greater, improvement than subjects in the CPR related-scene group. This may have been because of the greater variety and potential power of the unrelated reinforcers available to use in the individualized reinforcing scenes visualized by the subjects in the unrelated reinforcing scene condition.

Finger and Galassi (1977) compared CPR targeting the physiological component of anxiety with CPR targeting the cognitive component and a combined CPR condition. All treatment groups improved significantly, not only in the specific area targeted, but in the area targeted by the other CPR conditions as well. Subjects in the waiting-list control group did not improve.

Flannery (1972a) treated rat-phobic subjects with either standard CPR or a procedure in which the subject actually approached a rat, then visualized a reinforcing scene at each successively closer step. In other words, the target behavior was performed overtly, but the reinforcer was administered covertly. He found both treatments to be significantly more effective than an attention-placebo condition, but the subjects in the in vivo fear stimulus group surpassed the imagery group on most measures. The author concluded that imagery in CPR is about as effective as imagery in systematic desensitization.

In an experiment which employed both behavioral and self-report instruments to measure fear of rats, Kearney (1976) found CPR and systematic desensitization both to be superior to no treatment and a graduated exposure imagery condition. A group of subjects who received two additional sessions of progressive muscle relaxation training prior to and in addition to CPR, however, consistently showed nonsignificantly greater levels of improvement than either the CPR or systematic desensitization groups.

Blanchard and Draper (1973) employed a single-subject experimental design to evaluate the effectiveness of CPR in treating a client who had been referred to them because of a clinical level rodent phobia. The client's fear responses, which included leaving class crying during a discussion of mice, threatened her academic career as a psychology major.

The course of treatment included three hours of assessment and client support, followed by three hours of tape recorded CPR (distributed over six sessions). The third phase consisted of three 30-minute sessions similar to phase two, with the omission of the reinforcing scene. In the fourth condition, CPR was reinstated for three more sessions. The fifth phase was one week without treatment and the last phase was two 45-minute minute participant modeling sessions. Dependent variables consisted of approach behavior, physiological arousal, and four self-report measures. While the client reported no further problems with rats 4.5 months after treatment, the changes which occurred during treatment are interesting. The client showed the greatest improvement in approach behavior during the imagery and participant modeling phases, followed by slight improvement during the psychotherapy phase, and no change during no treatment. Physiological improvement took place during all conditions, except target imagery without reinforcing consequences (blood pressure increased), and no treatment (no change). Self-reports improved only during CPR and participant modeling conditions. This study demonstrated not only the importance of including the reinforcing scenes in CPR, but also the usefulness of operant designs in behavior therapy research.

Marshall et al. (1974) compared both CPR and CNR to an experimental variation of systematic desensitization and three other conditions in treating snake phobia. The authors reported that CPR and experimental desensitization were equally effective and superior to the control conditions. While the CNR group was also superior to the control groups, the improvement of the CNR subjects on behavioral tests, but not self-report measures, was significantly less than the improvement of the CPR and experimental desensitization subjects.

Cautela et al. (1974) tested the effectiveness of CM in treating fear of rats. Overt modeling and attention-placebo groups were also included. The subjects in the attention-placebo group spent their time exploring the origin and nature of their fears, under the expectation that this would lead to insight which would help change the fear. The results of the two modeling treatments were equivalent in three behavioral and one subjective measure. Subjects in the attention-placebo group showed slight improvement on a semantic differential and one behavioral test.

While both CM groups were superior to no-treatment and control groups, Kazdin (1973) found CM employing a coping model to be more effective than CM employing a mastery model in treating fear of snakes.

Also working with snake-fearful subjects, Thase and Moss (1976) found two versions of CM (standard CM and CM in which the subjects visualized themselves as the model) to be superior to a delayed-treatment control condition, but not as effective as guided participant modeling.

More recently, Tearnan et al. (1982) conducted an experiment in which two variations of CM were compared. The target behavior again was fear of snakes. In one CM group subjects were told to add coping self-instructions to the scenes of the model approaching the snake. The second CM group did not elaborate. Both treatments were equal and superior to an attention-control condition on the behavioral measures but the CM plus coping self-instructions treatment was superior to the other CM treatment.

Although treatment was limited to four sessions and 32 scene presentations, Gallagher and Arkowitz (1978) found CM more effective than two control conditions on one measure of test anxiety. Follow-up reports (length unspecified) suggested that treatment gains had not been maintained. Also, with limited trials (two sessions, 10 trials each), Chertock and Bornstein (1979) found several variations of CM to be effective in reducing behavioral components of children's dental fears. Improvement on self-report measures was more sporadic, and multiple versus single and coping versus mastery dimensions seemed unimportant.

Harris and Johnson (1983) reported using several variations of CM to reduce test anxiety. The variations included instructions versus no instructions in relaxation training and preceding CM scenes with scenes in which the subjects visualized themselves behaving competently in either test-related or test-unrelated situations. Self-report measures revealed significant decreases in test anxiety for all treatments. In addition, all groups, except the no-relaxation related-scene group, improved on grade point average while the waiting-list control group deteriorated significantly.

While treating test-anxious subjects, Bistline et al. (1980) compared

CM with cognitive restructuring and a condition which combined both treatments. Although all treatments were effective, subjects in the CM group showed greater improvement than those in the cognitive restructuring group. Adding the cognitive restructuring component to CM apparently did not increase its effectiveness.

CPR and CM have been almost exclusively the only covert conditioning procedures used in treating fear responses. Hayes and Barlow (1977), however, reported the treatment of a client with a public transportation phobia with a procedure labeled *flooding relief*. According to the authors, "Flooding relief is conceptualized as a straightforward operant procedure, designed to negatively reinforce appropriate behavior in response to environmental and behavioral cues" (pp. 745–746).

The conceptualization quoted above, together with the procedural description in the text, seems to qualify flooding relief as CNR. Treatment consisted of escape and avoidance scenes randomly alternated. Since the avoidance of public transportation resulted from the client's social fears of the reactions of other passengers to her facial disfigurement, an assertive response, rather than a relaxed response, was targeted. A multiple-baseline approach across public transportation situations was used. A six-month-follow-up revealed that improvement was maintained.

In general, the experimental evidence shows that both CPR and CM can be very powerful procedures for treating fear responses. While there are not yet as many studies of covert conditioning as there are of systematic desensitization, those experiments which have been conducted have yielded similar results, and those studies which have included both systematic desensitization and CPR have consistently demonstrated both to be equally effective.

Summary and Recommendations

CPR appears to be the most commonly employed covert conditioning procedure in the treatment of phobias. In using CPR to treat clinical-level phobias, a number of points should be considered. First, fear responses usually occur in more than one class of behavior. In addition to the client's overt behaviors, the therapist must remember to include the client's covert behaviors and physiological state of arousal as well.

There is some evidence (Kearney, 1976) to support the notion that if one class of behavior (e.g., overt motor behavior) is emphasized in scene development and presentation, it is likely that changes in that class will precede changes in other classes (e.g., attitudes).

Kearney (1976) has also shown that there can be added benefit to training individuals in progressive muscle relaxation before starting CPR. While it is not yet known whether the additional time could be better spent if used for more CPR trials, CPR plus relaxation appears to be slightly, but not significantly, more effective than the same number of desensitization sessions.

The therapist must also be sensitive to the need to frequently change reinforcing scenes so as to avoid reinforcer satiation. The use of too weak a reinforcer with too powerful a fear stimulus could conceivably result in the intended reinforcer beginning to elicit unpleasant responses from the client.

Fear responses commonly found in education settings (e.g., test anxiety, public speaking, small animals) can be more cost-effectively treated first in group settings and through automated treatment delivery. This can be followed up by individualized treatment as needed for remaining fear-related behaviors.

When practical, treatment in imagery should be followed by in vivo treatment. Clients can be taught to covertly administer reinforcers to themselves as they approach the fear stimulus. The SCT can also be taught to clients to help their progress with their in vivo practice.

In some relatively mild cases, once treatment is begun, improvement could come very quickly. Particularly in situations where the client has frequent opportunities to encounter the fear stimulus, improvement may seem to race on ahead of treatment. In other more complex cases, progress may be satisfactory at some points of treatment, followed by periods of no apparent progress. Should this occur, the therapist should consider revising the behavioral analysis and modifying the treatment procedures.

While CM has also been demonstrated to be effective in treating fear responses, its chief advantage vis-à-vis CPR is in cases where the client experiences too much difficulty visualizing himself/herself in the scenes. CM can be used to help get a particularly fearful client started in treatment, before switching to CPR.

In dealing clinically with severe fear responses, the therapist must take advantage of all that has been discovered about the treatment of fears and employ as many learning principles as possible. While both CPR and systematic desensitization have been shown to be effective with phobias, it is still an unsettled issue as to whether both procedures are applications of reciprocal inhibition or operant conditioning, or whether each is based on the learning principle suggested by its developer. The procedural differences between systematic desensitization and CPR were discussed in the earlier section devoted to CPR. Much of what has been learned through research on systematic desensitization can also be helpful with covert conditioning. For example, although CPR emphasizes the use of a logical-temporal hierarchy instead of a fear-ranked hierarchy, it may be useful when clients are having difficulty with particular items to go back to a previous step, introduce a new item to bridge a gap, or rearrange the items. Just as Sank (1976) found CPR to be a helpful addition when trying to help a flight-phobic subject to complete a particularly difficult systematic desensitization hierarchy step, there are times when elements of systematic desensitization can be helpful with covert conditioning.

Case Example

The client was a 40-year-old woman who was recently diagnosed as agoraphobic, but behavioral analysis revealed that she had been agoraphobic for at least 14 years. She was taking 5 mg of Valium four times a day. At the end of the first interview, she drove only within five miles of her house alone. She drove with other people in the car but did not stay in the car if someone else was driving. She did not go into any public place outside of a grocery store and a drug store near her home. Even in these situations, she had to have someone with her, even if only a young child.

Her husband's occupation was so demanding that he was rarely home until late evening. When he was home, he constantly criticized his wife for her poor housekeeping. He also frequently yelled and screamed at their 17-year-old daughter and 14-year-old son because of their poor table manners, inappropriate dress, and general lack of what he considered to be responsible behavior. Since the husband was often furious when the client made certain demands, she always acquiesced by withdrawing her demands in order to avoid having an anxiety attack.

The Agoraphobic Behavior Survey Schedule (Cautela, 1981b) revealed that the client's central fear was that she would be in a public place, become anxious, and then lose control and do something so outrageous that she would be carted off to the hospital. She said, "My greatest fear is that they will think that I am a raving lunatic." She also reported that she had never actually lost control in 14 years. When asked why she was still afraid of going into public places, even though she never did lose control, she replied that she always had been able to escape from or avoid anxiety-producing situations. It was explained to her that escaping from and avoiding anxiety-producing situations only reinforced her fear and never gave her the opportunity to find out that she never would lose control.

The therapist explained to her that in his many years of practice and treating agoraphobics, no client had ever lost control, and that she would never lose control and that, if she did, she would have her fee payments returned. The client and therapist agreed that the therapy goal would be to gradually desensitize her to all places that made her anxious or that she avoided. This treatment plan would expand her freedom, thereby enriching her life. It was also agreed to focus on having her be absolutely convinced that she would never lose control.

She was taught progressive muscle relaxation, and CPR was used to desensitize her to various anxiety-producing situations. Each week a tape was made involving a particular situation such as a supermarket, department store, fast-food establishment, restaurant, theater, and so forth. It was clear that, as each week progressed, it became easier to desensitize her to the next situation. There was no pressure put on her to follow through in vivo after she had practiced the scenes, although she was encouraged to do so if she felt comfortable trying.

A psychological assistant worked with her by shadowing, that is, following the client in a car to a particular destination, and then gradually increasing the time interval between the client starting and the associate following until the client could make the trip alone. CPR was done on the shadowing procedure to reduce the client's anxiety during the in vivo shadowing.

She found employing the SCT to be particularly helpful and effective whenever she started to get anxious and become concerned about losing control. She was instructed to use the SCT whenever she had any thought about even the possibility of losing control. CPR was employed by having her imagine she was getting anxious in a public situation but saying to herself, "Nothing is going to happen to me. I will not lose control" (reinforcement).

An important feature of the therapy was teaching the client assertive behavior toward her husband and two children, all of whom she felt were constantly bullying her.

Probably the most difficult part of the treatment was getting her to be assertive to her family even though she was able to be assertive to strangers and acquaintances. The husband and children were instructed to pay a lot of attention to her when she was not exhibiting agoraphobic behavior, and they were further instructed never to complain about the agoraphobic behavior or try to force her into a situation which she wanted to avoid. They agreed to cooperate, and more progress was actually made when she was reassured that no one would push her or force her to try situations until she felt she was ready.

She was seen on a weekly basis for 18 months. At the time of discharge, she would occasionally experience anxiety in a crowded department store or supermarket, but was easily able to reduce or eliminate the anxiety so that she did not escape the situation. She was free of all other symptoms. After 3 months, she started reducing her Valium to one a week. By the end of the seventh month she was not taking any drugs. A 2-year follow-up indicated that the client was maintaining the level of mobility she had effected at time of discharge.

It is important to note in this case that the fear of being trapped in a family situation was probably related to the feeling of being trapped in a place that would lead to unbearable anxiety from which there was no escape.

III

Efficacy Issues and Future Directions

10

The Efficacy of Covert Conditioning

Methodological Considerations

Whenever a new treatment approach is promulgated it must go through a series of stages to be evaluated and further developed. The first stage consists of anecdotal reports and case studies which describe the procedure and target behaviors to which it has been applied. The second stage involves relatively large group experiments in which the new procedure is compared with already established procedures and various controls. At this stage, evidence is gathered as to the level of effectiveness of the new procedure. If the procedure does seem to be effective, the third stage involves attempts to determine why the procedure works and what the essential components are.

One of the major problems in researching therapeutic techniques is the lack of standardization of the methods and procedures used. Understandably, different investigators emphasize different factors in their studies. Because of differing emphases, appropriate controls of other factors are sometimes neglected, resulting in potentially important variations in independent variables both within and between studies. Yet, because the same label might have been applied to variations of procedures used in different studies, inappropriate comparisons are sometimes made and conclusions drawn which are not justified by the studies actually conducted.

In addition, when various elements of a treatment procedure are rearranged, omitted, or replaced for experimental purposes, it does not necessarily follow that the newly constructed treatment will not have an effect. It simply means that the effects of the treatment actually administered might best be attributed to a learning operation other than that underlying either the original treatment or some other treatment with which it is being compared. For example, a study may be designed to compare the effectiveness of CPR and systematic desensitization in treating fear of snakes. In addition to CPR and desensitization groups, a third group in which the subjects practice images of snakes, but without either reinforcing scenes or relaxation, may be included as a control. Since the subjects in this group are rehearsing scenes of snakes without an unpleasant or punishing component, a form of CE may actually be in use, unknown to the investigator, accounting for the effectiveness of the supposed placebo treatment.

Furthermore, similar results of different treatments do not necessarily mean that the treatments are operating on the same learning principles or share the same "active ingredients." Just because systematic desensitization and CPR might be found to be equally effective in a given study, it does not necessarily follow that both procedures are really examples of reciprocal inhibition, positive reinforcement, or any other common factor.

Many learning factors, of course, contribute to each treatment procedure. This can include some factors that researchers may not anticipate or want to influence their results. For example, whenever a behavior is not being reinforced, it is being extinguished. Therefore, extinction is nearly always a factor in most treatment procedures, even those thought to be placebo or nonspecific. Also, reciprocal inhibition may contribute to the lessening of the emotional component when a maladaptive avoidance behavior is treated with CPR. (Similarly, positive reinforcement, in the form of relaxation, may increase the approach behavior when systematic desensitization is used to treat a maladaptive avoidance behavior.)

When considering the results of studies, it is important to remember that no matter what is done to subjects in the name of treatment, there are nearly always some individuals whose behavior is going to change anyway. When a statistical analysis is performed to detect, for example, a .05 level of significance, it is expected that one out of every twenty times treatment effects will be assumed when in reality there are none (cf. Barber, 1976, p. 21). Because of the dependence on the average changes of the behavior of groups (which can be greatly affected by extreme scores on post-test measures obtained by just one or two subjects), reliance on .05 level superiority of one treatment over another can be misleading when considering the usefulness and applicability of specific treatment procedures to individuals. Hugdahl and Öst (1981) have called for greater recognition of the distinction between statistical and clinical significance, which they describe as being more concerned with the effects of treatment procedures on individual cases rather than the average effects on groups of subjects.

Another consideration here is the choice of experimental design. Although the use of group factoral designs is appropriate at times, since covert conditioning is conceptualized as operantly based, more use should be made of those designs particularly suited to operant research, such as A-B-A and A-B-A-B designs.

From time to time researchers are criticized for conducting research on treating fears of small animals and nonclinical level problems. These kinds of studies do have their place, however, and while potential researchers should be cautioned not to make too overly enthusiastic statements about the generalizability of their results, they should not be discouraged from conducting them. Especially in the early stages of the development of a new procedure, or when investigating particular parameters or modifications of that procedure, studies which generally allow for greater ease of manipulation and control of variables are particularly valuable. Once the basic quantitative details are established, further qualitative research should be pursued, if it is warranted.

In planning experiments in which covert conditioning procedures are compared with other techniques, researchers should carefully consider the target behaviors they choose. Several procedures, thought to be based on differing learning principles, have been demonstrated to be effective in treating maladaptive avoidance behaviors. However, a procedure that is truly operant should modify a behavior whether it is maladaptive or not. In the circle size estimation study mentioned earlier (Wish, et al., 1970), no maladaptive behavior was involved, yet CPR was effective in modifying the target behavior. Before stating that CPR is simply a variant of systematic desensitization and therefore really an application of reciprocal inhibition, future investigators might do well to test the relative effectiveness of the two procedures in modifying neutral behaviors which do not have an emotional component. While an operant procedure should be effective in modifying a behavior which is emotionally neutral, reciprocal inhibition should not have a direct effect on approach behavior. That is, even if the avoidance component is removed, there must be additional motivation to perform the target behavior.

In designing research on covert conditioning, there are additional factors which should be controlled as a matter of course in most experiments. Two of these factors are the degree of subject in-

Table 10.1. Results of Studies of Covert Conditioning Techniques in Comparison to Group Results or Baseline Measures[a]

Studies	Results significantly different from controls	Results in the expected direction	Results not significantly different from controls	Total
Experiments				
Number	36	24	10	70
Percentage	51.4%	34.3%	14.3	100%
Dissertations				
Number	26	15	8	49
Percentage	53%	31%	16%	100%
Combined studies				
Number	62	39	18	119
Percentage	52%	33%	15%	100%

[a]From L. McCullough, *The Efficacy of Covert Conditioning.* Paper presented at the meeting of the Association for Advancement of Behavior Therapy, Chicago, November 1978. Reprinted with permission.

volvement (Wilson & Barber, 1978) and strength of the consequence. The Covert Conditioning Survey Schedule (Cautela, 1977a) can be useful in this regard.

Results

With regard to research already conducted, McCullough (1978) conducted the most extensive review of the covert conditioning literature we are aware of to date. Of 119 experiments and dissertations reviewed, 52 percent of the studies showed a significant difference while an additional 33 percent obtained results in the expected direction.* The remaining 15 percent showed no difference between covert conditioning and various control groups. This 15 percent, however, included studies in which both experimental and control groups changed significantly. McCullough's results are summarized in Table 10-1.

---

*McCullough used the term "in the expected direction" to refer to studies in which (1) the results approached significance ($p = .10$), (2) half the measures were significant ($p < .05$) and half approached significance, (3) there were single-case designs reporting successful results, and (4) covert conditioning results were consistently closer to significance than those of other treatments, but did not reach statistical significance.

In his 1979 presidential address to the Association for Advancement of Behavior Therapy, Barlow (1980) spoke of the decade of the empirical clinician. The importance of bridging the gap between scientists and practitioners was stressed, and he emphasized the value of clinicians' gathering and sharing various data. The use of relatively standardized assessment procedures and recording the specifics of treatment procedures can provide very valuable information about the application of various procedures to clinical populations.

With regard to covert conditioning procedures, data such as the client's imagery ability, level of reinforcement, and motivation for behavior change are important client variables. Also, the number of trials, in vivo exposure, and assignment of homework are treatment variables to consider.

Negative Results and Equivocal Research

Clinician's Dilemma

It is very disconcerting to the clinician who has used a particular procedure with some success with many clients to read in a review article that the procedure is not effective. Now, of course, the article could be interpreted as saying that if the clinician finds only successful results it is not due to the application of a particular procedure but due to variables such as placebo, spontaneous remission, and so forth. This presents quite a dilemma to the clinician who feels that his/her treatment success is due to skillful application of the components of the procedure in accordance with its theoretical underpinnings. Should he/she abandon procedures he/she has found effective because studies report the procedures not effective or no more effective than placebo or control groups?

The clinician should be wary of abandoning procedures he/she has found successful because of a few experiments that conclude that the procedure is not effective, or the evidence does not support its effectiveness. *All* the experimental evidence should be examined. There should also be a comparison of how the procedures used in experiments compare with clinical application of the procedures. For example, the clinician would not discharge a patient who has cut his smoking from two packs to eight cigarettes per day because experience teaches us that if a client is still smoking on discharge it is very likely that the client will smoke again. Yet it is usually the case that when researchers conduct experiments comparing the effects of different procedures on smoking behavior, they carry out a specific number of treatment sessions regardless of results. Then they conclude that on follow-up there are no differences between groups.

The usual findings by reviewers of behavioral treatment strategies (including biofeedback, cognitive behavior therapy, systematic desensitization, and covert conditioning) are that there is not enough evidence to support the assertions that all the components of the procedures are necessary for therapeutic effectiveness. Even so, these procedures are widely used by behavior therapists, described in detail in various texts, and are taught in many courses at many universities.

Why the some time discrepancy between interpretation of the data of reviewers and the belief of the practitioners who espouse the particular model? One could hold that there are common elements in all of these procedures which account for occasional success. Even if this were true, it would not argue against the use of the procedures.

In our examination of reviews, it is clear that the reviewer's bias is sometimes so strong that either the data are misinterpreted or significant articles are omitted from the review or both. One of the problems that occurs in reviewing the literature on treatment methodologies is that individuals of a similar bias quote each other, and it leaves the impression that a lot of authors have examined the evidence and agreed with the findings. But what often happens is the following: One biased author does the review (A). Another biased author (B) quotes author (A). A third biased author (C) quotes or refers to the findings of both (A) and (B), another biased author (D), then quotes or refers to the findings of authors (A, B, and C), but by this time the statement reads something like this: "Many investigators agree that. . . . "

Sometimes when investigators compare treatment modalities with a placebo, they find no differences between the experimental group and the placebo group. They then conclude that the treatment is not effective. This, of course, is a non sequitor. If the treatment was effective, it was effective irrespective of the placebo group findings. Also, just because there are no differences between the treatment group and the placebo group, it does not necessarily follow that the experimental treatment worked because of the placebo effect. Perhaps the placebo group was also a powerful treatment group. Even though some authors try to restrict their conclusions based on their findings in particular experiments reported, others go beyond the data and imply that the procedure is not effective, even though there are other experiments that have reported positive results with the procedure.

There is *no* procedure in the history of psychology that has been investigated to a reasonable extent where the experiments have all had positive results.

The above considerations should caution the clinician not to rely on a particular review for an evaluation of the assessment of treatment of the procedures. The clinician should have a general familiarity with the case illustrations and experimental evidence available concerning a particular assessment of the treatment procedure under consideration. Since this task is horrendous, more people rely on the review and interpret the findings as definitive. Unfortunately, there is no way out of this dilemma other than constantly trying to keep up with the literature in this field, even if this involves, in a number of cases, merely reading the abstract.

In addition to an examination of the experimental literature, the clinician can benefit from reading case illustrations. Case presentations can be useful in several ways:

1. To illustrate the diagnostic procedures.
2. To present details of treatment methodologies.
3. To stimulate other investigators to try the assessment of treatment procedures.
4. To stimulate research by testing the particular assessment procedure or treatment technique.
5. To stimulate research suggested by ideas presented in a discussion of the presented case.

Interpreting Empirical Data
Concerning Covert Conditioning

Interpretations of the equivocal and negative results of covert conditioning studies include these: (1) although covert conditioning procedures do work, they are really not covert conditioning but are effective because of some other principle, such as reciprocal inhibition, extinction, or cognitive factors and (2) covert conditioning does not work any better than placebo conditions. Our response to these criticisms is as follows:

1. Just because another procedure, treatment X, may appear to work as well as the particular covert conditioning technique being tested, it does not logically follow that the covert conditioning procedure must really either be a variation of treatment X or be effective because of the same learning, cognitive, or "dynamic" principal that is assumed to underlie treatment X. It is just as

reasonable to argue that covert conditioning is in fact occurring during the application of treatment X and further that it is more reasonable to consider treatment X to be a variation of covert conditioning than the reverse. Even if treatment X has a sound theoretical underpinning, based on something other than covert conditioning, there is no reason that under a given set of experimental conditions treatment X and covert conditioning cannot yield similar effective results.

2. Have the treatments labeled covert conditioning been properly applied in a manner consistent with knowledge of operant learning principles and was the placebo condition really a placebo? In other words, if an observer objectively viewed both conditions from an operant point of view, what learning principles would appear to be operating and what would their predicted effects be? If covert conditioning is truly analogous to operant conditioning, then what has been empirically established about operant conditioning should also be applicable to covert conditioning. Some authors seem to overlook the data on operant conditioning in conducting their experiments and interpreting the results. Lack of clinical experience with covert conditioning procedures during experiments can also lead to misapplications of the procedures.

This second point is particularly important since it has been suggested (Franks, 1980) that "in-house" people, or those trained directly by Cautela, seem to get results more supportive of covert conditioning than do those who have had to rely simply on the literature or an occasional workshop for their training. This should not be at all surprising since the in-house people and their future generations (that is, those whom they in turn train) should have the advantage of a more complete understanding of the theory and application of a family of complex therapy procedures and the underlying learning theory. The instruction and supervision received by these individuals may very well account for the more supportive results obtained in experiments they later conduct. It is not at all unreasonable to expect that a more complete understanding of a procedure will result in more accurate applications of that procedure. Would anyone be really surprised to find that some of the best research on systematic desensitization has been conducted by former students of Joseph Wolpe? It should be pointed out, however, that most covert conditioning studies have not been conducted by in-house people, for example, Alan Kazdin's studies on CM.

Common reasons for lack of positive results in covert conditioning studies may include insufficient trials, not considering reinforcer satiation, equating the term *reward* with reinforcer, and not con-

sidering appropriate behaviors to replace those targeted for deceleration. Clinical evidence suggests that 60 to 80 covert conditioning trials
are usually necessary to achieve reasonable results. While occasionally
fewer trials may bring out acceptable results (or even a greater number
of trials may be required), this should not be surprising since the total
number of overt and covert trials (nondirected covert conditioning) of
the inappropriate behaviors over the years has probably been much
higher. Most of the studies included in the McCullough (1978) review
cited earlier which did not obtain significant results had considerably
fewer trials. Incomplete treatment may be justified for experimental
purposes, when simply finding a trend in behavior change may be
sufficient to support or reject a hypothesis. Also, it is certainly
reasonable to vary the number of trials in hopes of experimentally
determining a general range of appropriate treatment length. The
experimenters must, however, remember that they are employing
partial, simplified treatments rather than the kind of covert conditioning that should occur in clinical contexts.

Researchers and clinicians using CPR must always be on guard for
signs of reinforcer satiation. Hungry rats will usually decrease their
rate of pressing levers for food when they are sated. Successful token
economy systems have several backup reinforcers available from
which participants can choose. This, of course, argues against the use
of single stimuli considered to be group "reinforcers" as well. While
standardized group target scenes can occasionally be employed
successfully, this is not the case with reinforcers. Similarly, the
effective consequences in covert conditioning procedures must be
frequently alternated and replaced. Once a stimulus has lost its
reinforcing quality, it may still appear pleasant or "rewarding," but by
definition it is no longer reinforcing and CPR is no longer taking place.
If the stimulus scene has, through overuse, become boring or aversive,
then CE or even covert sensitization may actually be occurring!

With regard to the use of the term *reinforcer* in the covert
conditioning model, Kazdin and Smith (1979) have pointed out that it
is inconsistent with operant theory to label events chosen to be
included in reinforcing scenes as reinforcers before their effects on
behavior have been demonstrated. It is, of course, true that even
though an individual considers a particular stimulus to be pleasurable, it still may not function as a reinforcer (i.e., actually increase the
likelihood of the target behavior being repeated in the future) in that
situation. This is a major factor which therapists and researchers must
consider when planning treatments and experiments and when
evaluating apparent lack of success. Since a functional definition

must consider the effects a given stimulus has on the frequency of the behavior upon which it is contingent, one cannot know in advance that something will or will not have the hoped-for therapeutic effect. But when directed, intentional, positive reinforcement is attempted, stimuli are selected in advance that are intended to function as reinforcers, whether the stimulus is a food pellet for a hungry rat or an image of an ice cream cone for a hungry client. Therefore, although strictly speaking it may not be correct to refer to consequent stimuli as reinforcers before their effects are known, it does seem to be a widespread practice, both in the psychological literature and in the everyday language of behavioral psychologists.

In using positive reinforcement it is a common practice to employ a continuous reinforcement schedule until the target behavior is established, then switch to an intermittent schedule to strengthen that behavior and make it more resistant to extinction. The same practice could be used with CPR. Occasionally, researchers compare treatment conditions in which subjects receive CPR on a continuous schedule with a condition in which CPR trials are alternated with another arrangement (e.g., the consequent scene may precede the target scene or be omitted altogether). Since the later condition in fact represents the application of a more powerful reinforcement schedule than in the former condition, it should not be surprising that the results may be at least as good. Just as the reinforcer must be individually determined for each client, the thinning out of the reinforcement schedule (number of reinforcements gradually reduced) must be approached on an individual basis as well. The failure to accelerate appropriate alternative behaviors is not a problem confined to seemingly ineffective applications of covert conditioning, but can occur any time a behavior is targeted for deceleration. This is more of an issue clinically than experimentally, and hopefully practitioners will give it due consideration and take appropriate actions in their clinical practices.

Experiments that are poorly designed, in which procedures are improperly or inadequately implemented, and/or whose results are improperly interpreted have the potential of contributing to a sort of "inoculation effect" by giving the unjustified impression that the procedures in question are ineffective and therefore do not warrant further research or use. Although this problem is by no means limited to covert conditioning research, it is still a major concern of ours and should also be of objective researchers and journal editors. A treatment should be evaluated fairly on the basis of research that is adequate in both quantity and quality. After a very extensive review of the covert sensitization literature, Little and Curran (1978) stated that "...most covert sensitization studies have inappropriately implemented the technique and/or have been methodologically flawed" (p. 513). Unfortunately the same statement applies to many of the studies conducted on the other covert conditioning procedures as well. Therefore, we will now review examples of covert conditioning research which, in our opinions, do not support the authors' conclusions.

Research Studies

Throughout this book we have cited numerous studies to demonstrate the efficacy of covert conditioning. In this section we will discuss the interpretation of experimental results, examine representative studies that report equivocal or negative results, and suggest guidelines for the conducting and reporting of future research.

Covert Positive Reinforcement: Operant Conditioning or Reciprocal Inhibition? As mentioned earlier, while CPR appears to be an effective behavior therapy procedure, there is still debate about its learning theory basis. The authors of a number of studies to be cited shortly offer a reciprocal inhibition explanation of CPR as an alternative to operant conditioning.

Among the first researchers to examine CPR were Marshall et al. (1974). Marshall et al. included a noncontingent CPR group (N-CPR) in their study in which the three steps of their CPR procedure (fear stimulus target scene, relaxation response, reinforcing scene) were presented in random order. The CPR group showed significantly greater improvement than the N-CPR group on behavioral measures, but there was no difference between the groups on self-report measures. The N-CPR group did, however, show significantly greater change on self-report measures than the various control groups. This Marshall et al. attributed to counterconditioning and then suggested a counterconditioning explanation of CPR as well.

A closer look at this experiment reveals that two-thirds of the aversive scene visualizations by subjects in the N-CPR group were followed immediately by either the imaginary reinforcing scene or the relaxation response. Since the relaxed state is usually pleasurable and therefore very likely to be reinforcing, it may be that Marshall et al. were alternating CPR with a procedure in which a covert scene was followed by an overt reinforcer—a relaxed state (the reverse of the procedure used by Wish et al., 1970, and Krop, et al., 1971). This would amount to putting the target behavior on a fairly rich intermittent reinforcement schedule. It might also be argued that the remaining one-third of the trials may have been effective in reducing fear of snakes. Trials such as these, in which a conditioned stimulus (e.g., snake) is presented without the unconditioned stimulus (any other aversive stimulus) may be analogous to classical extinction (Kearney, 1976).

It should also be noted that Marshall et al. did not have the subjects in their CPR group relax until after they finished visualizing the aversive scene. Subjects in the N-CPR group also relaxed after concluding the aversive scene on some trials. This does not seem consistent with the reciprocal inhibition principle, which requires the antagonistic (relaxation) response to occur simultaneously with the stimulus that gives rise to the anxiety response. This fact also weakens their counterconditioning explanation. As a matter of fact, if they used the same procedure in their desensitization group (one of the six conditions included in this experiment), it may be that three of their treatments were actually positive reinforcement and none were reciprocal inhibition. This study then does not seem to either prove a reciprocal inhibition basis of CPR or disprove an operant conditioning basis (especially since CPR was superior to N-CPR on behavioral measures).

Ladouceur (1974) compared CPR and a "reversed-CPR" (R-CPR) procedure in the treatment of rat phobia. The R-CPR procedure was one in which the reinforcing scene was presented immediately before the target scene. He found no significant difference between the treatment groups on a behavioral measure. Both groups were superior to a no-treatment control. Interestingly, Ladouceur states that the results contradict an operant conditioning explanation of CPR and support a reciprocal inhibition explanation.

With regard to the CPR treatment, according to Ladouceur, "Each R [response] in the 18 step sequence was imagined 3 times during a session. A different reinforcing scene was used at each session" (p. 5). This statement implies that the same reinforcing scene was used for 54 consecutive trials in the course of a single treatment session. Even if the scene chosen for a given session functioned as a reinforcer at the beginning of the session, clinical experience and what is known about reinforcer satiation suggest that perhaps, in fact, there were not as many CPR trials administered as the investigator intended. In other words, as the reinforcing quality of the intended reinforcing scene diminished, the subjects may actually have been experiencing CE trials.

Actually, all that was demonstrated was that these two treatments were equally effective in this experiment. If, as Ladouceur seems to imply, reciprocal inhibition is the reason for the success of the R-CPR procedure, then all that was shown was that reciprocal inhibition was as effective as a second procedure, which may or may not best be explained by reciprocal inhibition and may or may not have been CPR.

As in the Marshall et al. study cited above, the relaxed state (assumed to be elicited by the reinforcing stimulus) in the CPR treatment was not in effect until after the completion of the target response, thus weakening the reciprocal inhibition argument. In the R-CPR treatment, the assumed relaxed state immediately preceded the target response and may have carried over into the scene presentation, thus, in effect, functioning as a systematic desensitization trial. Another, more parsimonious explanation for the success of the R-CPR group is extinction (Evans, 1973). In any event, even if reciprocal inhibition were operating in the R-CPR treatment, it does not follow that just because a second technique achieves the same results, it is necessarily based on the same learning principles. In order to discredit the explanation for one procedure, in this case CPR, it is not enough to prove something else works too; the evidence for the first procedure must also be discredited.

After conducting two later experiments, Ladouceur (1977, 1978) wrote that neither counterconditioning nor positive reinforcement provides an adequate explanation of CPR. He concluded that extinction offers a more satisfactory explanation.

In the 1977 experiment, Ladouceur basically replicated his 1974 study, adding two control groups and a 1 month follow-up. Dependent variables were scores on a Rat Attitude Survey, Behavioral Avoidance Test, and Fear Thermometer. The Fear Thermometer was administered in conjunction with the Behavioral Avoidance Test as follows: "At the step on which the subject refused to proceed further with the Behavioral Avoidance Test she was asked to rate her fear on a 100-point scale using the Fear Thermometer . . . " (p. 548). A common assumption of this sort of fear assessment is that once a certain level of fear (e.g., level X) is reached, subjects will be unwilling to approach closer to the fear stimulus. Since level X is the level assumed to stop a subject, regardless of the distance from the fear stimulus (whether it be 10 feet at pre-test or 3 feet at post-test), asking subjects to rate their fear at the spot at which they stop approaching the stimulus can be misleading, since that level will usually be level X. Differences in the numerical rating assigned to specific instances of level X fear are, therefore, more likely to reflect the reliability or lack thereof of this particular self-report meausure than differences in level of fear actually experienced. If a significant difference is to occur, then the subject must actually complete the hierarchy. Instead, as suggested by Kearney (1976), the post-test Fear Thermometer rating should be made at the same point (e.g., 8 feet) as it was made during the pre-test, thereby allowing for a more meaningful comparison of pre-test and post-test scores without the confounding of the measure through the introduction of the second variable, distance from the fear stimulus. Thus, it is not surprising that the author found no significant differences on the Fear Thermometer.

On the Rat Attitude Survey, however, which measured degree of comfort in rat-related situations, Ladouceur found " ... that the two covert positively reinforced groups significantly increased ($p < .01$) from pre- to post-test. However, only the former group maintained this positive increase at the follow-up" (p. 549). Data are not presented to enable the determination of which CPR group is the "former" group, or that with more lasting effectiveness, but Ladouceur's earlier description of the standard CPR group prior to the noncontingent CPR group suggests that perhaps it was the standard CPR group, which alone yielded statistically significant results on this measure at the 1-month follow-up. In the noncontingent condition, "All the reinforcing scenes were presented first for approximately 20 min., next phobic scenes were imagined for 20 min ... " (p. 548). Subjects in this condition therefore essentially received 20-minute treatment sessions of either imaginal flooding or desensitization without formal relaxation instructions, depending on the order of item presentation. This component would, of course, have also been operating in the reversed CPR condition. All three treatment groups improved on the BAT (Behavioral Avoidance Test), whereas subjects in the control groups did not. Ladouceur interpreted these results as supporting the efficacy of CPR, but casting doubt on the adequacy of the operant theoretical basis.

In the 1978 experiment Ladouceur compared two methods of hierarchy arrangement in three treatment procedures: CPR, systematic desensitization, and what was essentially a covert classical extinction condition. The two methods of hierarchy arrangement were chronological sequence and progressive sequence, or the arrangement of items according to increasing level of anxiety. Although all six treatment conditions were effective in reducing fear, Ladouceur felt that the results cast doubt on the theoretical underpinnings of both systematic desensitization and CPR, with exposure now being the most plausible explanation of their success. He found that across all treatment conditions, subjects who were presented with scenes in chronological sequence required an average of 148.1 presentations to reduce their *suds* (subjective unit of disturbance, Wolpe, 1982) ratings to 10, whereas subjects who visualized scenes according to increasing level of anxiety arousal only needed 96.5 scene visualizations to achieve the same reduced *suds* level. An implication of this finding is that although CPR, systematic desensitization, and other procedures may be effective with the chronological scene presentation, clinical application of CPR in the treatment of phobias may be more effective if the scenes are presented progressively, thereby taking advantage of both reciprocal inhibition and operant conditioning principles simultaneously.

The author explains this result, however, by stating that " . . . a progressive presentation of the anxiety evoking situation may increase the perception of self-efficacy (see Bandura, 1977)" (p. 419). This seems to conflict with Ladouceur's statement that "Taken together, these results supports Marks' (1975) position which asserts that *exposure per se* to the anxiety evoking stimuli is the crucial element in many therapeutic methods aimed at reducing anxiety" (p. 418). Exposure, which one would assume is an application of extinction, does not require the hypothesizing of notions of self-efficacy or other less parsimonious hypothetical constructs for an explanation. Extinction would be expected to take place more smoothly in a progressive hierarchy than a chronological hierarchy. Therefore, the invocation of a subjective sense of self-efficacy, which may simply be nondirected covert conditioning trials of successful behavior anyway, is an additional unnecessary obstruction which adds nothing useful in terms of explanation.

Bajtelsmit and Gershman (1976) conducted a study expressly for the purpose of investigating the operant conceptualization of CPR. The six groups in their study included standard CPR, a procedure in which subjects imagined anxiety-eliciting scenes in gradually increasing hierarchical order followed by reinforcing scenes (CPR$_2$), CPR followed by a distracting auditory stimulus (CPR$_3$), a reversed CPR procedure followed by the auditory stimulus (CPR$_4$), attention focusing discussion (AF), and no treatment. All five treatment groups showed significant change on almost all of the self-report anxiety measures. Behavioral measures used were of test performance, not test anxiety.

Bajtelsmit and Gershman concluded that their results supported the effectiveness of CPR but conflicted with an operant explanation of CPR. Disregarding possible difficulties with the self-reporting of anxiety (Bernstein, 1973; Bernstein & Nietzel, 1974), there are other problems with this contention.

The success of the CPR treatment in anxiety studies may be partially explainable by counterconditioning as Bajtelsmit and Gershman suggest, but as mentioned in the discussion of Ladouceur's reversed CPR group, that does not mean that all effective procedures operate on the same principle. Bajtelsmit and Gershman also attribute the success of the CPR_2 group to counterconditioning. They go on to write that if operant conditioning were operating, an increase in anxiety should have resulted in this group.

While the above results and conclusion may logically follow from the use of the CPR_2 procedure as Bajtelsmit and Gershman describe it, this is hard to determine from the available information. There are a number of additional factors which should be taken into consideration. For example, the authors do not mention how the anxiety was included in the scene. Did the subjects imagine they were anxious, relaxed, coping, or not coping? It does not seem likely that subjects were asked to imagine they were anxious in these scenes since they had been told the program was "directed at alleviating test anxiety." The authors mention that the scenes were presented in a hierarchy. Therefore, it seems likely that little, if any, anxiety was elicited. Earlier studies (Cooke, 1966; Schubot, 1966) have shown that anxiety can be reduced by presenting scenes in a hierarchical order without including the relaxation response. If extinction were operating in the CPR_2 group, the reinforcing scene may have been presented immediately after a neutral rather than anxious response. This might then have resulted in the covert reinforcement of the neutral emotional response to the test-related situations. Although it seems that this study demonstrated that a number of different procedures, including CPR, can be effective in reducing self-reports of test anxiety, it did not discredit the operant theoretical basis of CPR.

Covert Positive Reinforcement: Other Alternative Explanations
Some authors offer alternative theories to either operant or reciprocal inhibition explanations. Hurley (1976), for one, has challenged both operant and reciprocal inhibition explanations of CPR. Working with a group of 40 snake-phobic subjects, she compared CPR with a Covert Exposure procedure, in which no reinforcing scene followed the target scene, and Covert Noncontiguity, in which both target scenes and reinforcing scenes were imagined, but with a 1- to 2-minute break intervening. There were no significant differences between these treatments, but all three were superior to an attention-placebo group. Hurley states that these results are inconsistent with a reinforcement explanation of CPR and implies they are also inconsistent with a reciprocal inhibition explanation. She offers a response prevention

(Wilson & Davison, 1972) explanation as an alternative. Hurley's Covert Exposure treatment appears similar to the Wish et al. (1970) neutral scene group. It will be recalled that in the Wish et al. study this procedure was not as effective as the covert reinforcer. Also, the goal for Wish et al. was not fear reduction, but the alteration of the estimation of circle sizes in a consistent manner. It may be that Hurley's Covert Exposure and Covert Noncontiguity procedures worked because of response prevention. Perhaps they were effective because of extinction. Whatever the case may be, this does not disprove the operant conditioning basis of CPR.

Steffen (1977) reported two studies involving the use of CPR with a word-naming task. Subjects in the first study were 50 hospitalized adult males diagnosed as suffering from schizophrenia, chronic, undifferentiated type. All subjects were asked to speak 200 words, of their own choosing, with the single limitation that the words did not form sentences. There were five treatment conditions. The first 10 subjects simply emitted the 200 words. For the second group the experimenter spoke the word *scene* after all plural nouns emitted by the subject for words 51 through 150. Subjects in the third group were instructed to visualize the most pleasurable scene they identified on the RSS whenever they heard the word *scene*. The experimenter then spoke the word *scene* on 10 random occasions during the emission of words 51 through 150. Group 4 subjects were instructed to visualize the least pleasurable scene they identified on the RSS in response to the word *scene*. The experimenter then said "scene" after every plural noun these subjects spoke during words 51 through 150. The fifth condition, CPR, was similar to group 4, except that the most pleasurable scene was substituted for the least pleasurable scene. Results showed that there was no difference between groups in the number of plural nouns emitted during the first 50 words (baseline). During the post-treatment stage, words 151 through 200, however, subjects in the CPR condition showed a significantly greater increase in plural-noun emissions than all the other groups, which did not differ from each other.

The second experiment basically replicated the first, with the substitution of 25 male and 25 female paid college students for the schizophrenic subjects. In this experiment, however, only the male CPR subjects showed a treatment effect. The author then dismisses the operant bases of CPR writing that, "The failure to find a significant change in plural-noun responding for female subjects is somewhat problematic for the assumption that an operant model provides adequate explanation of the process of change in covert reinforcement" (Steffen, 1977, p. 293). Although the author then hints that some kind of cognitive model might provide a better explanation of CPR, he neglects to suggest a specific cognitive model which would require the use of a procedure precisely consistent with an operant basis of CPR in order to be effective.

Aside from the obvious question of inquiring as to the relative baseline rates of plural-noun emissions (and therefore opportunities for reinforcing that behavior) of male and female subjects (this information was not provided by the author nor were the data from which it could be gleaned), one wonders whether it is the author's intention to imply that, because of some kind of sex-determined cognitive differences, females as a group cannot respond to covert conditioning. Several other studies have, of course, demonstrated that female subjects are just as capable as male subjects of benefiting from covert conditioning (e.g., Kearney, 1984).

In a later experiment, in which CPR was applied to test anxiety, Lurie and Steffen (1980) found a covert rehearsal condition (CPR without the reinforcing scene) to be superior to CPR and three other conditions, including delayed treatment. The authors used these results to dismiss the operant basis of CPR in favor of a cognitive mediational model. If this were true, however, the CPR and cognitive information control groups should also have shown similar improvement. Perhaps a more reasonable explanation for these results lies in the fact that the four graduate students serving as therapists were each given exclusive treatment responsibility for all subjects in one of the experimental conditions. In other words, all subjects in each group were exposed to only one therapist, who treated no subject in any other group. Thus, the results of this study are confounded by therapist variable factors. With this in mind, it may be that the effectiveness of the covert rehearsal group is attributable to covert classical extinction.

Turkat and Adams (1982) conducted an experiment "to assess experimentally the efficacy of covert positive reinforcement in modifying pain, as well as its theoretical basis" (p. 191). Dependent variables included self-reports, physiological measures, and tolerance of finger pressure pain. Subjects who reported muscle contraction headaches were assigned to one of six groups: CPR imagining exposure to the pain stimulus, CPR plus instructions that CPR was not very effective, CPR plus instructions that CPR was very effective, CPR imagining that pain was experienced, attention placebo, and no treatment. After baseline (of headache) and pre-test (of finger pressure pain) measures, subjects received their "training" in the various CPR procedures, which consisted of listening to a treatment or control tape. Subjects were then readministered the experimental pain test, with the additional instructions to use the self-control procedure to control the pain. No significant difference was found between any of the groups on finger pressure pain or headache, although all groups reported fewer headaches at a two-week follow up. Turkat and Adams (1982) concluded that:

> The results of the present investigation indicate that the covert positive reinforcement technique was no more effective than placebo and no treatment in modifying clinical and experimental pain. The covert positive reinforcement procedure has previously been reported to be effective in modifying a variety of phenomena. However, insufficient dependent measures were used and many uncontrolled variables were present in these investigations, so as to limit their utlility in generating cause-effect relationships. . . . The present investigation differed from these studies in a variety of methodological aspects which may account for the discrepant findings of covert positive reinforcement's effectiveness. (p. 199)

The implication here is that Turkat and Adams (1982) consider their study to be better designed than many of the studies more supportive of CPR. While the present study may be well designed in general, there are major weaknesses with it as a study of CPR. One of the "methodological aspects which may account for the discrepant findings" (p. 199) is the lack of learning trials provided to subjects. CPR "treatment" consisted of having subjects listen to a single playing of an audiotape between pre and post finger pain tests. The authors did not specify either the length of the tape treatment session or the number of trials contained on the tape. Most experimental CPR treatment tapes reported in the literature, however, last about 30 minutes. Assuming a typical 30-minute treatment session used to maximum efficiency with 3-minute CPR trials, we have a situation in which subjects received a total of only 10 conditioning trials each. Even if there were twice as many trials involved, this is far short of the 60 to 80 trials which an inspection of the CPR literature suggests is minimally adequate for satisfactory results. Even if the attempted reinforcement were overt rather than covert, there seem to be far too few conditioning trials for learning to take place. If there were a reasonable number of trials, however, we are still faced with another problem. That is, what is the behavior to be learned? According to the authors' view of CPR, "In this procedure, the individual imagines being exposed to the pain stimulus, that the individual experiences no pain and then imagines a reinforcing scene of the individual's choice"

(p. 194) and "With this technique, the individual imagines performing the target behavior (e.g., pain insensitivity) and then reinforces this behavior by imagining a pleasant image" (p. 191). We disagree with the authors' apparently considering insensitivity to pain to be a behavior. Since insensitivity to pain is also a characteristic of, or something that can be "done" by, pencils, rocks and cadavers, it does not pass Ogden Lindsley's "dead man's rule" and cannot be considered a behavior. Therefore there was no behavior to be reinforced! Our suggestion is to teach an alternative or incompatible response to replace the pain behaviors. When the SCT is employed, muscle relaxation is the alternative response. Other coping strategies may be to relabel the sensation or to try to identify the component sensations (e.g., pressure, warmth). This is the method used by other researchers who have found CPR useful in modifying pain responses (e.g., Bennett & Cautela, 1981; Scott & Leonard, 1978).

Another possibility is that the authors were attempting to use a differential reinforcement of other behavior (DRO) procedure to decrease the pain response. This is also unlikely though, since apparently no unreinforced pain response trials were included to allow differential learning to take place.

With regard to application of the various treatment strategies to headaches, subjects were instructed "to practice the specific treatment strategy twice daily regardless of whether they were experiencing pain" (Turkat & Adams, p. 194). However, it is unclear how much practice actually took place. Although the authors do include the subjects' reports of practice frequency in a table, the reported mean frequency of daily practices for the CPR group was 2.88 practices/per day during the first follow-up week and 1.54 practices/per day during the second follow-up week, which appears consistent with instructions. According to the same table, however, the CPR subjects reported 2.13 practices/per week during both weeks. Since the weekly frequencies are clearly not muliples of the daily frequencies, something is amiss with the data reported, thus making it useless to comment upon.

In the Turkat and Adams experiment described above, there seems to be a fundamental misunderstanding of the theoretical basis of covert conditioning and a subsequent misapplication of the CPR procedure. However, it may be that the improvement which was found in all groups may very well have come about because the various CPR and other "treatments" served as cognitive distraction strategies, even though they were not given the opportunity to function as behavioral learning procedures. In addition, both an auditory stimulus which was sounded every 10 seconds once pain was reported and the subject's task of then reporting the level of perceived pain also most likely served as distractions interfering with the perception of pain by all subjects, even those in the no-treatment condition.

Covert Negative Reinforcement   In an attempt to investigate the operant basis of CNR, Zemore et al. (1978) compared standard CNR, a CNR like condition with a second pause between the aversive and target scene, and a no-treatment condition in treating snake-phobic subjects. Both treatment conditions were equally effective and superior to no treatment. The authors suggest extinction as a more reasonable explanation for the success of both treatments and state that " . . . the classical conditioning paradigm would seem a more appropriate basis for explaining the success of covert negative reinforcement than an operant-conditioning paradigm" (p. 961). While this may be true (and extinction does seem to be the most parsimonious explanation for the success of the CNR-pause treatment), once again we must state that it does not logically follow that simply demonstrating two treatments to be equally effective proves that they must operate according to the same learning principles.

Covert Sensitization   Foreyt and Hagen (1973) conducted a frequently referred to study in which covert sensitization, a placebo-control (suggestion) condition, and no treatment were compared in treating obesity. A careful reading of this report reveals what appears to be a very thorough, well designed, and well controlled experiment. Each subject received a reasonable number of trials (270). Although the authors reported that some of the subjects in the covert sensitization group " . . . could not capture strong feelings of nausea" (p. 19), which is necessary in vomiting scenes, the sample description of a covert sensitization scene included in the text seems to be well constructed. Interestingly, the description of the sample placebo control scene included very closely resembles a lengthy CPR flow scene, which might be predicted to actually increase the eating of the targeted foods!

There were no significant differences in weight between any of the groups, and the weight loss that did take place was not significant in any of the conditions. However, in response to a Food Palatability Scale devised by the authors, subjects in both the covert sensitization and placebo control groups reported decreased liking for their favorite, targeted foods. The authors conclude that "If, as the data indicate, suggestion, rather than conditioning was operating for the covert sensitization placebo group, it is reasonable to assume that suggestion was also a critical independent variable for the covert sensitization group" (Foreyt & Hagen, 1973, p. 22).

As mentioned above, the only dependent variables employed in this study were weight and the Food Palatability Scale. Although there was some weight loss in all groups, including the no-treatment group, there was no significant difference between any of the groups in weight loss, so this study did not demonstrate covert sensitization, suggestion, placebo treatment, or anything else to be effective in bringing about weight loss. What did change were the reports of the subjects in the covert sensitization and placebo conditions as to the palatability, not the consuming, of targeted foods. This suggests that either the decrease in palatability was not great enough to lead to a meaningful decrease in consumption of the targeted foods, that substantial decreases in consumption of the targeted foods was accompanied by increases in consumption of nontargeted foods (in order to maintain weight level), or that subject self-reports were not accurate (a possibility pointed out by the authors), perhaps in response to demand factors built into the conduct of this experiment. A post-treatment questioning of subjects revealed that while many subjects in both treatment groups reported decreased desire for targeted foods, subjects in the covert sensitization group generally also reported sensations of nausea when exposed to targeted foods.

With regard of the role of expectancy in covert sensitization, the study by Barlow et al. (1972) described in the chapter of this book devoted to covert sensitization showed that covert sensitization can be effective in spite of subject expectations to the contrary. This does not, of course, rule out the influence of subject expectations, and we encourage practitioners to make use of this phenomenon in their clinical applications of covert conditioning. In the Foreyt and Hagen study described above, however, it seems that since there were no significant weight changes, no reported changes in the dietary habits of the subjects, and only self-report changes in the demand direction which are somewhat questionable in that they may or may not have accurately described changes in subjects' experienced palatability responses to targeted foods, no claims for the effectiveness of anything should be made based on this study. Since this does appear to be such a well designed and conducted experiment in so many areas, however, it might well be worth replicating, with the inclusion of additional assessments of the subjects' actual eating and exercise habits. Since covert sensitization is very specific in its effects and only the eating of specific foods was targeted, it would be informative to see what happens to the subjects' consumption of other foods.

Davidson and Denney (1976) conducted what at first appears to be a well designed and controlled study of the usefulness of covert sensitization in treating nail biting. Thirty-three college students were assigned to either standardized covert sensitization, information only, information plus covert sensitization, or waiting-list control groups. The single dependent variable used was the total length of all 10 fingernails. Measurements were taken before treatment, after 6 weeks of treatment, and at the end of a 5-week follow-up period. Based on these measurements, Davidson and Denney (1976) found that only the information group showed significant improvement from pre-test to post-test. The authors concluded that:

> Contrary to prediction, covert sensitization did not contribute significantly to the improvement in nail length measures over the course of treatment. Furthermore, on the basis of specific comparisons between each treatment group and the control group, covert sensitization may have actually detracted from the effectiveness of information alone. (p. 516)

A careful reading of the report of this experiment leaves several questions unanswered, the answers to which might affect the interpretations of results. First of all, Davidson and Denney reported that, "The covert sensitization tapes lasted about 15 minutes, the first beginning with a brief rationale describing aversive conditioning. All eight tapes included brief relaxation exercises, followed by an aversive scene and an aversion-relief scene" (Davidson & Denney, 1976, p. 514). The use of one aversive scene together with the obvious limited amount of time available during each session (15 minutes minus relaxation exercises) suggests one covert sensitization plus one CNR trial per session. Over the course of eight sessions this amounts to 8 covert sensitization trials plus 8 CNR trials for a total of 16 covert conditioning trials in all, considerably fewer than clinical observations suggest as adequate. The first question then, is, were subjects limited to 16 covert conditioning trials, distributed over 6 weeks of treatment, for an average of .38 trials per day?

Second, although it is true that standardized tape recordings have proven to be an effective method in delivering CPR treatment for experimental purposes, another factor has to be considered. When the target scenes employed are generally the same for all subjects, the consequent scenes are usually individualized, and individualized consequent scenes are presented to individual subjects within the context of the standardized, tape recorded treatment (cf. Kearney, 1976; Kearney, 1984). While it is not perfectly clear from a reading of the report of the present study, it appears that all subjects visualized the same nausea-aversive component of the treatment scenes. If this is true, it seems fair to ask, what was the justification for choosing this scene for use with all subjects? Was, for example, the Fear Survey Schedule or Aversive Scene Survey Schedule administered to some or all of the subjects prior to scene development?

Also, there are questions that can be asked about the choice and control of the dependent variable, fingernail length. Were subjects given any direct instructions regarding normal fingernail grooming during the course of treatment or follow-up period? It seems that 11 weeks is quite a while to expect individuals to go without normal fingernail cutting or filing, unless specific instructions are given to the contrary. Uncontrolled adjustment of fingernail length by subjects would, of course, invalidate the dependent variable. How much growth was biologically possible during the 6- and 11-week periods, respectively? Should a control group of non-biters who also did not trim their nails have been included for comparison purposes? Do we know, in the combined information-covert sensitization treatment condition, for example, whether it was possible for any additional growth to have been measured?

Although Davidson and Denney (1976) report that covert sensitization was not effective at the end of the five-week treatment period, they also add that "Subjects in the three treatment groups improved significantly from the pre-test to the follow-up test, and there was no differential effect among the three treatments" (p. 516). Since changes in the dependent variable of this study are not immediately observable, as would be the case with, for example, the amount of time the subject's fingers are in his/her mouth, might it not be that covert sensitization was simply slower in bringing about its maximum effect than was the information condition?

Another question worthy of consideration deals with the appropriateness of the choice of nail biting as the target behavior for a covert sensitization study. As stated above, the authors suggested that the addition of covert sensitization may actually have detracted from the effectiveness of information in inhibiting nail biting. Nail biting is often thought of as an anxiety response, a behavior which, at least in the short run, may help to reduce the individual's level of anxiety. Since covert sensitization is a punishment procedure, increased anxiety on the part of the subject is a very common side effect of its use. It may be, then, that increased anxiety resulting from the visualization of the aversive scene may have served as a discriminative stimulus to occasion an increase in nail biting behavior, a behavior which in the past served to decrease anxiety. In a more recent study, Meade (1979) found that CPR was significantly more effective than no treatment in increasing fingernail length.

Covert Extinction   In an attempt to test the effectiveness of CE in reducing cigarette-smoking behavior, Götestam and Melin (1983) assigned 21 volunteers to one of three conditions: CE, relaxation, or waiting-list control. Three classes of subject behavior were assessed: overt behavior, that is, number of cigarettes smoked; covert physio-logical behavior, that is, pulse rate; and covert psychological behavior, that is, craving for cigarettes. Subjects in all groups were told to stop smoking in six days and "given some convenient strategies to facilitate the smoking cessation" (p. 28). In addition, subjects in the CE group received 5 therapist-directed trials on each of six days, for a total of 30 CE trials. Prior to treatment, subjects reported a range of 4 to 32 years of smoking 12 to 30 cigarettes each day for a minimum possible number of reinforcing cigarette smoking trials of 17,520 (assuming conservatively that only one puff per cigarette was reinforcing). Subjects were asked to practice CE outside of the formal sessions, but no mention is made of the actual number of additional trials completed by the subjects.

Although all three groups significantly decreased their amount of cigarette consumption ($p < .01$) immediately after treatment, there was no difference between groups. At a one-month follow-up, however, the waiting-list group had relapsed, but, for some unexplained reason, the treatment groups showed both significant improvement from pre-test to follow-up and significant relapse from post-test to follow-up.

> Tukey's test showed significant decrease in smoking for all groups ($p < .01$) from baseline to first and second treatment, and for the treatment groups from baseline to follow-up. There were also significant changes (increased smoking) for all three groups from end of treatment to follow-up ($p < .01$). (Götestam & Melin, 1983, p. 29)

Both treatment groups showed significant improvement on pulse rate, but the changes in craving were not significant. The authors conclude that CE "is a procedure which has no specific therapeutic efficacy, which surpasses other unspecific efforts" (p. 31).

Future research may demonstrate that CE does have no specific therapeutic effect. However, the advisability of taking subjects with a strong reinforcement history such as a minimum of 17,520 re-inforcement trials distributed over at least a 4-year period, switching them to a schedule of 10 to 14 reinforcers (based on data presented on cigarettes smoked during treatment) to 5 extinction trials (or possibly

10, if subjects did as much homework as in office therapy) for a 3-day period, and then thinning the schedule still further to a 2 or 3 reinforcers per 5 or 10 extinction trials during the second 3-day stage of treatment is questionable. Finally, drawing conclusions generalized to all applications of the employed procedure cannot be justified. Actually, such a step-by-step switch to a leaner reinforcement schedule would be predicted to make the target behavior, cigarette smoking, more resistant to extinction. The relatively few extinction trials used is surprising. In their earlier successful application of CE to amphetamine addiction (Götestam & Melin, 1974), the authors used 100 to 200 trials, subjects (with one exception) did not have access to the drugs abused during treatment, and they had considerably fewer substance-abuse trials in their history compared to the subjects in the 1983 study.

As mentioned above, there was a significant decrease in the number of cigarettes actually consumed by both the CE and relaxation groups. It does not logically follow, however, that the same factor or "unspecified factors" were responsible for all the decreases. Also, based on the substantial, but not significant, decrease in consumption by the waiting-list group, it appears that the instructions to stop smoking and/or the unspecified "convenient strategies to facilitate the smoking cessation" (p. 28) may very well have had an effect and thereby confounded the effects of both CE and relaxation training.

Summary. The 13 studies reviewed in this section are far from a complete report of studies which have not been supportive of the covert conditioning model. The sample of studies we have included was chosen because these studies are representative of experiments whose results are not entirely favorable to covert conditioning, and they include several studies commonly referred to by other authors attempting to discredit either the efficacy of covert conditioning or its theoretical basis.

In almost every study just reviewed, however, the covert conditioning procedures were effective, although perhaps not more so than the other conditions. It is, in fact, rare to find a study in which covert conditioning was not effective. It is more usual to find that covert conditioning and one or more of the other treatments included in a particular experiment were similarly effective.

Studies designed to test behavior therapy procedures usually involve several dependent variables to help determine the effectiveness of the various procedures under investigation. This of course often leads to situations in which some treatments turn out to have statistically significant superior results as compared to other conditions on some measures but not on all measures. In discussing the results of these studies, the authors' own biases are a deciding factor in whether to conclude that a given treatment was or was not effective. In some cases the same objective data can be used to both support and refute a treatment's effectiveness.

In the preceding section different interpretations and conclusions were drawn from experiments conducted and evaluated by other investigators. Examining the results, in 7 of the 13 studies reviewed, the covert conditioning procedures were at least as effective as the other treatment and/or placebo conditions employed. In an eighth report (Steffen, 1977), which consisted of two experiments, CPR was the only treatment to show a significant effect in the first experiment and the only treatment to show an effect with male subjects in the second experiment. Covert conditioning was found to be effective, but no more so than no treatment in two studies, leaving only four experiments in which the authors concluded that covert conditioning was not at all effective. This summary is presented in Table 10-2.

General Considerations

With regard to the CPR studies reviewed, the most common approach seems to be for authors to rearrange the order of the steps in CPR, get

Table 10-2. Effectiveness of Covert Conditioning in Investigations Reviewed in Chapter 10

A. Covert conditioning at least as effective as other treatment and/or placebo conditions
1. Bajtelsmit & Gershman (1976)
2. Hurley (1974)
3. Ladouceur (1974)
4. Ladouceur (1977)
5. Ladouceur (1978)
6. Marshall, Boutillier, & Minnes (1974)
7A. Steffen (1977) (Experiment I and Experiment II male subjects)
8. Zemore, Ramsay, & Zemore (1978)
B. Covert conditioning effective, but no more effective than no treatment
9. Götestam & Melin (1983)
10. Turkat & Adams (1982)
C. Covert conditioning not effective
11. Davidson & Denney (1976)
12. Lurie & Steffen (1980)
13. Foreyt & Hagen (1973)
7B. Steffen (1977) (Experiment II female subjects)

significant results, attribute the results to reciprocal inhibition, and then proceed to refer to CPR as a variant of systematic desensitization. There are some faults with this line of logic. First, both the reciprocal inhibition principle as such and reciprocal inhibition as an explanation of desensitization are still often questioned. The reciprocal inhibition explanation of desensitization needs to be more firmly established before it is offered as an explanation for other procedures. Second, when two techniques get similar results, it does not necessarily follow that they are both variants of the same procedure or operate according to the same principle. It is not enough to prove something else works to discredit the operant basis of CPR; the existing evidence for the operant basis must be refuted. Third, the argument is often made that the pleasurable scene elicits a relaxed state functionally equivalent to relaxation training. Therefore, CPR is really a variant of desensitization. It may very well be that CPR does have reciprocal inhibition components that do contribute to its success in treating anxiety-related behaviors. However, the opposite argument can also be made. That is, that the relaxed state brought about in desensitization is reinforcing.* Therefore, desensitization is really a variant of CPR. The volumes of evidence establishing operant conditioning together with the questions surrounding reciprocal inhibition at the present time certainly make this a more parsimonious possibility.

Further support for the operant basis of CPR may be found in the kinds of behaviors the technique has been used to change. True tests of the operant underpinning of CPR should involve behaviors without an anxiety component. Whereas desensitization works by changing the emotional responses elicited by various stimuli and thereby allows subjects sufficiently motivated to engage in various motor behaviors (e.g., give a speech, approach a dog, take an examination), CPR has been successfully used to directly modify behaviors without an emotional component (Epstein & Peterson, 1973; Rhodes, 1978; Wish et al., 1970). Reduction of avoidance behaviors, which is the prime use of desensitization, is not the same as the increase of approach behaviors. Direct fear reduction is classical conditioning, whereas the increase of approach behavior, even if accompanied by reduction of avoidance and other fear responses, is operant.

Attributing the total effectiveness of the procedures in question to one learning principle is probably too simplistic. It is very likely that

---

* This position does have some empirical support (cf. Edmonds, 1975) and is consistent with the interaction assumption.

neither CPR nor systematic desensitization, nor any other behavior therapy procedure, for that matter, owes all of its effectiveness to one, and only one, learning principle. In other words, there probably is no perfectly "pure" technique. Perhaps most, if not all, of the learning principles (as well as expectancy, demand, and other variables often offered as explanations) contribute to the successes of covert conditioning, systematic desensitization, and the various transformations of these procedures used in experiments. This would help explain the continued successes with the many transformations which seem to lend support to any number of explanations of the various procedures.

Saying that covert conditioning can be effective is not the same as saying that it is *always* effective. There are some incidents of ineffectiveness for every treatment. Sometimes the ineffectiveness is easily attributable to faulty application of the treatment, sometimes it is not.

Wilson and O'Leary (1980, p. 267) hold that overt conditioning is more powerful than cognitive-based procedures. With regard to covert conditioning, however, we have shown that there is more than one way of explaining results which are sometimes interpreted as not supporting either the covert conditioning assumptions or procedures. There is also some evidence to suggest that at times the effects of overt and covert conditioning can be similar (see Brownell & Barlow, 1976). Based on all the available evidence, it seems that it cannot be claimed that covert conditioning is consistently either more or less effective than overt conditioning.

Covert Conditioning Research Guidelines

In conducting research on covert conditioning, it would be helpful if experimental conditions, other than the independent variable, could be standardized. Scott and Rosenstiel (1975) have pointed out that a major problem in CPR research, which is true of research on the other procedures as well, is that instructions to subjects regarding imagination are not presented in a consistent fashion. Perhaps it would be useful if standardized scripts of therapist verbal behavior were developed for experimental use, somewhat like the Stanford Hypnotic Susceptibility Scales (Weitzenhoffer & Hilgard, 1959), which are frequently used in hypnosis research. Due to current unavailability of such an aid, researchers should include samples of the therapists' instructions to their subjects (or clients in case studies) in their reports.

Parameters of other variables, such as duration of target scene and consequence scene presentation (5 to 15 seconds seems to be long enough for most subjects to obtain clear imagery, yet brief enough to avoid fatigue), subject rating of scene clarity and pleasantness/ aversiveness, and length of the interval between trials, should be reported. Researchers should also report the number of different reinforcers and how they were alternated.

One of the most important topics that should be included in reports deals with the trials. In addition to the total number of trials practiced (60 to 80 trials appears to be numerically adequate in most situations), how were they scheduled? Were homework sessions assigned, and if so, how many additional trials did the subjects actually receive in this manner? Lack of sufficient treatment has been commented on as a common flaw in covert conditioning research by Little and Curran (1978), who also make other useful suggestions for future covert conditioning research.

An additional research guideline we would like to suggest is that, when possible, researchers include an overt operant conditioning condition equivalent to the covert conditioning condition. For example, if a subject imagines approaching a rat and follows that scene with an imaginary 15 seconds viewing of a rock concert, why not include a condition in which subjects approach the rat in vivo and view 15 seconds of a videotape of the same concert? Experimental designs of this sort could shed greater light on both the validity of the homogeneity assumption and the relative strengths of overt and covert conditioning. Moreover, through experiments in which the number of reinforcers and/or trials and order of stimulus presentations are manipulated, we would have a yardstick for comparison with overt procedures. Also, this would help control for situations in which conditions intended as placebos are in fact, unknown to the experimenter, effectively operating, according to operant principles (or any other principles), to change behavior.

From time to time the question of subjects' expectations is raised. In experiments designed to test the efficacy of various treatment procedures in modifying maladaptive behaviors, the experimenter cannot reasonably be expected to keep the subjects naive with regard to the purpose of the experiment. In other studies, however, when neutral behaviors, such as circle size estimation and verbal responses, are targeted, subjects can and often should be kept naive as to the experiment's purpose. After reviewing three covert conditioning studies dealing with neutral behaviors (Ascher, 1973; Cautela et al., 1971; Wish et al., 1970), Scott and Rosenstiel (1975) found that only 2 of the 92 subjects participating could report the true purpose of the experiment, yet the results of all three studies were supportive of covert conditioning.

Even if subject expectations did seem to make a difference, as outlined earlier in this book, a good case can be made for explaining expectations in terms of nondirected covert conditioning. What this means is simply that some individuals, without formal instructions from the therapist, covertly rehearse certain sequences of events. A cognitive psychologist might label this phenomenon as subject expectancy, whereas another psychologist might consider this to be additional covert conditioning trials. Therefore, subjects who appear to respond much more quickly to treatment than others have had the advantage of additional informal, nondirected, treatment. This may account for the apparently unexplainable response to treatment conditions which nonbehavioral psychologists explain by conjuring up explanatory fictions such as "expectancy factors" or "nonspecific factors"—which are really nonexplanations that themselves demand explanation!

11

Future of
Covert Conditioning

Covert conditioning has been, and continues to be, one of the most widely researched, discussed, and used therapeutic approaches in behavior therapy. The literature review which was conducted for the bibliography section of this book uncovered well over 400 published and otherwise available sources of information about covert conditioning.

A few years ago Wade et al. (1979) surveyed members of the Association for Advancement of Behavior Therapy (AABT) regarding their views and practices. One of the questions in the survey asked respondents to indicate which treatment procedures they frequently use. Covert conditioning was reported to be used by the sixth greatest percentage of therapists, as indicated by their responses to the open-ended study.*

In 1979, *Advances in Behaviour Research and Therapy* devoted an entire issue to covert conditioning (Kazdin & Smith, 1979). According to the authors, "In recent years, the number of covert conditioning techniques and their respective empirical literature have proliferated. The purpose of the present paper is to review and evaluate research on covert conditioning" (p. 57). The authors reviewed much of the published experimental work on the various covert conditioning

---

* The six most widely used treatment procedures, as indicated by the percentages of therapists, were operant conditioning (60.7%), systematic desensitization (48.6%), modeling (33.5%), relaxation training (22.6%), assertion training (20.2%), and covert conditioning (17.9%). For a listing of the 13 most frequently reported treatments, see Wade et al., (1979).

procedures and pointed out numerous important areas for future research.

A further indication of increasing interest in covert conditioning is the recent establishment within the Association for Advancement of Behavior Therapy of the Covert Conditioning Special Interest Group. Several members of the Association for Behavior Analysis have also expressed a desire to form a covert conditioning special interest group within that organization.

Some Areas of Future Applications and Research

Covert conditioning is now well into its second decade. Although there is little doubt that covert conditioning procedures can be effective in modifying a wide range of behaviors, there is still some debate about why covert conditioning works. As future research is planned to further investigate covert conditioning's effectiveness and parameters, it seems appropriate that, in keeping with the operant conceptualization of covert conditioning, more use be made of the A-B-A-B operant design. Some of the parameters which may be further investigated and some of the areas to which covert conditioning is being newly applied are discussed in the following sections.

Covert Conditioning Procedures

Nearly all of the applications of CNR have relied on the use of covert escape conditioning. In addition to its potential clinical usefulness, the development of covert avoidance conditioning has an important theoretical consideration. That is, additional evidence could well be gathered pertinent to the operant conceptualization of covert conditioning in general and CNR in particular.

Covert avoidance conditioning might more easily employ a single evolving scene rather than the switching of two scenes, as is more frequently used in other covert conditioning techniques. In covert sensitization a single, evolving scene is generally used. Recently completed CPR research (Kearney, 1984) demonstrated the effectiveness of a flow of scenes in which the reinforcing consequences follow naturally after the target behavior, within the same scene. The effectiveness of this variation, which needs to be more firmly established, will be an obvious benefit to clients who have difficulty switching scenes.

Another area of possible future research on CNR, in this case escape conditioning, might also involve the use of flow scenes. It is unclear whether it is necessary, helpful, irrelevant, or harmful to have temporal overlap of the aversive stimulus and the behavior which follows it in order for learning to take place. If one reaches to turn off a radio emitting noxious sounds, certainly a chain of behavior is underway prior to the actual cessation of the aversive stimulus. The completion of the final link in the chain, the clicking off of the on–off switch, immediately results in the cessation of the noise. In the case of a record player, however, there is usually a delay of a few seconds (and therefore obvious overlap) between the completion of the last behavior in the chain (engaging the reject switch) and the automatic lifting of the needle from the record. In these examples, the behaviors negatively reinforced were responsible for terminating the noxious stimuli, as is usually the case in the laboratory. However, just as superstitious behavior can be developed by random positive reinforcement, there is no reason why behavior that just happens to be in the right place at the right time cannot also be shaped by negative reinforcement, even if the behavior in question was not responsible for the cessation of the noxious stimuli.

To help clear up some of these points, a possible future experiment could employ four groups: overt conditioning—overlap; overt conditioning—nonoverlap; covert conditioning—overlap; covert conditioning—nonoverlap. The flow scene procedure could be used with the covert conditioning overlap treatment.

In clinical applications of CM, the reinforcers chosen are intended to be pleasurable to the client. Scenes are constructed so that the consequences also appear reinforcing to the model. However, since reinforcers are idiosyncratic, it is quite possible that an observer might perceive a model as being reinforced by a behavioral consequence, but would not find that stimulus personally reinforcing. The reverse of this scenario, that is, when the consequence is not reinforcing to the model but is attractive to the observer, is another possible situation that is occasionally encountered in everyday life. One would expect that the former arrangement would not likely increase the rate at which the observer performs the target behavior, whereas the latter arrangement would increase the rate of behavior. But, to our knowledge, this hypothesis has not yet been tested on either the covert or overt level.

General Level of Reinforcement

In reviewing the CPR literature for this book, it became apparent that there is a considerable amount of variability in the number of different reinforcing scenes employed and the number of trials for which each is used with experimental subjects. If covert conditioning is truly analogous to operant conditioning, then the matter of reinforcement satiation must always be a concern. Research into this topic could have both theoretical and practical implications if what is known about overt operant reinforcement is to be taken into consideration in the interpretation of results.

The questions above are related to another area of growing interest, the issue of level of reinforcement. This will see considerable research in the future, the results of which may have important implications for the clinical application of covert conditioning. By level of reinforcement, we refer to the number and quality of stimuli that an individual is experiencing which are capable of functioning as reinforcers for that particular individual. We are concerned with the individual's perception of the experienced stimuli as reinforcing or nonreinforcing. Reinforcement level is determined by the degree of positive and negative scanning of past events, the number of current reinforcing events at present in the individual's life, and the anticipation of future reinforcing or aversive activities.

The therapist should be sensitive to the concurrent amount of reinforcement received by the client on a daily basis. The reinforcement experienced by the individual for any particular time sample has been designated the General Level of Reinforcement (GLR; Cautela, 1984). The General Level of Reinforcement has been defined as the number, quality, and duration of reinforcements per unit of time. The GLR is related to a number of significant clinical factors:

1. The lower the GLR, the more likely it is that the individual experiences stress or depression.
2. Whenever maladaptive approach behavior, such as drug abuse, smoking, or sexual deviation, is the presenting complaint, it is often more difficult to achieve client cooperation. If the client is already at a low level of reinforcement, removal of reinforcers related to the problem behavior results in further distress and depression. This is also true of some anxiety-related behavior, for example, agoraphobia, which has operant components. The clinical strategy for treatment of any problematic behavior should include an increase in the GLR.
3. At a low GLR, the organism is in a state of deprivation of reinforcement. Therefore, any reinforcement received will be more powerful than a reinforcement received when the GLR is high. This means that when the problematic behavior is

reinforced, each reinforcement has a greater effect on the problematic behavior.

One important advantage of the SCT is that while the procedure is used to decrease problematic behavior, it also increases reinforcement by including the imagining of a pleasant scene. The GLR theory, of course, substantiates the therapist's strategy of always reinforcing a noncompatible response when the punishment procedure is used. That is, when covert sensitization is employed, CPR for incompatible responses should be utilized as well.

Clinical observations suggest that the lower the GLR, the more difficult it is to eliminate behaviors maintained by reinforcement. If an individual is receiving relatively less general reinforcement at a given point in time, a given stimulus is likely to be more powerful as a reinforcer than at other times when the individual is experiencing a greater amount of reinforcement. CPR obviously offers an alternative or supplementary means to increase an individual's GLR. Potential areas of research include investigating the role of nondirected covert conditioning with regard to depression, phobic thoughts, physical complaints, and psychological complaints.

Covert Classical Conditioning

To date, the development of covert conditioning has been limited to operant applications. However, there is no reason why this focus could not be expanded to include the development of covert classical conditioning. The necessity of the scenes used in covert conditioning to be able to evoke various states of arousal has already been stressed. The reliance of other imagery-based techniques, such as systematic desensitization (Wolpe, 1958), implosive therapy (Stampfl & Levis, 1967), flooding, and emotive imagery (Lazarus & Abramovitz, 1962), on the ability of imagery to elicit appropriate emotional responses suggests a classical conditioning component to these techniques. There is speculation that some of the attention-placebo treatments used in phobia research may actually be applications of covert classical extinction (Kearney, 1976).

King (1973) developed a theory of classical conditioning according to which the conditioned response is brought about by a conditioned stimulus image of the unconditioned stimulus. Yaremko and Werner (1974) researched conditioning GSR to imagerial stimuli using a procedure that could be considered covert classical conditioning.

Covert Conditioning and Brain Research

It was mentioned earlier that, in some cases, clients who report having difficulty with imagery can be helped by emphasizing various sense modalities. It may be that certain individuals with relatively severe sensory problems, including those often labeled learning disabled, perceptually handicapped, neurologically impaired, or brain damaged, may respond better to instructions to emphasize, for example, auditory or tactile sense modalities rather than visual. In some cases, imagery instructions may be more effective if delivered visually (e.g., slides or sign language) or tactiley (e.g., hand writing) than in the more common, oral–auditory manner.

The right cerebral cortex is assumed to be the predominant center for imagery (Baker & Glackman, 1981, p. 178). In a discussion of imagery and brain hemisphere function, Singer and Pope (1978) state that visual and auditory imagery are associated with the right hemisphere, whereas language is associated with the left hemisphere. Since tests such as the Wechsler Scales and Luria-Nebraska Neuropsychological Battery are sometimes used in the investigation of perceptual and hemispheric functioning, it may be possible to identify in advance clients who are more likely to respond favorably to treatments that emphasize, for example, visual imagery as opposed to cognitive self-statements. Hartlage (1980) has already presented some data to suggest that behavioral procedures in general show a clearer superiority over insight-oriented therapy in the treatment of strong right-hemisphere-dominant clients with specific complaints than in the treatment of left-hemisphere-dominant clients. The matching of clients with therapeutic procedures is a fascinating and important area for psychotherapy in general. However, it appears to be particularly pertinent and useful in covert conditioning, since there are so many options available in the use of covert conditioning and its applications can be so flexible and varied. This is certainly a field worthy of considerable future research.

Dreams

Dream behavior is covert behavior that involves thoughts, images, and feelings. The covert conditioning procedure is particularly suitable for the modification of dream behavior. According to the interaction hypothesis, nightmares can be modified by employing CPR to desensitize individuals to various components of the nightmares. This usually results in the elimination of nightmares. We have been employing covert conditioning to modify nightmare behavior for the last 10 years. Also, we have used covert conditioning procedures to influence dream content. The client is instructed to apply the covert conditioning procedure just before going to sleep. In approximately 60 percent of the cases, the clients report they have dreams involving the content of the procedure. For example, if covert sensitization is being employed on drinking alcohol, the subject might dream that he/she is having an accident while under the influence of alcohol. The dream behavior, of course, acts like another covert conditioning trial.

Behavioral Medicine

Perhaps the most rapidly expanding area within behavior modification is the field of behavioral medicine. Biofeedback and overt operant procedures are widely recognized as having useful applications in behavioral medicine. Scattered throughout this book, however, are examples of the use of covert conditioning in the successful treatment of organic dysfunction. Some of the organic problems mentioned, which covert conditioning has helped to ameliorate, have been heroin addiction (Wisocki, 1973b), pain (Cautela, 1977c; Stevens, 1982), amphetamine addiction (Götestam & Melin, 1974), alcoholism (Olson, Ganley, Devine, & Dorsey, 1981), agoraphobia (Flannery, 1972a), and TMJ syndrome (Cleveland, 1982). In addition, there have been numerous other applications of covert conditioning to organic dysfunction which have not yet been published. These include depression, amyotropic lateral sclerosis, Reynaud's disease, seizures, headaches, and asthma. As more work is published and empirical support for the interaction assumption grows, still further research on covert conditioning of organic dysfunction will be encouraged. An earlier theoretical paper (Cautela, 1977b) may serve as a basis for applications of covert conditioning in the treatment of cancer.

Sport Psychology

Another growing field in which covert conditioning is beginning to be applied is sport psychology. Two specific areas of potential usefulness are in the management of performance-hindering anxiety (e.g., the SCT, CPR) and skill acquisition (e.g., CM, CPR). Anecdotally, we are aware of instances in which athletes have employed CM to assist in adherence to training regimens and CPR to improve running form. In a recent study, Woolfolk, Parrish, and Murphy (1983) found that subjects who visualized successfully putting golf balls were able to overtly putt golf balls significantly more successfully than control-group subjects. A third group of subjects who visualized unsuccess-fully putting golf balls deteriorated in their overt performance.

During the 1984 Winter Olympics several athletes were interviewed regarding their use of imagery. Rosalyn Sumners, who went on to win the silver medal in figure skating, mentioned that after rehearsing her performance in imagery, she then imagined a scene of standing on the winner's platform receiving a medal.

Behavioral Hygiene

One of our goals in therapy is to ensure that the client is familiar with behavioral assessment and can employ the covert conditioning procedure as needed to modify his/her behaviors. Individuals can be taught covert conditioning procedures as preventive measures to decrease the probability of developing problematic behaviors. It would be especially valuable to teach children how to employ covert conditioning procedures as a means of self-control to prevent the escalation of aversive experiences into phobic behaviors—for example, employing the SCT after a frightening experience with a dog.

Another example of behavioral hygiene is employing covert con-ditioning to increase social skills. If individuals notice that they are engaged in detrimental behavioral excesses such as eating or drinking, they can employ covert conditioning to avoid the development of problematic behaviors such as alcoholism. Individuals can monitor their behavior daily. Then, daily, just before retiring, apply the covert conditioning procedure to modify any undesirable behaviors that may have occurred during the day. For example, if they were unable to assert themselves during the day, they can do some CPR scenes in which they assert themselves and feel comfortable in doing so. If they were anxious in a social situation, they can employ CM or covert rehearsal on the social situation that occurred during the day, but this time they feel calm and comfortable.

In addition to applications of covert conditioning to new areas, there should be more replications of previously conducted covert con-ditioning studies. The lack of replications is certainly not limited to covert conditioning research, and we do understand both the relative difficulty of getting replications published and the appropriateness of conducting original research for doctoral dissertations. But many universities require graduate students to complete other research projects prior to the dissertation. Devoting more of these projects to replications of all kinds of psychological research would benefit both the students and the psychological community as a whole.

Although these may be some of the directions covert conditioning will take in the decade ahead, other directions will be defined by necessity. Case studies will be presented and published describing applications of covert conditioning to new target behaviors and in innovative ways to meet the immediate needs of real clients.

As the nonprofessional community becomes more aware and makes more use of behavioral principles in general, covert conditioning should also become better known. Judging by the popular media, it seems that the general population is currently interested in the use of imagery. There is no shortage of imagery-based procedures being proposed for self-improvement and self-control purposes. Those procedures which are most effective and with the firmest theoretical underpinnings should survive while interest in others extinguishes. Covert conditioning, which is empirically solidly established and well suited for self-control use, may evolve into a popular behavioral hygiene strategy of the next decade if the current trends continue.

IV

References and Bibliography

References

Ader, R. (1980). Psychosomatic psychoimmunological research. *Psychosomatic Medicine, 42*, 307–321.

Alford, G.S., Webster, J.S., & Sanders, S.H. (1980). Covert aversion of two interrelated deviant sexual practices: Obscene phone-calling and exhibitionism: A single case analysis. *Behavior Therapy, 11*, 15–25.

Alford, G.S., Wedding, D., & Jones, S., (1983). "Turn-ons" and "turn-offs": The effects of competitory covert imagery on penile tumescence responses to diverse extrinsic sexual stimulus materials. *Behavior Modification, 7*, 112–125.

Anant, S.S. (1966a). The treatment of alcoholics by a verbal aversion technique: A case report. *Manas, 13*, 79–86.

Anant, S.S. (1966b). The use of verbal aversion techniques with a group of alcoholics. *Saskatchewan Psychologist*, 28–30.

Anant, S.S. (1967a). A note on the treatment of alcoholics by a verbal aversion technique. *Canadian Psychologist, 8*, 19–22.

Anant, S.S. (1967b). The treatment of alcoholics and drug addicts by a verbal aversion technique. *Psychotherapy and Psychosomatics, 15*, 6.

Anant, S.S. (1968a). Former alcoholics and social drinking: An unexpected finding. *The Canadian Psychologist, 9*, 35.

Anant, S.S. (1968b). Treatment of alcoholics and drug addicts by verbal aversion techniques. *International Journal of the Addictions, 3*, 381–388.

Anant, S.S. (1968c). The use of verbal aversion (negative conditioning) with an alcoholic: A case report. *Behavior Research and Therapy, 6*, 395–396.

Anant, S.S. (1968d). Verbal aversion therapy with a promiscuous girl: A case report. *Psychological Reports, 22*, 795–796.

Ascher, L.M. (1973). An analog study of covert positive reinforcement. In R.D. Rubin, J.P. Brady, & J.R. Henderson (Eds.), *Advances in behavior therapy* (Vol. 4). *Proceedings of the 5th Conference of the Association for the Advancement of Behavior Therapy*. New York: Academic Press.

193

Ascher, L.M., & Cautela, J.R. (1972). Covert negative reinforcement: An experimental test. *Journal of Behavior Therapy and Experimental Psychiatry*, *3*, 1–5.

Ascher, L.M., & Cautela, J.R. (1974). An experimental study of covert extinction. *Journal of Behavior Therapy and Experimental Psychiatry*, *5*, 233–238.

Ashem, B., & Donner, L. (1968). Covert sensitization with alcoholics. A controlled replication. *Behavior Research and Therapy*, *6*, 7–12

Ayllon, T., & Azrin, N.H. (1968). *The token economy*. Englewood Cliffs, NJ: Prentice-Hall.

Azrin, N.H., Hutchinson, R.R., & Hake, D.F. (1966). Extinction induced aggression. *Journal of the Experimental Analysis of Behavior*, *9*, 191–204.

Bajtelsmit, J.W., & Gershman, L. (1976). Covert positive reinforcement: Efficacy and conceptualization. *Journal of Behavior Therapy and Experimental Psychiatry*, *7*, 207–212.

Baker, P., & Glackman, W.G. (1981). Brain hemisphericity and response to the imaginal processes inventory. In E. Klinger (Ed.), *Imagery, concepts, results, and applications* (Vol. 2). New York: Plenum.

Bandura, A. (1965). Influence of models' reinforcement contingencies on the acquisition of imitative responses. *Journal of Personality and Social Psychology*, *1*, 589–595.

Bandura, A. (1969). *Principles of behavior modification*. New York: Holt, Rinehart & Winston.

Bandura, A. (1970). Modeling theory. In W.S. Sahakian (Ed.), *Psychology of learning: Systems, models, and theories*. Chicago: Markham.

Bandura, A. (1971a). *Psychological modeling: Conflicting theories*. New York: Lieber-Atherton.

Bandura, A. (1971b). Psychotherapy based upon modeling principles. In A.E. Bergin & S.L. Garfield (Eds.), *Handbook of psychotherapy and behavior change*. New York: Wiley.

Bandura, A. (1977). Self-efficacy: Toward a unifying theory of behavior change. *Psychological Review, 84*, 191–215.

Bandura, A., & Menlove, F.L. (1968). Factors determining vicarious extinction of avoidance behavior through symbolic modeling. *Journal of Personality and Social Psychology*, *8*, 99–108.

Bandura, A., Ross, D., & Ross., S.A. (1963). Imitation of film-mediated aggressive models. *Journal of Abnormal and Social Psychology, 66*, 3–11.

Barber, T.X. (1976). *Pitfalls in human research*. New York: Pergamon.

Barlow, D.H. (1980). Behavior therapy: The next decade. *Behavior Therapy, 11*, 315–328.

Barlow, D.H., Agras, W.S., Leitenberg, H., Callahan, E.J., & Moore, R.C. (1972). The contributions of therapeutic instructions to covert sensitization. *Behavior Research and Therapy, 10*, 411–415.

Barlow, D.H., Leitenberg, H., & Agras, W.S. (1969). Experimental control of sexual deviation through manipulation of the noxious scene in covert sensitization. *Journal of Abnormal Psychology, 74*, 596–601.

Barlow, D.H., Reynolds, E.J., & Agras, W.S. (1973). Gender identity change in a transsexual. *Archives of General Psychiatry, 28*, 569–576.

Baron, M.G. (1975). An operant analysis of imagery: The parameters of covert reinforcement (Doctoral dissertation, Boston College, 1975). *Dissertation Abstracts International, 36*, 1469B. (University Microfilms No. 75-20, 696.)

Baron, M.G., & Cautela, J.R. (1983–84). Imagery assessment with normal and special needs children. *Imagination, Cognition, and Personality, 3*(1), 17–33.

Bauer, R.M., & Craighead, W.E. (1979). Psychophysiological responses of the imagination of fearful and neutral situations: The effects of imagery instructions. *Behavior Therapy, 10*, 389–403.

Baugh, B.L. (1977). Generalization effects of covert conditioning and instruction in the suppression of eating behaviors (Doctoral dissertation, University of Texas at Austin, 1976). *Dissertation Abstracts International, 37*, 4127B. (University Microfilms No. 77, 3861.)

Beck, A.T. (1976). *Cognitive therapy and the emotional disorders.* New York: International Universities Press.

Bellack, A.S. (1974). Covert aversion relief and treatment of homosexuality. *Behavior Therapy, 5*, 435–437.

Bellack, A.S., Glanz, L.M., & Simon, R. (1976). Self-reinforcement style and covert imagery in the treatment of obesity. *Journal of Consulting and Clinical Psychology, 44*, 490–491.

Bennett, A.K., & Cautela, J.R. (1981). The use of covert conditioning in the modification of pain: Two experimental tests. *Journal of Behavior Therapy and Experimental Psychiatry, 12*, 315–320.

Bernstein, D.A. (1973). Situational factors in behavioral fear assessment: A progress report. *Behavior Therapy, 4*, 41–48.

Bernstein, D.A., & Nietzel, M.T. (1974). Behavioral avoidance tests: The effects of demand characteristics and repeated measures on two types of subjects. *Behavior Therapy, 5*, 183–192.

Binder, C.V. (1975). A note on covert processes and the natural environment. *Behavior Therapy, 6*, 568.

Bistline, J.L., Jaremko, M.E., & Sobleman, S. (1980). The relative contributions of covert reinforcements and cognitive restructuring to test anxiety reduction. *Journal of Clinical Psychology, 36*, 723–728.

Blanchard, E.B., & Draper, D.O. (1973). Treatment of a rodent phobia by covert reinforcement: A single subject experiment. *Behavior Therapy, 4*, 559–564.

Blanchard, E.B., & Epstein, L.H. (1977). Clinical applications of biofeedback. In M. Herson, N.M. Eisler, & P.M. Maller (Eds.), *Progress in behavior modification*, (Vol. 4). New York: Academic Press.

Blanchard, E.B., Libet, J.M., & Young, L.D. (1973). Apneic aversion and covert sensitization in the treatment of a hydrocarbon inhalation addiction: A case study. *Journal of Behavior Therapy and Experimental Psychiatry, 4*, 383–387.

Bornstein, P.H., & Devine, D.A. (1980). Covert modeling-hypnosis in the treatment of obesity. *Psychotherapy: Theory, Research, and Practice, 17,* 272–276.

Brownell, K.D., & Barlow, D.H. (1976). Measurement and treatment of two sexual deviations in one person. *Journal of Behavior Therapy and Experimental Psychiatry, 7,* 349–354.

Brownell, K.D., Hayes, S.C., & Barlow, D.H. (1977). Patterns of appropriate and deviant sexual arousal: The behavioral treatment of multiple sexual deviation. *Journal of Consulting and Clinical Psychology, 45,* 1144–1155.

Brunn, A.C., & Hedberg, A.G. (1974). Covert positive reinforcement as a treatment procedure for obesity. *Journal of Community Psychology, 2,* 117–119.

Burdick, M.R. (1972). An exploration of the aversion therapy technique of covert sensitization with selected cases of exhibitionism (Doctoral dissertation, University of Minnesota, 1972). *Dissertation Abstracts International, 33,* 2805B. (University Microfilms No. 72-32282.)

Capehart, J., Viney, W., & Hulicka, I.N. (1958). The effect of effort upon extinction. *Journal of Comparative and Physiological Psychology, 51,* 505–507.

Carney, R.M., & Hong, B.A. (1982). Effects of covert sensitization on facial EMG: A pilot study. *Perceptual and Motor Skills, 55,* 655–658.

Catania, A.C. (1979). *Learning.* Englewood Cliffs, NJ: Prentice Hall.

Cautela, J.R. (1966). Treatment of compulsive behavior by covert sensitization. *Psychological Record, 16,* 33–41.

Cautela, J.R. (1967). Covert sensitization. *Psychological Reports, 20,* 459–468.

Cautela, J.R. (1969). Behavior therapy and self-control. In C.M. Franks (Ed.), *Behavior therapy: Appraisal and status* (pp. 323–340). New York: McGraw-Hill.

Cautela, J.R. (1970a). Covert negative reinforcement. *Journal of Behavior Therapy and Experimental Psychiatry, 1,* 273–278.

Cautela, J.R. (1970b). Covert reinforcement. *Behavior Therapy, 1,* 33–50.

Cautela, J.R. (1970c). Treatment of smoking by covert sensitization. *Psychological Reports, 26,* 415–420.

Cautela, J.R. (1971a). Covert extinction. *Behavior Therapy, 2,* 192–200.

Cautela, J.R. (1971b, September). *Covert modeling.* Paper presented at the Fifth Annual Meeting of the Association for Advancement of Behavior Therapy, Washington, DC.

Cautela, J.R. (1972). *Covert sensitization scenes: A compilation of typical scenes used in the application of covert sensitization to a variety of maladaptive behaviors.* Unpublished manuscript, Boston College.

Cautela, J.R. (1976). Covert response cost. *Psychotherapy: Theory, Research, and Practice, 13,* 397–404.

Cautela, J.R. (1977a). *Behavior analysis forms for clinical intervention.* Champaign, IL: Research Press.

Cautela, J.R. (1977b). Toward a Pavlovian theory of cancer. *Scandinavian Journal of Behavior Therapy, 6,* 117–142.

Cautela, J.R. (1977c). The use of covert conditioning in modifying pain behavior. *Journal of Behavior Therapy and Experimental Psychiatry, 8,* 45–52.

Cautela, J.R. (1980, November). *The application of covert conditioning to organic dysfunction.* Invited address to the Fourteenth Annual Meeting of the Association for Advancement of Behavior Therapy, New York.

Cautela, J.R. (1981a). Behavioral treatment of elderly patients with depression. In J.F. Clarkin & H.G. Glazer (Eds.), *Depression: Behavioral and directive treatment strategies.* New York: Garland Press.

Cautela, J.R. (1981b). *Behavioral analysis forms for clinical intervention* (Vol. 2). Champaign, IL: Research Press.

Cautela, J.R. (1981c). *Organic dysfunction survey schedules.* Champaign, IL: Research Press.

Cautela, J.R. (1983). The self-control triad: Description and clinical applications. *Behavior Modification, 7,* 299–315.

Cautela, J.R. (1984). General level of reinforcement. *Journal of Behavior Therapy and Experimental Psychiatry, 15,* 109–114.

Cautela, J.R., & Baron, M.G. (1973). Multifaceted behavior therapy of self-injurious behavior. *Journal of Behavior Therapy and Experimental Psychiatry, 4,* 125–131.

Cautela, J.R., and Baron, M.G. (1977). Covert conditioning: A theoretical analysis. *Behavior Modification, 1,* 351–368.

Cautela, J.R., & Bennett, A.K. (1981). Covert conditioning. In R. Corsini (Ed.), *Handbook of innovative psychotherapies.* New York: Wiley.

Cautela, J.R., & Flannery, R.B., Jr. (1973). Seizures: Controlling the uncontrollable. *Journal of Rehabilitation, 39,* 34–39.

Cautela, J.R., Flannery, R.B., Jr., & Hanley, S. (1974). Covert modeling: An experimental test. *Behavior Therapy, 5,* 494–502.

Cautela, J.R., & Kastenbaum, R. (1967). A reinforcement survey schedule for use in therapy, training, and research. *Psychological Reports, 20,* 1115–1130.

Cautela, J.R., & Kearney, A.J. (1984). Endorphins/enkephalins. In R. Corsini (Ed.), *Wiley Encyclopedia of Psychology.* New York: Wiley.

Cautela, J.R., & McCullough, L. (1978). Covert conditioning: A learning theory perspective on imagery. In J.L. Singer & K.S. Pope (Eds.), *The power of human imagination.* New York: Plenum.

Cautela, J.R., & Upper, D. (1975). The process of individual behavior therapy. In M.H. Eisen & R.M. Eilser (Eds.), *Progress in behavior modification* (pp. 275–305). New York: Academic Press.

Cautela, J.R., & Upper, D. (1976). The behavioral inventory battery: The use of self-report measures in behavioral analysis and therapy. In M. Hersen & A.S. Bellack (Eds.), *Behavioral assessment: A practical handbook.* Oxford: Pergamon Press.

Cautela, J.R., & Wall, C.C. (1980). Covert conditioning in clinical practice. In E. Foa & A. Goldstein (Eds.), *Handbook of behavioral interventions*. New York: Wiley.

Cautela, J.R., Walsh, K., & Wish, P. (1971). The use of covert reinforcement in the modification of attitudes toward the mentally retarded. *Journal of Psychology, 77*, 257–260.

Cautela, J.R., & Wisocki, P.A. (1969a). The use of imagery in the modification of attitudes toward the elderly: A preliminary report. *Journal of Psychology, 73*, 193–199.

Cautela, J.R., & Wisocki, P.A. (1969b). The use of male and female therapists in the treatment of homosexual behavior. In R.D. Rubin & C. Franks (Eds.), *Advances in behavior therapy, 1968*. New York: Academic Press.

Chertock, S.L., & Bornstein, P.H. (1979). Covert modeling treatment of children's dental fears. *Child Behavior Therapy, 1*, 249–255.

Clark, D.F. (1965). A note on avoidance conditioning techniques in sexual disorder. *Behavior Research and Therapy, 3*, 203–206.

Cleveland, P. (1982). Comparison of covert conditioning, relaxation, training, biofeedback and placebo as treatments for myofacial pain (or TMJ) dysfunction syndrome (Doctoral dissertation, Boston College, 1981). *Dissertation Abstracts International, 42*, 3818B. (University Microfilms No. DA8203959.)

Cohen, J. (1967). The interaction of responses in the brain to semantic stimuli. *Psychophysiology, 2*, 187–196.

Cooke, G. (1966). The efficacy of two desensitization procedures: An analog study. *Behavior Research and Therapy, 4*, 17–24.

Craig, K.D., & Best, J.A. (1977). Perceived control over pain: Individual differences and situational determinants. *Pain, 3*, 127–135.

Cyborg Corporation. (1979). *EMG-J33 Handbook*. Boston, MA: Cyborg Corporation.

Davidson, A.M., & Denney, D.R. (1976). Covert sensitization and information in the reduction of nailbiting. *Behavior Therapy, 7*, 512–518.

Davidson, R.J., & Schwartz, G.E. (1977). Brain mechanisms subserving self-enervated imagery: Electrophysiological specificity and patterning. *Psychophysiology, 14*, 598–602.

Davison, G.C. (1966). Differential relaxation and cognitive restructuring in therapy with a "paranoid schizophrenic" or "paranoid state." *Proceedings of the 74th Annual Convention of the American Psychological Association, 1*, 177–178.

Day, W.F. (1969). Radical behaviorism in reconciliation with phenomenology. *Journal of Experimental Analysis of Behavior, 12*, 315–328.

DeBerry, S. (1981). An evaluation of multi-model behavior therapy, covert sensitization, and long term follow-up in the treatment of obesity. *The Behavior Therapist, 4*(5), 17–18.

DeLancey, A.L. (1979). The effects of covert reinforcement and social skills training with psychiatric patients (Doctoral dissertation, Boston College,

1979). *Dissertation Abstracts International, 40,* 1358B. (University Microfilms No. 79-20, 481.)

Denholtz, M.S. (1973). An extension of covert procedures in the treatment of male homosexuals. *Journal of Behavior Therapy and Experimental Psychiatry, 4,* 305.

Denny, D.R., Sullivan, B.J., & Thiry, M.C. (1977). Participant modeling and self-verbalization in training in reduction of spider fears. *Journal of Behavior Therapy and Experimental Psychiatry, 8,* 247–253.

Devine, D.A. (1978). Hypnosis and covert modeling in the treatment of obesity (Doctoral dissertation, University of Montana, 1977). *Dissertation Abstracts International, 38,* 3859B–3896B. (University Microfilms No. 77-28, 775.)

Dinsmoor, J.A. (1968). Escape from shock as a conditioning technique. In M. Jones (Ed.), *Miami Symposium on the Prediction of Behavior, 1967: Aversive Stimulation.* Miami: University of Miami Press.

Dougher, M.J. (1984, November). *An experimental test of Cautela's operant explanation of covert conditioning procedures.* Paper presented at the 18th Annual Meeting of the Association for Advancement of Behavior Therapy, Philadelphia.

Drummond, P., White, K., & Ashton, R. (1978). Imagery vividness affects habituation rate. *Psychophysiology, 15,* 193–195.

Edmonds, R.M. (1975). Relaxation as a reinforcer in desensitization (Doctoral dissertation, University of Pittsburgh, 1974). *Dissertation Abstracts International, 36,* 906B. (University Microfilms No. 75-18, 223.)

Elkins, R.L. (1976). A note on aversion therapy for alcoholism. *Behavior Research and Therapy, 4,* 159–160.

Ellis, A. (1962). *Reason and emotion in psychotherapy.* New York: Lyle Stuart.

Ellis, A. (1970). *The essence of rational psychotherapy: A comprehensive approach to treatment.* New York: Lyle Stuart.

Ellis, A. (1979). A note on the treatment of agoraphobics with cognitive modification versus prolonged exposure in vivo. *Behavior Research and Therapy, 17,* 162–163.

Emmelkamp, P.M.G., & Walta, C. (1978). Effects of therapy set on electrical aversion therapy and covert sensitization. *Behavior Therapy, 9,* 185–188.

Epstein, L.H., & Abel, G.G. (1977). Analysis of biofeedback training effects for tension headache patients. *Behavior Therapy, 8,* 37–47.

Epstein, L.H., & Peterson, G.L. (1973). Differential conditioning using covert stimuli. *Behavior Therapy, 4,* 96–99.

Eshleman, J.W. (1983). All the known precision teaching references. *Journal of Precision Teaching, 4*(3), 56–67.

Evans, I.M. (1973). The logical requirements for explanations of systematic desensitization. *Behavior Therapy, 4,* 506–514.

Feldman, M.P. (1966). Aversion therapy for sexual deviations: A critical review. *Psychological Bulletin, 65,* 65–79.

Finger, R., & Galassi, J.P. (1977). Effects of modifying cognitive vs. emotionality responses in the treatment of test anxiety. *Journal of Consulting and Clinical Psychology, 45,* 280–287.

Finke, R.A. (1980). Levels of equivalence in imagery and perception. *Psychological Review, 87,* 115–132.

Flannery, R.B., Jr. (1972a). Covert conditioning in the behavioral treatment of an agoraphobic. *Psychotherapy: Theory, Research, and Practice, 9,* 217–220.

Flannery, R.B., Jr. (1972b). A laboratory analogue of two covert reinforcement procedures. *Journal of Behavior Therapy and Experimental Psychiatry, 3,* 171–177.

Flannery, R.B., Jr. (1972c). Use of covert conditioning in the behavioral treatment of a drug dependent college dropout. *Journal of Counseling Psychology, 19,* 547–550.

Fordyce, W.E. (1973). An operant conditioning method for managing chronic pain. *Postgraduate Medicine, 53,* 123–128.

Fordyce, W.E. (1976a). Behavioral concepts in chronic pain and illness. In P.O. Davidson (Ed.), *Behavioral management of anxiety, depression, and pain.* New York: Bruner/Mazel.

Fordyce, W.E. (1976b). *Behavior methods for chronic pain and illness.* St. Louis: Mosby.

Foreyt, J.P., & Hagen, R.L. (1973). Covert sensitization: Conditioning or suggestion? *Journal of Abnormal Psychology, 82,* 17–23.

Forster, F.M. (1966). Conditioning in sensory evoked seizures. *Conditional Reflex, 1,* 224.

Franks, C.M. (1980). Covert conditioning—The evidence not yet overt (Review of *Covert Conditioning*). *Contemporary Psychology, 25*(12), 1005–1006.

Freund, K. (1960). Some problems in the treatment of homosexuality. In H.J. Eysenck (Ed.), *Behavior therapy and the neuroses* (pp. 312–326). London: Pergamon.

Gallagher, J.W., & Arkowitz, H. (1978). Weak effects of covert modeling treatment of test anxiety. *Journal of Behavior Therapy and Experimental Psychiatry, 9,* 23–26.

Gantt, W.H. (1976). New-Pavlovianism. In D.I. Mostofsky (Ed.), *Behavior control and modification of physiological activity* (pp. 249–267). Englewood Cliffs, NJ: Prentice Hall.

Gershman, L. (1970). Case conference: A transvestite fantasy treated by thought-stopping, covert sensitization and aversive shock. *Journal of Behavior Therapy and Experimental Psychiatry, 1,* 153–161.

Gerson, P., & Lanyon, R.I. (1972). Modification of behavior with an aversion-desensitization procedure. *Journal of Consulting and Clinical Psychology, 38,* 399–402.

Glenn, S.S. (1983). Maladaptive functional relations in client verbal behavior. *The Behavior Analyst, 6,* 47–56.

Glick, B.S. (1972). Aversive imagery therapy using hypnosis. *American Journal of Psychotherapy, 26,* 432–436.

Gold, S., & Neufeld, I. (1965). A learning theory approach to the treatment of homosexuality. *Behavior Research and Therapy, 2,* 201–204.

Goldiamond, I. (1976a). Fables, armadyllics, and self-reinforcement. *Journal of Applied Behavior Analysis, 9,* 521–525.

Goldiamond, I. (1976b). Self-reinforcement. *Journal of Applied Behavior Analysis, 9,* 509–514.

Goldstein, A.P., Sprakfin, R.P., & Gershaw, N.J. (1976). *Skill training for community living: Applying structured learning therapy.* New York: Pergamon.

Götestam, K.G., & Melin, L. (1974). Covert extinction of amphetamine addiction. *Behavior Therapy, 5,* 90–92.

Götestam, K.G., & Melin, L. (1983). An experimental study of covert extinction on smoking cessation. *Addictive Behaviors, 8,* 27–31.

Groden, J. (1982). Procedures to increase social interaction among autistic adolescents: A multiple baseline analysis (Doctoral dissertation, Boston College, 1982). *Dissertation Abstracts International, 43,* 525B. (University Microfilms No. 8215479.)

Groden, J., & Cautela, J.R. (1984). Use of imagery procedure with students labeled "trainable retarded." *Psychological Reports, 54,* 595–605.

Guidry, L.S., & Randolph, D.L. (1974). Covert reinforcement in the treatment of test anxiety. *Journal of Counseling Psychology, 21,* 260–264.

Harbert, T.L., Barlow, D.H., Hersen, M., & Austin, J.B. (1974). Measurement and modification of incestuous behavior: A case study. *Psychological Reports, 34,* 79–86.

Harris, G., & Johnson, S.B. (1980). Comparison of individualized covert modeling self-control desensitization, and study skills training for the alleviation of test anxiety. *Journal of Consulting and Clinical Psychology, 48,* 186–194.

Harris, G., & Johnson, S.B. (1983). Coping imagery and relaxation instructions in a covert modeling treatment for test anxiety. *Behavior Therapy, 14,* 144–157.

Hartlage, L.C. (1980, November). *Neuropsychological approaches to matching patients with maximally effective psychotherapeutic techniques.* Paper presented at the Fourteenth Annual Meeting of the Association for Advancement of Behavior Therapy, New York.

Hay, W.M., Barlow, D.H., & Hay, L.R. (1981). Treatment of a sterotypic cross-gender motor behavior using covert modeling in a boy with gender identity confusion. *Journal of Consulting and Clinical Psychology, 49,* 388–394.

Hay, W.M., Hay, L.R., & Nelson, R.O. (1977). The adaptation of covert modeling procedures to the treatment of chronic alcoholism and obsessive-compulsive behavior: Two case reports. *Behavior Therapy, 8,* 70–76.

Hayes, S.C., & Barlow, D.H. (1977). Flooding relief in a case of public transportation phobia. *Behavior Therapy, 8,* 742–746.

Hayes, S.C., Brownell, K.D., & Barlow, D.H. (1978). The use of self-administered covert sensitization in the treatment of exhibitionism and sadism. *Behavior Therapy, 9,* 283–289.

Hayes, S.C., Brownell, K.D., & Barlow, D.H. (1983). Heterosexual skills training and covert sensitization. Effects on social skills and sexual arousal in sexual deviants. *Behavior Research and Therapy, 21,* 383–392.

Hefferline, R.F., & Perera, T.B. (1963). Proprioceptive discrimination of a covert operant without its observation by the subject. *Science, 139,* 834–835.

Hersen, M., Kazdin, A.E., Bellack, A.S., & Turner, S.M. (1979). Effects of live modeling and rehearsal on assertiveness in psychiatric patients. *Behavior, Research and Therapy, 17* 369–377.

Homme, L.E. (1965). Perspectives in psychology: XXIV Control of coverants, the operants of the mind. *Psychological Record, 15,* 501–511.

Hugdahl, K., & Öst, L.G. (1981). On the difference between statistical and clinical significance. *Behavioral Assessment, 3,* 289–295.

Hughes, R.C. (1977). Covert sensitization treatment of exhibitionism. *Journal of Behavior Therapy and Experimental Psychiatry, 8,* 177–179.

Hull, C.L. (1943). *Principles of behavior.* New York: Appleton.

Hull, C.L. (1952). *A behavior system.* New York: Wiley.

Hurley, A.D. (1976). Covert reinforcement: The contributions of the reinforcing stimulus to treatment outcome. *Behavior Therapy, 7,* 374–378.

Hutchinson, R.R. (1977). By-products of aversive control. In W.K. Honig & J.E.R. Staddon (Eds.), *Handbook of operant behavior.* Englewood Cliffs, NJ: Prentice-Hall.

James, B. (1962). Case of homosexuality treated by aversion therapy. *British Medical Journal, 1,* 768–770.

Janda, L.H., & Rimm, D.C. (1972). Covert sensitization in the treatment of obesity. *Journal of Abnormal Psychology, 80,* 37–42.

Jungemann, G.T. (1981). *Dakota teacher.* Sioux Falls, SD: N-sight Communications.

Kazdin, A.E. (1972). Response cost: The removal of conditioned reinforcers for therapeutic change. *Behavior Therapy, 3,* 533–546.

Kazdin, A.E. (1973). Covert modeling and the reduction of avoidance behavior. *Journal of Abnormal Psychology, 81,* 87–95.

Kazdin, A.E. (1974a). Comparative effects of some variations of covert modeling. *Journal of Behavior Therapy and Experimental Psychiatry, 5,* 225–231.

Kazdin, A.E. (1974b). Covert modeling, model similarity and the reduction of avoidance behavior. *Behavior Therapy, 5,* 325–340.

Kazdin, A.E. (1974c). The effect of model identity and fear-relevant similarity on covert modeling. *Behavior Therapy, 5,* 624–635.

Kazdin, A.E. (1974d). Effects of covert modeling and model reinforcement on assertive behavior. *Journal of Abnormal Psychology, 83,* 240–252.

Kazdin, A.E. (1975). Covert modeling, imagery assessment, and assertive behavior. *Journal of Consulting and Clinical Psychology, 43,* 716–724.

Kazdin, A.E. (1976a). Assessment of imagery during covert modeling of assertive behavior. *Journal of Behavior Therapy and Experimental Psychiatry, 7,* 213–219.

Kazdin, A.E. (1976b). Effect of covert modeling, multiple models, and model reinforcement on assertive behavior. *Behavior Therapy, 7*, 211–222.

Kazdin, A.E. (1977). Research issues in covert conditioning. *Cognitive Therapy and Research, 1*, 45–48.

Kazdin, A.E. (1978). Covert modeling: The therapeutic application of imagined rehearsal. In J.L. Singer & K.S. Pope (Eds.), *The power of human imagination* (pp. 255–278). New York: Plenum.

Kazdin, A.E. (1979). Imagery elaboration and self-efficacy in the covert modeling treatment of unassertive behavior. *Journal of Consulting and Clinical Psychology, 47*, 725–733.

Kazdin, A.E. (1980). Covert and overt rehearsal and elaboration during treatment in the development of assertive behavior. *Behavior Research and Therapy, 18*, 191–201.

Kazdin, A.E. (1982). The separate and combined effects of covert and overt rehearsal in developing assertive behavior. *Behavior Research and Therapy, 20*, 17–25.

Kazdin, A.E., & Mascitelli, S. (1982). Covert and overt rehearsal and homework practice in developing assertiveness. *Journal of Consulting and Clinical Psychology, 2*, 250–258.

Kazdin, A.E., and Smith, G.A. (1979). Covert conditioning: A review and evaluation. *Advances in Behaviour Research and Therapy, 2*, 57–98.

Kearney, A.B. (1984). *A comparison of the relative efficacy of related versus unrelated reinforcing scenes in the use of covert positive reinforcement for the treatment of test anxiety.* Unpublished doctoral dissertation, Boston College.

Kearney, A.J. (1976). A comparison of systematic desensitization and covert positive reinforcement in the treatment of a fear in laboratory rats (Doctoral dissertation, Boston College, 1976). *Dissertation Abstracts International, 37*, 809A. (University Microfilms No. 76-13, 935.)

Kendrick, S.R., & McCullough, J.P. (1972). Sequential phases of covert reinforcement and covert sensitization in the treatment of homosexuality. *Journal of Behavior Therapy and Experimental Psychiatry, 3*, 229–231.

King, D.L. (1973). An image of classical conditioning. *Psychological Reports, 33*, 403–411.

Kolvin, I. (1967). Aversive imagery treatment in adolescents. *Behavior Research and Therapy, 5*, 245–248.

Kornetsky, C. (1976). *Drugs affecting behavior.* New York: Wiley.

Kostka, M.P., & Galassi, J.P. (1974). Group systematic desensitization vs. covert positive reinforcing in the reduction of test anxiety. *Journal of Consulting Psychology, 21*, 464–468.

Kroger, W.S. (1963). *Clinical and experimental hypnosis.* Philadelphia and Toronto: J.B. Lippincott.

Kroger, W.S., & Fezler, W.D. (1976). *Hypnosis and behavior modification: Imagery conditioning.* Philadelphia: J.B. Lippincott.

Krop, H., Calhoun, B., & Verrier, R. (1971). Modification of the "self-concept" of emotionally disturbed children by covert reinforcement. *Behavior Therapy, 2,* 201–204.

Krop, H., Messinger, J., & Reiner, C. (1973). Increasing eye contact by covert reinforcement. *Interpersonal Development, 4,* 51–57.

Ladouceur, R. (1974). An experimental test of the learning paradigm of covert positive reinforcement in deconditioning anxiety. *Journal of Behavior Therapy and Experimental Psychiatry, 5,* 3–6.

Ladouceur, R. (1977). Rationale of covert reinforcement: Additional evidence. *Psychological Reports, 4,* 547–550.

Ladouceur, R. (1978). Rationale of systematic desensitization and covert reinforcement. *Behavior Research and Therapy, 16,* 411–420.

Lande, S.D. (1980). A combination of organic reconditioning and covert sensitization in the treatment of a fire fetish. *Journal of Behavior Therapy and Experimental Psychiatry, 11,* 291–296.

Lang, P.J. (1977). Imagery in therapy: An information processing analysis of fear. *Behavior Therapy, 8,* 862–886.

Latimer, P.R., & Sweet, A.A. (1984). Cognitive versus behavioral procedures in cognitive-behavior therapy: A critical review of the evidence. *Journal of Behavior Therapy and Experimental Psychiatry, 15,* 9–22.

Lawson, R. (1960). *Learning and behavior.* New York: Macmillan.

Lazarus, A.A. (1973). Multimodal behavior therapy: Treating the basic id. *Journal of Nervous and Mental Disease, 156,* 404–411.

Lazarus, A.A. (1976). *Multimodal behavior therapy* (Vol. 1). New York: Springer.

Lazarus, A.A., & Abramovitz, A. (1962). The use of "emotive imagery" in the treatment of children's phobias. *Journal of Mental Science, 108,* 191–195.

Levin, S.M., Barry, S.M., Gambaro, S., Wolfinsohn, & Smith, A. (1977). Variations of covert sensitization in the treatment of pedophilic behavior: A case study. *Journal of Consulting and Clinical Psychology, 45,* 896–907.

Levine, J.D., Gordon, N.C., & Fields, H.L. (1978, Sept. 23). The mechanism of placebo analgesia. *Lancet, 2,* 654–657.

Lewis, B.J. (1979). Treatment of a schizoid personality using hypnoperant therapy. *American Journal of Clinical Hypnosis, 22,* 42–46.

Little, L.M., & Curran, J.P. (1978). Covert sensitization: A clinical procedure in need of some explanations. *Psychological Bulletin, 85,* 513–531.

Lowe, M.R. (1978). The use of covert modeling in social skills training with depressed patients (Doctoral dissertation, Boston College, 1978). *Dissertation Abstracts International, 38,* 6163B-6164B. (University Microfilms No. 7807239.)

Lowe, S.E. (1978). The comparative effectiveness of ideal self, ideal person, and real self as models in covert modeling procedures (Doctoral dissertation, Boston College, 1978). *Dissertation Abstracts International, 39,* 988B. (University Microfilms No. 7813783.)

Lubar, J.R., & Bahler, W.W. (1976). Behavioral management of epileptic seizures following E.E.G. biofeedback training of sensori-motor rhythm. *Biofeedback and Self-Regulation 1,* 77–104.

Lurie, E.S., & Steffen, J.J. (1980). Effective components of covert reinforcement. *Journal of Psychology, 106,* 241–248.

MacCulloch, M.J., Feldman, M.P., & Pinschoff, J.M. (1965). The application of anticipatory avoidance learning to the treatment of homosexuality: Avoidance response latencies and pulse rate changes. *Behavior Research and Therapy, 3,* 21–44.

Mahoney, M.J. (1970). Toward an experimental analysis of covert control. *Behavior Therapy, 1,* 510–521.

Mahoney, M.J. (1974). *Cognition and behavior modification.* Cambridge, MA: Ballinger.

Mahoney, M.J. (1976). Terminal terminology: A self-regulated response to Goldiamond. *Journal of Applied Behavior Analysis, 9,* 515–517.

Mahoney, M.J., Thoresen, C.E., & Danaher, B.G. (1972). Covert behavior modification: An experimental analog. *Journal of Behavior Therapy and Experimental Psychiatry, 3,* 7–14.

Maletzky, B.M. (1973). "Assisted" covert sensitization: a preliminary report. *Behavior Therapy, 4,* 117–119.

Maletzky, B.M. (1974). "Assisted" covert sensitization for drug abuse. *International Journal of the Addictions, 9,* 411–429.

Maletzky, B.M. (1977). "Booster" sessions in aversion therapy: The permanency of treatment. *Behavior Therapy, 8,* 460–463.

Maletzky, B.M. (1980a). "Assisted" covert sensitization in the treatment of exhibitionism. In D.J. Cox & R.J. Daitzman (Eds.), *Exhibitionism: Description, assessment, and treatment.* New York: Garland Press.

Maletzky, B.M. (1980b). Self-referred versus court referred sexually deviant patients: Success with assisted covert sensitization. *Behavior Therapy, 11,* 306–314.

Maletzky, B.M. & George, F.S. (1973). Treatment of homosexuality by "assisted" covert sensitization. *Behavior Research and Therapy, 11,* 655–657.

Manno, B., & Marston, A.R. (1972). Weight reduction as a function of negative reinforcement (sensitization) versus positive covert reinforcement. *Behavior Research and Therapy, 10,* 201–207.

Marks, I. (1975). Behavioral treatments of phobic and obsessive-compulsive disorders: A critical appraisal. In M. Hersen, R.M. Eisler, & P.M. Miller (Eds.), *Progress in behavior modification* (Vol. I). New York: Academic Press.

Marquis, J.N. (1970). Orgasmic reconditioning: Changing sexual object choice through controlling masturbation fantasies. *Journal of Behavior Therapy and Experimental Psychiatry, 1,* 263–272.

Marshall, W.L., Boutillier, J., & Minnes, P. (1974). The Modification of phobic behavior by covert reinforcement. *Behavior Therapy, 5,* 469–480.

Marshall, W.L., & Christie, M.M. (1982). The enhancement of social self-esteem. *Canadian Counsellor, 16*(2), 82–89.

Marshall, W.L., Christie, M.M., Lanthier, R.D., & Cruchley, J. (1982). The nature of the reinforcer in the enhancement of social self-esteem. *Canadian Counsellor, 16*(2), 90–96.

May, J.R. (1977). A psychophysiological study of self and externally regulated phobic throughts. *Behavior Therapy, 8,* 849–861.

McAndrew, J.F. (1981). The relative efficacy of covert and overt conditioning in modifying verbal and pain tolerance behavior (Doctoral dissertation, University of Minnesota, 1980). *Dissertation Abstracts International, 41,* 2771B. (University Microfilms No. 8102123.)

McConaghy, N., Armstrong, M.S., & Blaszczynski, A. (1981). Controlled comparison of aversive therapy and covert sensitization in compulsive homosexuality. *Behavior Research and Therapy, 19,* 425–434.

McCullough, L. (1978, November). *The efficacy of covert conditioning.* Paper presented at the meeting of the Association for Advancement of Behavior Therapy, Chicago.

McGlynn, F.D., Reynolds, E.J., & Linder, L.H. (1971). Experimental desensitization following therapeutically oriented and physiologically oriented instructions. *Journal of Behavior Therapy and Experimental Psychiatry, 2,* 13–18.

McGuire, R.J., & Vallance, M. (1964). Aversion therapy by electrical shock: A simple technique. *British Medical Journal, 1,* 151–153.

McMahon, C.E., & Hastings, J.L. (1980). The role of imagination of the disease process. Post-Cartesian history. *Journal of Behavioral Medicine, 3,* 205–217.

Meade, L.S. (1979). Covert positive reinforcement in the treatment of nailbiting: Target-relevant versus target-irrelevant consequences (Doctoral dissertation, University of North Carolina at Greensboro, 1978). *Dissertation Abstracts International, 39,* 3530B–3531B. (University Microfilms No. 7824896.)

Mealiea, W.L., & Nawas, N.M. (1970). Systematic desensitization vs. implosive therapy. *Proceedings of the 78th Annual Convention of the American Psychological Association, 5,* 511–512.

Meichenbaum, D.H. (1971). Examination of model characteristics in reducing avoidance behavior. *Journal of Personality and Social Psychology, 17,* 298–307.

Meichenbaum, D.H. (1974). *Cognitive behavior modification.* Morristown, NJ: General Learning Press.

Meichenbaum, D.H. (1977). *Cognitive behavior modification.* New York: Plenum.

Melvin, K.B., & Brown, J.S. (1964). Neutralization of an aversive light stimulus as a function of number of paired presentations with food. *Journal of Comparative and Physiological Psychology, 58,* 350–353.

Melzack, R. (1975). The McGill Pain Questionnaire: Major properties and scoring methods. *Pain, 1,* 277–299.

Miller, N.E. (1935). *The influence of past experience upon the transfer of subsequent training.* Unpublished doctoral dissertation, Yale University.

Miller, R.C., & Berman, J.S. (1983). The efficacy of cognitive behavior therapies: A quantitative review of the research evidence. *Psychological Bulletin, 94*(1), 39–53.

Miller, W.R. (1982). Treating problem drinkers: What works? *The Behavior Therapist, 5*(1), 15–18.

Mostofsky, D.I. (1976). (Ed.), *Behavior control and modification of physiological activity.* Englewood Cliffs, NJ: Prentice Hall.

Nesse, M., & Nelson, R. (1977). Variations of covert modeling on cigarette smoking. *Cognitive Therapy and Research, 1,* 343–354.

Nietzel, M.T., Martorano, R.D., & Melnick, J. (1977). The effects of covert modeling with and without reply training on the development and generalization of assertive response. *Behavior Therapy, 8,* 183–192.

Nigel, A.J. (1976). Use of covert reinforcements in the acquisition of dental behavior (Doctoral dissertation, Universtiy of Cincinnati, 1975). *Dissertation Abstracts International, 36,* 4172B–4173B. (University Microfilms No. 75-25, 922.)

O'Brien, J.S., Raynes, A.E., & Patch, V.D. (1972). Treatment of heroin addiction with aversion therapy, relaxation training, and systematic desensitization. *Behavior Research and Therapy, 10,* 77–80.

Olds, J. (1956). Pleasure centers in the brain. *Scientific American, 195,* 105–116.

Olson, R.P., Ganley, R., Devine, V.T., & Dorsey, G.C., Jr. (1981). Long-term effects of behavioral vs. insight-oriented therapy with inpatient alcoholics. *Journal of Consulting and Clinical Psychology, 49,* 866–877.

Park, T.P. (1979). Covert positive reinforcement: The contribution of the reinforcing stimulus in reducing public speaking anxiety (Doctoral dissertation, University of South Dakota, 1978). *Dissertation Abstracts International, 39,* 5574B. (University Microfilms No. 7904903.)

Paul, G.L. (1969). Outcome of systematic desensitization, II. In C.M. Franks (Ed.). *Behavior therapy: Appraisal and status* (pp. 105–159). New York: McGraw-Hill.

Pavlov, I.F. (1927). *Conditioned reflexes: An investigation of the physiological activity of the cerebral cortex* (G.V. Anrep, trans.). London: Oxford University Press.

Poetter, R.A. (1978). The effects of covert negative reinforcement on students' attending behavior (Doctoral dissertation, Ohio University, 1977). *Dissertation Abstracts International, 38,* 3901B–3902B. (University Microfilms No. 7730272.)

Polakow, R.L. (1975). Covert sensitization treatment of a probational barbiturate addict. *Journal of Behavior Therapy and Experimental Psychiatry, 6,* 53–54.

Premack, D. (1959). Toward empirical behavior laws: I. Positive reinforcement. *Psychological Review, 66,* 219–233.

Ramsey, G.T. (1978). A program of weight loss and weight maintenance employing behavioral and somatic awareness training (Doctoral dissertation, Virginia Commonwealth University, 1978). *Dissertation Abstracts International, 39,* 1496B. (University Microfilms No. 7814875.)

Rehm, L.P., & Rozensky, R.H. (1974). Multiple behavior therapy techniques with a homosexual client: A case study. *Journal of Behavior Therapy and Experimental Psychiatry, 5,* 53–57.

Reynolds, G.S. (1968). *A primer of operant conditioning.* Glenview, IL: Scott, Foresman.

Rhodes, R.S. (1978). Covert positive reinforcement: A test of the experimental paradigms (Doctoral dissertation, University of Mississippi, 1978). *Dissertation Abstracts International, 39,* 3002B–3003B. (University Microfilms No. 7824062.)

Richardson, A. (1969). *Mental imagery.* New York: Springer.

Roberts, J.R., & Weerts, T.C. (1982). Cardiovascular responding during anger and fear imagery. *Psychological Reports, 50,* 219–230.

Rogers, M.P., Reich, P., Strom, T.B., & Carpenter, C.B. (1976). Behaviorally conditioned immunosuppression: Replication of a recent study. *Psychosomatic Medicine, 38,* 447–451.

Rohrer, J.H. (1947). Experimental extinction as a function of the distribution of extinction trials and response strength. *Journal of Experimental Psychology, 37,* 473–493.

Rohrer, J.H. (1949). A motivational state resulting from nonreward. *Journal of Comparative and Physiological Psychology, 42,* 476–485.

Rosenthal, T.L., & Reese, S.L. (1976). The effects of covert and overt modeling on assertive behavior. *Behavior Research and Therapy, 14,* 463–469.

Rosenzweig, M.R., & Bennett, E.L. (1980). How plastic is the nervous system? In J.M. Ferguson & C.B. Taylor (Eds.), *The comprehensive handbook of behavioral medicine* (Vol. 1). New York: S.P. Medical and Scientific Books.

Sanders, S.H., & Hammer, D. (1979). An empirical test of three alternative explanations for covert reinforcement effects. *Psychological Reports, 44,* 611–622.

Sank, L.I. (1976). Counterconditioning for a flight phobia. *Social Work, 21,* 318–319.

Schubot, E.D. (1966). *The influence of hypnotic and muscular relaxation in systematic desensitization of phobias.* Unpublished doctoral dissertation, Stanford University.

Schuele, J.G., & Wiesenfield, A.R. (1983). Automatic response to self-critical thought. *Cognitive Therapy and Research, 7,* 189–194.

Schwartz, G.E., & Higgins, J.D. (1971). Cardiac activity preparatory to overt and covert behavior. *Science, 173,* 1144–1146.

Schwartz, G.E., & Weiss, S.M. (1977). *Proceedings of the Yale Conference on Behavioral Medicine* (DHEW Publication No. NIH 78-1424). Washington, DC: US Government Printing Office.

Scott, D.S., & Leonard, C.F. (1978). Modification of pain threshold by covert reinforcement procedure and a cognitive strategy. *Psychological Record, 28,* 49–57.

Scott, D.S., & Rosenstiel, A.K. (1975). Covert positive reinforcement studies: Review, critique, and guidelines. *Psychotherapy: Theory, Research, and Practice, 12,* 374–384.

Scott, J., & Huskisson, E.C. (1976). Graphic representation of pain. *Pain, 2,* 175–184.

Scott, R.W., Blanchard, E.B., Edmundsen, E.D., & Young, L.D. (1973). A shaping procedure for heart control in chronic tachycardia. *Perceptual and Motor Skills, 37,* 327–338.

Seligman, M.E.P., & Wiess, J.M. (1980). Part IV. Questions from the audience. In M. Weinraub & A. Schulman (Eds.), Coping behavior, learned helplessness, physiological change, and learned inactivity. *Behavior Research and Therapy, 18,* 483.

Shatus, E.L. (1974). Treatment of disruptive classroom behavior in male, hospitalized delinquents using two covert procedures (Doctoral dissertation, University of Southern Mississippi, 1973). *Dissertation Abstracts International, 34,* 4057B–4058B. (University Microfilms No. 74-3958.)

Singer, J.L., & Pope, K.S. (1978). The use of imagery and fantasy techniques in psychotherapy. In J.L. Singer & K.S. Pope, (Eds.), *The power of human imagination.* New York: Plenum.

Skinner, B.F. (1953). *Science and human behavior.* New York: Macmillan.

Skinner, B.F. (1963). Behaviorism at fifty. *Science, 140,* 951–958.

Skinner, B.F. (1969). *Contingencies of reinforcement.* New York: Appleton-Century-Crofts.

Snowden, L.R. (1978). Personality tailored covert sensitization of heroin abuse. *Addictive Behaviors, 3,* 43–49.

Solomon, R.L. (1948). Efforts and extinction rate: A confirmation. *Journal of Comparative and Physiological Psychology, 41,* 93–101.

Solyom, L., & Miller, S. (1965). A differential conditioning procedure as the initial phase of the behavior therapy of homosexuality. *Behavior Research and Therapy, 3,* 147–160.

Stampfl, T., & Levis, D.J. (1967). Essentials of implosion therapy: A learning theory based psychodynamic behavioral therapy. *Journal of Abnormal Psychology, 72,* 496–503.

Steffen, J. (1971). Covert reinforcement with schizophrenics. Paper presented at the Annual Meeting of the Association for Advancement of Behavior Therapy, Washington, DC.

Steffen, J.J. (1977). Covert reinforcement: Two studies and a comment. *Psychological Reports, 40,* 291–294.

Stevens, M.J. (1982). The effects of covert positive reinforcement in modifying cold-pressor pain (Doctoral dissertation, University of Missouri-Columbia, 1981). *Dissertation Abstracts International, 43,* 81A. (University Microfilms No. DA8213876.)

Stevens, T.G. (1974). The effects of varying covert reinforcement and covert behavior rehearsal instructions on friendly assertive behavior: An automated self-control procedure (Doctoral dissertation, University of Hawaii, 1973). *Dissertation Abstracts International, 34,* 4678B. (University Microfilms No. 74-7514.)

Sulzer, B., & Mayer, R.G. (1972). *Behavior modification procedures for school personnel.* New York: Holt, Rinehart, and Winston.

Tearnan, B.H., Lahey, B.B., Thompson, J., & Hammer, D. (1982). The role of coping self-instructions combined with covert modeling in specific fear reduction. *Cognitive Therapy and Research, 6,* 185–190.

Tepfer, K.S., & Levine, B.A. (1977). Covert sensitization with internal aversive cues in the treatment of chronic alcoholism. *Psychological Reports, 41*, 92–94.

Thase, M.E., & Moss, M.K. (1976). The relative efficacy of covert modeling procedures and guided participant modeling on the reduction of avoidance behavior. *Journal of Behavior Therapy and Experimental Psychiatry, 7*, 7–12.

Thompson, M.S., & Conrad, P.L. (1977). Multifaceted behavioral treatment of drug dependence: A case study. *Behavior Therapy, 8*, 731–737.

Thoresen, C.E., & Wilbur, C.S. (1976). Some encouraging thoughts about self-reinforcement. *Journal of Applied Behavioral Analysis, 9*, 518–520.

Thorpe, J., Schmidt, E., & Castell, D. (1964). A comparison of positive and negative (aversive) conditioning in the treatment of homosexuality. *Behavior Research and Therapy, 1*, 357–362.

Tondo, T.R., & Cautela, J.R. (1974). Assessment of imagery in covert reinforcement. *Psychological Reports, 34*, 1271–1280.

Tondo, T.R., Lane, J.R., & Gill, K., Jr. (1975). Suppression of specific eating behaviors by covert response cost: An experimental analysis. *Psychological Record, 25*, 187–196.

Turkat, I.D., & Adams, H.E. (1982). Covert positive reinforcement and pain modification: A test of efficacy and theory. *Journal of Psychosomatic Research, 26*, 191–201.

Vernon, W.M. (1969). Comparative aversiveness of self-delivered shock. *Proceedings of the 77th Annual Convention of the American Psychological Association, 4*, 813–814.

Wadden, T.A., & Flaxman, J. (1981). Hypnosis and weight loss: A preliminary study. *International Journal of Clinical and Experimental Hypnosis, 29*, 162–173.

Wade, T.C., Baker, T.B., & Hartmann, D.P. (1979). Behavior therapists' self-reported views and practices. *Behavior Therapist, 2*, 3–6.

Wade, T.C., Malloy, T.E., & Proctor, S. (1977). Imaginal correlates of self-reported fear and avoidance behavior. *Behavior Research and Therapy, 15*, 17–22.

Wasserman, T.H. (1978). The elimination of complaints of stomach cramps in a 12-year-old child by covert positive reinforcement. *The Behavior Therapist, 1*(3), 13–14.

Watson, J.B. (1913). Psychology as the behaviorist views it. *Psychological Review, 20*, 158–177.

Watson, J.B., & Rayner, P. (1920). Conditioned emotional reactions. *Journal of Experimental Psychology, 3*, 1–14.

Watson, L.J. (1977). The effects of covert modeling and covert reinforcement on acquisition of job interview skills by youth offenders (Doctoral dissertation, West Virginia University, 1976). *Dissertation Abstracts International, 37*, 4229B–4230B. (University Microfilms No. 77-2556.)

Wayner, E.A., Flannery, G.R., & Singer, G. (1978). Effects of taste aversion conditioning on the primary antibody response to sheep red blood cells and brucella abortus in albino rats. *Physiological Behavior, 21*, 995–1000.

Weiner, H. (1965). Real and imagined cost effects upon human fixed-interval responding. *Psychological Reports, 17,* 659–662.

Weisenberg, M. (1977). Pain and pain control. *Psychological Bulletin, 84,* 1008–1044.

Weiss, T., & Engel, B.T. (1971). Operant conditioning of heart rate in patients with premature ventricular contractions. *Psychosomatic Medicine, 37,* 301–321.

Weitzenhoffer, A.M., & Hilgard, E.R. (1959). *Stanford hypnotic susceptibility scale.* Palo Alto, CA: Consulting Psychologists Press.

Welgan, P.R. (1974). Learned control of gastric acid secretions in ulcer patients. *Psychosomatic Medicine, 36,* 411–419.

White, O.R. (1971). *A glossary of behavioral terminology.* Champaign, IL: Research Press.

Wilson, G.T., & Davison, G.C. (1972). Processes for fear reduction in systematic desensitization. I: Animal studies. *Psychological Bulletin, 78,* 28–31.

Wilson, G.T., & O'Leary, K.D. (1980). *Principles of behavior therapy.* Englewood Cliffs, NJ: Prentice-Hall.

Wilson, G.T., & Tracey, D.A. (1976). An experimental analysis of aversive imagery versus electrical aversive conditioning in the treatment of chronic alcoholics. *Behavior Research and Therapy, 14,* 41–51.

Wilson, S.C., & Barber, T.X. (1978). The creative imagination scale—as a measure of hypnosis. *American Journal of Clinical Hypnosis, 20,* 235–249.

Wish, P.A., Cautela, J.R., & Steffen, J.J. (1970). Covert reinforcement: An experimental test. *Proceedings of the Annual Convention of the American Psychological Association, 5,* 513–514.

Wisocki, P.A. (1970). Treatment of the obsessive-compulsive behavior by covert sensitization and covert reinforcement: A case report. *Journal of Behavior Therapy and Experimental Psychiatry, 1,* 233–239.

Wisocki, P.A. (1971). An application of covert reinforcement for the treatment of test anxiety (Doctoral dissertation, Boston College, 1971). *Dissertation Abstracts International, 32,* 1229B–1230B. (University Microfilms No. 71-19, 792.)

Wisocki, P.A. (1973a). A covert reinforcement program for the treatment of test anxiety : A brief report. *Behavior Therapy, 4,* 264–266.

Wisocki, P.A. (1973b). The successful treatment of heroin addiction by covert conditioning techniques. *Journal of Behavior Therapy and Experimental Psychiatry, 4,* 55–61.

Wisocki, P.A. (1976). A behavioral treatment program for social inadequacy. Multiple methods for a complex problem. In J. Krumboltz & C. Thoresen (Eds.), *Counseling methods* (pp. 287–301). New York: Holt, Rinehart, & Winston.

Wisocki, P.A. (1977). The successful treatment of a heroin addict by covert conditioning techniques: An updated report. In D. Upper (Ed.), *Perspectives in behavior therapy* (pp. 31–44). Kalamazoo, MI: Behaviordelia.

Wolpe, J. (1958). *Psychotherapy by reciprocal inhibition.* Stanford, CA: Stanford University Press.

Wolpe, J. (1982). *The practice of behavior therapy* (3rd ed.). New York: Pergamon.

Wolpe, J., & Lang, P. (1964). A fear survey schedule for use in behaviour therapy. *Behavior Research and Therapy, 2,* 27–30.

Woolfolk, R.L., Parrish, M.W., & Murphy, S.M. (1983, December). *The effects of positive and negative imagery on motor skill performance.* Paper presented at the Seventeenth Annual Meeting of the Association for Advancement of Behavior Therapy, Washington, DC.

Yaremko, R.M., & Butler, M.C. (1975). Imagined experience and attenuation of the galvanic skin response to shocks. *Bulletin of Psychonomic Science, 5,* 317–318.

Yaremko, R.M., Glanville, B.B., & Leckart, B.T. (1972). Imagery-medicated habituation of the orienteering reflex. *Psychonomic Science, 27,* 204–206.

Yaremko, R.M., & Werner, M. (1974). Cognitive conditioning: Imagerial stimulus contiguity and third interval conditional GSR. *Pavlovian Journal of Biological Science, 9,* 215–221.

Zeisset, R.M. (1968). Desensitization and relaxation in the modification of psychiatric patients' interview behavior. *Journal of Abnormal Psychology, 73,* 18–24.

Zemore, R., Ramsay, B., & Zemore, J. (1978). Success of covert negative reinforcement is not the result of operant conditioning. *Psychological Reports, 43,* 955–961.

Zielinski, J.J., & Williams, L.J. (1979). Covert modeling vs behavior rehearsal. The training and generalization of assertive behavior: A crossover design. *Journal of Clinical Psychology, 35,* 855–863.

Criteria for Inclusion and Exclusion in the Bibliography

The items cited in this bibliography include controlled studies, case reports, literature reviews, theoretical articles, and a few works which do not quite fit into any of these categories. As we reviewed many of the works under consideration for inclusion, two observations became clear to us. First, occasionally an author who had referred to a procedure used as covert conditioning would go on to describe a procedure that was clearly not an example of covert conditioning in the way we have used the term. Second, from time to time authors have described procedures which seemed to us to be obvious examples of covert conditioning, but did not refer to these procedures as covert conditioning.

In order to present an accurate and substantially complete bibliography of covert conditioning, we used the following guidelines for inclusion:

1. Papers in which a procedure used is either labeled covert conditioning or is given the name of any one of the seven specific covert conditioning procedures.
2. Papers in which a procedure used clearly relies on the use of appropriate contingent imaginary consequences (or at least verbal instructions to imagine the consequences). A few articles that fall into this category were published before the first covert conditioning article by Cautela (1966). Although Cautela was the first to systematize and conceptualize these procedures as covert conditioning and to develop the consistent language so useful in science, in some cases covert conditioning procedures were first

suggested by others (e.g., Kazdin, 1972, predicted the future development of CRC).

3. Not included were examples of the general use of imagery, noncontingent imagery, or other specific behavioral procedures, such as systematic desensitization, implosive therapy, covert assertion, coverant control, and emotive imagery.

4. Not included were works in which there is only a brief, or passing, mention of covert conditioning.

5. Not included were any of the ever-increasing number of textbooks with sections devoted to covert conditioning.

6. Nearly all of the references listed are published articles or books, doctoral dissertations, master's theses, or papers presented at professional meetings. Although some of the other sources included are unpublished manuscripts, we listed those which seem to be cited in the literature from time to time, suggesting a reasonable likelihood of availability. In cases where a particular work is available from more than one source (e.g., journal article and book of readings) we have listed the original source.

Although our goal has been to compile as complete a listing of sources of information about covert conditioning as possible, we know we can never have a totally complete listing. Certainly, there are papers in press, or in preparation, and dissertations being written as we write this book. In attempting to compile such a list both incorrect inclusions and omissions are likely. The goal of such a project should be to be as complete as possible, thereby allowing the users of the bibliography to decide whether or not the included material is appropriate for their purposes. A non-included source would of course not be available for the user's decision. Therefore in those relatively few instances when the appropriateness of the inclusion of a given item was unclear, we chose to lean toward being overly inclusive rather than being overly exclusive.

From time to time we expect to be updating this bibliography. Therefore, we would like to request some help from you, our readers. If you are aware of any sources which should have been included, but were overlooked, please let us know. If you feel strongly that an included source should not have been included, please let us know. As mentioned above, there were some gray areas. If you become aware of sources in the future which should probably be included in an updated edition, please let us know. In compiling this listing we found several errors in citations, published in journals, which we tried to correct. If you find any additional errors in our listing (anything from misspelling to incorrect journals) please contact us.

Also, we hope to assemble as complete a depository as possible of covert conditioning papers. We would be grateful for copies, or reprints, or any past or future papers, and ask any authors whose work is listed in the bibliography (or should be) to consider this as a formal request for reprints. We would also like to receive copies of unpublished manuscripts on covert conditioning. Eshleman (1983) has recently made a computerized data base of all known precision teaching references available to interested persons. We hope to be able to offer a similar service in the not too distant future.

Finally, we would be thankful for any other comments or suggestions regarding the format and content of this book.

Topical Index

In order to make the locating of appropriate references easier, the sources listed in this section have been categorized in three ways. The three categories are:

1. Procedure (e.g., CE, CM, CPR).
2. Target behavior (e.g., addictions, organic dysfunctions, phobias).
3. Type of source (e.g., case studies, experiments, reviews).

For example, someone wishing to find a listing of all case reports (source) of the use of covert extinction (procedure) in the treatment of addictions (target behavior) would simply cross reference the three categories by checking which sources are listed under the three appropriate headings: Covert Extinction, Addictions, and Case Studies. Rather than duplicate the References section of this book, the sources are here listed by number, which corresponds to the alphabetical arrangement of sources in the bibliography. Under Procedure, covert extinction articles 20, 69, 155, 179, 180, 181, 362 are listed. Next, in checking Target Behavior—Addictions, the researcher finds that sources 2, 3, 8, 14, 155, 179, 180, 181, 283, and 364 are listed. However, only five of the sources listed under covert extinction are also listed under Addictions, 155, 179, 180, 181, and 364. Lastly, in checking Source Format—Case study, the researcher finds numerous listings. However, the only numbers that appear in all three lists are 158, 179, and 181, thereby locating the only two case study reports of the use of CE to treat addictions as sources number 179 and 181.

Procedures

1. Covert Classical Conditioning: 35, 135, 249, 440.

2. Covert Conditioning (more than one procedure or not specified): 3, 4, 33, 34, 36, 61, 62, 68, 71, 73, 74, 75, 76, 77, 80, 81, 82, 83, 84, 85, 86, 89, 90, 91, 93, 94, 95, 96, 97, 98, 99, 101, 102, 112, 113, 129, 151, 160, 167, 175, 176, 185, 186, 188, 193, 194, 204, 206, 210, 217, 219, 235, 242, 247, 250, 262, 263, 271, 272, 277, 278, 279, 280, 281, 291, 292, 297, 301, 302, 310, 317, 321, 324, 330, 331, 357, 358, 360, 362, 366, 374, 376, 381, 393, 396, 403, 406, 411, 416, 418, 421, 423, 424, 425, 426, 431, 433, 435.

3. Covert Extinction: 20, 69, 155, 179, 180, 181, 362.

4. Covert Modeling: 41, 44, 47, 70, 79, 92, 104, 105, 106, 107, 121, 130, 132, 160, 162, 169, 182, 196, 197, 199, 200, 207, 222, 225, 226, 227, 228, 229, 230, 231, 232, 233, 234, 236, 237, 238, 239, 240, 241, 274, 275, 303, 304, 305, 315, 316, 341, 351, 352, 354, 376, 378, 379, 380, 383, 385, 397, 400, 406, 431, 442.

5. Covert Negative Reinforcement: 1, 19, 36, 37, 63, 101, 147, 201, 292, 317, 327, 360, 424, 441.

6. Covert Positive Reinforcement: 7, 16, 17, 18, 23, 24, 32, 38, 39, 40, 41, 44, 45, 51, 64, 65, 66, 87, 100, 106, 109, 115, 117, 118, 119, 120, 121, 127, 129, 131, 134, 135, 149, 151, 152, 154, 157, 159, 160, 161, 183, 187, 189, 192, 193, 194, 204, 213, 214, 218, 243, 244, 245, 246, 247, 250, 252, 253, 254, 255, 256, 257, 258, 259, 266, 273, 276, 291, 292, 293, 294, 296, 298, 301, 306, 317, 321, 322, 326, 331, 335, 336, 343, 344, 348, 349, 350, 353, 355, 356, 358, 361, 362, 365, 370, 371, 372, 375, 376, 386, 387, 388, 391, 394, 398, 404, 405, 406, 417, 418, 419, 421, 422, 423, 424, 426, 428, 430, 431, 432, 433, 434, 436, 437, 438, 439.

7. Covert Response Cost: 78, 362, 389, 408.

8. Covert Sensitization: 2, 5, 6, 8, 9, 10, 11, 12, 13, 14, 15, 21, 22, 25, 26, 27, 28, 29, 30, 31, 33, 35, 36, 37, 38, 42, 43, 46, 48, 49, 50, 52, 53, 54, 55, 56, 57, 58, 59, 60, 66, 67, 72, 88, 89, 103, 108, 110, 111, 114, 116, 122, 123, 124, 125, 126, 129, 133, 134, 136, 137, 138, 139, 140, 141, 142, 143, 144, 145, 146, 148, 150, 151, 153, 156, 158, 163, 164, 165, 166, 168, 170,

171, 172, 173, 174, 177, 178, 184, 190, 191, 193, 194, 195, 198, 202, 203, 204, 205, 208, 209, 211, 212, 215, 216, 220, 221, 223, 224, 227, 248, 250, 251, 260, 261, 264, 265, 267, 268, 269, 270, 282, 283, 284, 285, 286, 287, 288, 289, 290, 291, 295, 299, 300, 301, 303, 307, 308, 309, 311, 312, 313, 314, 318, 319, 320, 321, 323, 325, 328, 329, 331, 332, 333, 334, 337, 338, 339, 340, 342, 345, 346, 347, 358, 359, 360, 363, 364, 367, 368, 369, 373, 374, 377, 382, 384, 385, 390, 392, 399, 402, 407, 409, 410, 412, 413, 414, 415, 418, 420, 421, 423, 426, 427, 429, 430, 433, 436, 437.

Target Behavior

1. Addictions (alcohol, cigarettes, drugs, food, etc.): 2, 3, 8, 9, 10, 11, 12, 13, 14, 21, 22, 25, 35, 36, 38, 42, 46, 47, 51, 66, 67, 71, 74, 97, 108, 110, 111, 125, 126, 131, 132, 133, 136, 137, 138, 139, 140, 141, 142, 143, 144, 145, 146, 148, 150, 155, 156, 162, 163, 164, 165, 166, 168, 172, 173, 175, 176, 178, 179, 180, 181, 198, 200, 205, 209, 211, 215, 216, 220, 251, 261, 268, 269, 282, 283, 290, 291, 295, 299, 303, 307, 308, 309, 312, 313, 314, 315, 319, 320, 323, 328, 329, 331, 332, 333, 337, 338, 339, 342, 345, 346, 347, 364, 366, 367, 368, 369, 373, 374, 377, 382, 384, 385, 389, 390, 392, 399, 400, 401, 402, 409, 410, 413, 414, 415, 420, 421, 423, 426, 427, 429, 433.

2. Organic Dysfunctions: 1, 7, 39, 40, 56, 82, 83, 109, 115, 121, 213, 298, 355, 357, 362, 375, 393, 394, 405, 412.

3. Other (not otherwise classified, neutral experimental behaviors, etc.): 1, 7, 16, 19, 20, 23, 32, 33, 34, 43, 57, 65, 84, 89, 100, 101, 116, 117, 118, 120, 121, 122, 123, 134, 152, 154, 158, 160, 170, 183, 184, 186, 188, 190, 191, 193, 194, 200, 202, 204, 208, 218, 219, 223, 224, 243, 246, 254, 255, 256, 260, 263, 265, 274, 275, 281, 299, 306, 310, 311, 317, 318, 325, 327, 335, 340, 353, 354, 355, 358, 360, 361, 365, 370, 381, 386, 387, 388, 391, 398, 404, 408, 417, 418, 428, 430, 432, 434, 436, 437, 439, 440.

4. Phobias: 24, 41, 44, 45, 86, 92, 104, 105, 106, 107, 112, 119, 130, 135, 149, 157, 159, 161, 169, 182, 189, 196, 197, 201, 214, 222, 225, 227, 229, 230, 244, 245, 252, 253, 257, 258, 259, 273, 276, 292, 296, 326, 348, 349, 350, 378, 379, 380, 383, 412, 419, 422, 441.

5. Sexual Dysfunctions: 1, 5, 6, 15, 26, 27, 28, 29, 30, 31, 37, 48, 49, 50, 52, 53, 54, 55, 102, 103, 114, 129, 171, 174, 177, 195, 199, 202, 203, 212, 247, 264, 282, 284, 285, 286, 287, 288, 289, 300, 334, 359, 416.

Source

Bibliography

1. Abraham, H.A. (1968). Hypnosis used in the treatment of somatic manifestations of a psychotic disorder. *American Journal of Clinical Hypnosis, 10*, 304.
2. Abrams, D.B. (1979). Clinical developments in the behavioral treatment of obesity. *Clinical Behavior Therapy Review, 1*(2), 1, 3–14.
3. Abramson, E.E. (1973). A review of behavioral approaches to weight control. *Behaviour Research and Therapy, 11*, 547–556.
4. Agras, W.S. (1972). Covert conditioning. *Seminar in Psychiatry, 4*, 157–163.
5. Alford, G.S., Webster, J.S., & Sanders, S.H. (1980). Covert aversion of two interrelated deviant sexual practices: Obscene phone-calling and exhibitionism: A single case analysis. *Behavior Therapy, 11*, 15–25.
6. Alford, G.S., Wedding, D., & Jones, S. (1983). "Turn-ons" and "turn-offs": The effects of competitory covert imagery on penile tumescence responses to diverse extrinsic sexual stimulus materials. *Behavior Modification, 7*, 112–125.
7. Altamura, L.S., & Chitwood, P.R. (1974). Covert reinforcement and self-control procedures in systematic desensitization of gagging behavior. *Psychological Reports, 35*, 563–566.
8. Anant, S.S. (1966). The treatment of alcoholics by a verbal aversion technique: A case report. *Manas, 13*, 79–86.
9. Anant, S.S. (1966). The use of verbal aversion techniques with a group of alcoholics. *Saskatchewan Psychologist*, 28–30.
10. Anant, S.S. (1967). A note on the treatment of alcoholics by a verbal aversion technique. *Canadian Psychologist, 8*, 19–22.
11. Anant, S.S. (1967). The treatment of alcoholics and drug addicts by a verbal aversion technique. *Psychotherapy and Psychosomatics, 15*, 6.
12. Anant, S.S. (1968). Former alcoholics and social drinking: An unexpected finding. *The Canadian Psychologist, 9*, 35.

13. Anant, S.S. (1968). Treatment of alcoholics and drug addicts by verbal aversion techniques. *International Journal of the Addictions, 3,* 381–388.

14. Anant, S.S. (1968). The use of verbal aversion (negative conditioning) with an alcoholic: A case report. *Behavior Research and Therapy, 6,* 395–396.

15. Anant, S.S. (1968). Verbal aversion therapy with a promiscuous girl: A case report. *Psychological Reports, 22,* 795–796.

16. Angstadt, K.R. (1979). A comparison of overt and covert techniques in self-management (Doctoral dissertation, University of Maryland, 1978). *Dissertation Abstracts International,* 428B. (University of Microfilms No. 7915793.)

17. Ascher, L.M. (1971, September). *An analog study of covert positive reinforcement.* Paper presented at the meeting of the Association for Advancement of Behavior Therapy, Washington, DC.

18. Ascher, L.M. (1973). An analog study of covert positive reinforcement. In R.D. Rubin, J.P. Brady, & J.D. Henderson (Eds.), *Advances in behavior therapy* (Vol. 4, pp. 127–138). New York: Academic Press.

19. Ascher, L.M., & Cautela, J.R. (1972). Covert negative reinforcement: An experimental test. *Journal of Behavior Therapy and Experimental Psychiatry, 3,* 1–5.

20. Ascher, L.M., & Cautela, J.R. (1974). An experimental study of covert extinction. *Journal of Behavior Therapy and Experimental Psychiatry, 5,* 233–238.

21. Ashem, B., & Donner, L. (1968). Covert sensitization with alcoholics. A controlled replication. *Behavior Research and Therapy, 6,* 7–12.

22. Ashem, B., Poser, E., & Trudell, P. (1972). The use of covert sensitization in the treatment of overeating. In R.D. Rubin, H. Fensterheim, J.D. Henderson, & L.P. Ullmann (Eds.), *Advances in behavior therapy* (Vol. 3). New York: Academic Press.

23. Aubut, L., & Ladouceur, R. (1978). Modification of self-esteem by covert positive reinforcement. *Psychological Reports, 42,* 1305–1306.

24. Bajtelsmit, J.W., & Gershman, L. (1976). Covert positive reinforcement: Efficacy and conceptualization. *Journal of Behavior Therapy and Experimental Psychiatry, 7,* 207–212.

25. Barbarin, O.A. III (1975). A comparison of overt and symbolic aversion in the self-management of chronic smoking behavior (Doctoral dissertation, Rutgers University, 1975). *Dissertation Abstracts International, 36,* 2457B–2458B. (University Microfilms No. 75-24, 655.)

26. Barlow, D.H., Agras, W.S., & Leitenberg, H. (1970, September). *A preliminary report on the contribution of therapeutic instructions to covert sensitization.* Paper presented at the meeting of the Association for Advancement of Behavior Therapy, Miami, FL.

27. Barlow, D.H., Agras, W.S., & Leitenberg, H. (1970, September). *Experimental investigations in the use of covert sensitization in the*

modification of sexual behavior. Paper presented at the meeting of the Association for Advancement of Behavior Therapy, Miami, FL.

28. Barlow, D.H., Agras, W.S., & Leitenberg, H., Callahan, E.J., & Moore, R.C. (1972). The contribution of therapeutic instructions to covert sensitization. *Behaviour Research and Therapy, 10,* 411–415.

29. Barlow, D.H., Leitenberg, H., & Agras, W.S. (1968). *Preliminary report of the experimental control of sexual deviation by manipulation of the US in covert sensitization.* Paper presented at the meeting of the Eastern Psychological Association, Washington, DC.

30. Barlow, D.H., Leitenberg, H., & Agras, W.S. (1969). Experimental control of sexual deviation through manipulation of the noxious scene in covert sensitization. *Journal of Abnormal Psychology, 74,* 596–601.

31. Barlow, D.H., Reynolds, E.J., & Agras, W.S. (1973). Gender identity change in a transsexual. *Archives of General Psychiatry, 28,* 569–576.

32. Baron, M.G. (1975). An operant analysis of imagery: The parameters of covert reinforcement (Doctoral dissertation, Boston College, 1975). *Dissertation Abstracts International, 36,* 1469 B. (University Microfilms No. 75-20, 696.)

33. Baron, M.G., & Cautela, J.R. (1977). Eliminating the self-injurious behavior of a young psychiatric patient. In D. Upper (Ed.), *Perspectives in behavior therapy* (pp. 103–125). Kalamazoo, MI: Behaviordelia.

34. Baron, M.G., & Cautela, J.R. (1983–84). Imagery assessment with normal and special needs children. *Imagination, Cognition, and Personality, 3*(1), 17–33.

35. Barrett, T.J., & Sachs, L.B. (1974). Test of the classical conditioning explanation of covert sensitization. *Psychological Reports, 34,* 1312–1314.

36. Baugh, B.L. (1977). Generalization effects of covert conditioning and instruction in the suppression of eating behaviors (Doctoral dissertation, University of Texas at Austin, 1976). *Dissertation Abstracts International, 37,* 4127B. (University Microfilms No. 77, 3861.)

37. Bellack, A.S. (1974). Covert aversion relief and treatment of homosexuality. *Behavior Therapy, 5,* 435–437.

38. Bellack, A.S., Glanz, L.M., & Simon, R. (1976). Self-reinforcement style and covert imagery in the treatment of obesity. *Journal of Consulting and Clinical Psychology, 44,* 490–491.

39. Bennett, A.K., & Cautela, J.R. (1979, December). *The use of covert conditioning in the modification of pain: Two experimental tests.* Paper presented at the meeting of the Association for Advancement of Behavior Therapy, San Francisco.

40. Bennett, A.K., & Cautela, J.R. (1981). The use of covert conditioning in the modification of pain: Two experimental tests. *Journal of Behavior Therapy and Experimental Psychiatry, 12,* 315–320.

41. Bernal, G., Wisocki, P.A., & Tennen, H. (1974, November). *Imagerial rehearsal or reinforcement in a covert behavioral technique: A single*

subject experiment. Paper presented at the Eighth Annual conference of the Association for Advancement of Behavior Therapy, Chicago.

42. Bier, R.S. (1979). Assisted covert sensitization and smoking cessation (Doctoral dissertation, University of Texas at Dallas, 1978). *Dissertation Abstracts International, 39*, 4019B. (University Microfilms No. 7902523.)

43. Binder, C.V. (1975). A note on covert processes and the natural environment. *Behavior Therapy, 6*, 568.

44. Bistline, J.L., Jaremko, M.E., & Sobleman, S. (1980). The relative contributions of covert reinforcements and cognitive restructuring to test anxiety reduction. *Journal of Clinical Psychology, 36*, 723–728.

45. Blanchard, E.B., & Draper, D.O. (1973). Treatment of a rodent phobia by covert reinforcement: A single subject experiment. *Behavior Therapy, 4*, 559–564.

46. Blanchard, E.B., Libet, J.M., & Young, L.D. (1973). Apneic aversion and covert sensitization in the treatment of a hydrocarbon inhalation addiction: A case study. *Journal of Behavior Therapy and Experimental Psychiatry, 4*, 383–387.

47. Bornstein, P.H., & Devine, D.A. (1980). Covert modeling-hypnosis in the treatment of obesity. *Psychotherapy: Theory, Research, and Practice, 17*, 272–276.

48. Brownell, K.D., & Barlow, D.H. (1976). Measurement and treatment of two sexual deviations in one person. *Journal of Behavior Therapy and Experimental Psychiatry, 7*, 349–354.

49. Brownell, K.D., & Barlow, D.H. (1980). The behavioral treatment of sexual deviation. In A. Goldstein & E.B. Foa (Eds.), *Handbook of behavioral interventions: A clinical guide* (pp. 604–672). New York: Wiley.

50. Brownell, K.D., Hayes, S.C., & Barlow, D.H. (1977). Patterns of appropriate and deviant sexual arousal: The behavioral treatment of multiple sexual deviation. *Journal of Consulting and Clinical Psychology, 45*, 1144–1155.

51. Brunn, A.C., & Hedberg, A.G. (1974). Covert positive reinforcement as a treatment procedure for obesity. *Journal of Community Psychology, 2*, 117–119.

52. Burdick, M.R. (1972). An exploration of the aversion therapy technique of covert sensitization with selected cases of exhibitionism (Doctoral dissertation, University of Minnesota, 1972). *Dissertation Abstracts International, 33*, 2805B. (University Microfilms No. 72-32282.)

53. Callahan, E.J. (1972). *Aversion therapy for sexual deviation: A series of within-Ss examinations*. Unpublished doctoral dissertation, University of Vermont.

54. Callahan, E.J. (1976). Covert sensitization for homosexuality. In J.D. Krumboltz & C.E. Thoresen (Eds.), *Counseling methods* (pp. 234–245). New York: Holt, Rinehart & Winston.

55. Callahan, E.J., & Leitenberg, H. (1973). Aversion therapy for sexual deviation: Contingent shock and covert sensitization. *Journal of Abnormal Psychology, 81,* 60–73.

56. Carney, R.M., & Hong, B.A. (1982). Effects of covert sensitization on facial EMG: A pilot study. *Perceptual and Motor Skills, 55,* 655–658.

57. Cautela, J.R. (1966). Treatment of compulsive behavior by covert sensitization. *Psychological Record, 16,* 33–41.

58. Cautela, J.R. (1967, September). *Behavior therapy and the need for behavioral assessment.* Paper presented at the meeting of the American Psychological Association, Washington, DC.

59. Cautela, J.R. (1967). Covert sensitization. *Psychological Reports, 20,* 459–468.

60. Cautela, J.R. (1968). Behavior therapy and the need for behavioral assessment. *Psychotherapy: Theory, Research, and Practice, 5,* 175–179.

61. Cautela, J.R. (1969). Behavior therapy and self-control. In C.M. Franks (Ed.), *Behavior therapy: Appraisal and status* (pp. 323–340). New York: McGraw-Hill.

62. Cautela, J.R. (1969). The use of imagery in behavior modification. In R. Rubin & C. Franks (Eds.), *Advances in behavior therapy,* New York: Academic Press.

63. Cautela, J.R. (1970). Covert negative reinforcement. *Journal of Behavior Therapy and Experimental Psychiatry, 1,* 273–278.

64. Cautela, J.R. (1970). Covert reinforcement. *Behavior Therapy, 1,* 33–50.

65. Cautela, J.R. (1970). The modification of behaviors that influence the probability of suicide in elders. *Proceedings of the 78th Annual Convention of the American Psychological Association, 5,* 934.

66. Cautela, J.R. (1970). The treatment of alcoholism by covert sensitization. *Psychotherapy: Theory, Research, and Practice, 7,* 86–90.

67. Cautela, J.R. (1970). Treatment of smoking by covert sensitization. *Psychological Reports, 26,* 415–420.

68. Cautela, J.R. (1971). Covert conditioning. In A. Jacobs & L.B. Sacks (Eds.), *The psychology of private events* (pp. 109–130). New York: Academic Press.

69. Cautela, J.R. (1971). Covert extinction. *Behavior Therapy, 2,* 192–200.

70. Cautela, J.R. (1971, September). *Covert modeling.* Paper presented at the Fifth Annual Meeting of the Association for Advancement of Behavior Therapy, Washington, DC.

71. Cautela, J.R. (1972). Covert conditioning of addictive behaviors. In D. Upper & D.S. Goodenough (Eds.), *Behavior modification with the individual patient. Proceedings of the Third Annual Brockton Symposium on Behavior Therapy, 3,* 3–24.

72. Cautela, J.R. (1972). *Covert sensitization scenes: A compilation of typical scenes used in the application of covert sensitization to a variety of maladaptive behaviors.* Unpublished manuscript, Boston College.

73. Cautela, J.R. (1972). Rationale and procedures for covert conditioning. In R.D. Rubin, H. Fensterheim, J. Henderson, & L.P. Ullman (Eds.), *Advances in behavior therapy* (Vol. 4, pp. 85–96). New York: Academic Press.

74. Cautela, J.R. (1972). The treatment of over-eating by covert conditioning. *Psychotherapy: Theory, Research, and Practice, 9,* 211–216.

75. Cautela, J.R. (1973). Covert processes and behavior modification. *Journal of Nervous and Mental Disease, 157,* 27–36.

76. Cautela, J.R. (1975). Processus de conditionnement par provocation d'images et modification du comportement (in French). In G. Trudel & Y. Lemontagne (Eds.), *Modification du comportement en milieu clinique et en education* (pp. 9–18). Maquette: Roland Marquis.

77. Cautela, J.R. (1975). The use of covert conditioning in hypnotherapy. *International Journal of Clinical and Experimental Hypnosis, 23,* 15–27.

78. Cautela, J.R. (1976). Covert response cost. *Psychotherapy: Theory, Research, and Practice, 13,* 397–404.

79. Cautela, J.R. (1976). The present status of covert modeling. *Journal of Behavior Therapy and Experimental Psychiatry, 7,* 323–326.

80. Cautela, J.R. (1977). *Behavior analysis forms for clinical intervention.* Champaign, IL: Research Press.

81. Cautela, J.R. (1977). Covert conditioning: Assumptions and procedures. *Journal of Mental Imagery, 1,* 53–64.

82. Cautela, J.R. (1977). The use of covert conditioning in modifying pain behavior. *Journal of Behavior Therapy and Experimental Psychiatry, 8,* 45–52.

83. Cautela, J.R. (1980, November). *The application of covert conditioning to organic dysfunction.* Invited address to the Fourteenth Annual Meeting of the Association for Advancement of Behavior Therapy, New York.

84. Cautela, J.R. (1981). The behavioral treatment of elderly patients with depression. In J.F. Clarkin & H.G. Glazer (Eds.), *Depression: Behavioral and directive treatment strategies.* New York: Garland.

85. Cautela, J.R. (1981). *Behavioral analysis forms for clinical intervention* (Vol. 2). Champaign, IL: Research Press.

86. Cautela, J.R. (1982). Covert conditioning with children. *Journal of Behavior Therapy and Experimental Psychiatry, 13,* 209–214.

87. Cautela, J.R. (1983). The self-control triad: Description and clinical applications. *Behavior Modification, 7,* 299–315.

88. Cautela, J.R., & Avitable, M. (1967, September). *Physiological concomitants of covert sensitization.* Paper presented at the Annual Meeting of the Association for Advancement of Behavior Therapy, Washington, DC.

89. Cautela J.R., & Baron, M.G. (1973). Multifaceted behavior therapy of self-injurious behavior. *Journal of Behavior Therapy and Experimental Psychiatry, 4,* 125–131.

90. Cautela, J.R., & Baron, M.G. (1977). Covert conditioning: A theoretical analysis. *Behavior Modification, 1*, 351–368.
91. Cautela, J.R., & Bennett, A.K. (1981). Covert conditioning. In R. Corsini (Ed.), *Handbook of innovative psychotherapies*. New York: Wiley.
92. Cautela, J.R., Flannery, R.B., Jr., & Hanley, S. (1974). Covert modeling: An experimental test. *Behavior Therapy, 5*, 494–502.
93. Cautela, J.R., & Kearney, A.J. (1984). Covert conditioning. In R. Corsini (Ed.), *Wiley encyclopedia of psychology* (Vol. 1, pp. 305–306). New York: Wiley.
94. Cautela, J.R., & Kearney, A.J. (1986). *The Covert Conditioning Handbook*. New York: Springer.
95. Cautela, J.R., & Mansfield, L. (1977). A behavioral approach to geriatrics. In W.D. Gentry (Ed.), *Geropsychology: A model of training and clinical service* (pp. 21–42). Cambridge, MA: Ballinger.
96. Cautela, J.R., & McCullough, L. (1978). Covert conditioning: A learning theory perspective on imagery. In J.L. Singer & K.S. Pope (Eds.), *The power of human imagination*. New York: Plenum.
97. Cautela, J.R., & Rosenstiel, A.K. (1975). The use of covert conditioning in the treatment of drug abuse. *The International Journal of the Addictions, 10*, 277–303.
98. Cautela, J.R., & Upper, D. (1975). The process of individual behavior therapy. In M.H. Eisen & R.M. Eilser (Eds.), *Progress in behavior modification* (pp. 275–305). New York: Academic Press.
99. Cautela, J.R., & Wall, C.C. (1980). Covert conditioning in clinical practice. In E. Foa & A. Goldstein (Eds.), *Handbook of behavioral interventions*. New York: Wiley.
100. Cautela, J.R., Walsh, K. & Wish, P. (1971). The use of covert reinforcement in the modification of attitudes toward the mentally retarded. *Journal of Psychology, 77*, 257–260.
101. Cautela, J.R., & Wisocki, P.A. (1969). The use of imagery in the modification of attitudes toward the elderly: A preliminary report. *Journal of Psychology, 73*, 193–199.
102. Cautela, J.R., & Wisocki, P.A. (1969). The use of male and female therapists in the treatment of homosexual behavior. In R.D. Rubin & C. Franks (Eds.), *Advances in behavior therapy, 1968*. New York: Academic Press.
103. Cautela, J.R., & Wisocki, P.A. (1971). Covert sensitization for the treatment of sexual deviations. *Psychological Record, 21*, 37–48.
104. Chertock, S.L. (1977). Covert modeling treatment of children's dental fears (Doctoral dissertation, University of Montana, 1976). *Dissertation Abstracts International, 37*, 5826B. (University Microfilms No. 77-10, 674.)
105. Chertock, S.L., & Bornstein, P.H. (1979). Covert modeling treatment of children's dental fears. *Child Behavior Therapy, 1*, 249–255.
106. Chewning, M., Wood, S., & Jaremko, M.E. (1980, November). *Active ingredients in the cognitive-behavioral treatment of clinical significant*

anxiety. Paper presented at the 14th Annual Convention of the Association for Advancement of Behavior Therapy, New York.

107. Chudy, J.F., Jones, G.E., & Dickson, A.L. (1983). Modified desensitization approach for the treatment of phobic behavior in children. A quasi-experimental case study. *Journal of Clinical Child Psychology, 12,* 198–201.

108. Clarke, J.C., & Hayes, K. (1984). Covert sensitization, stimulus relevance and the equipotentiality premise. *Behavior Research and Therapy, 22,* 451–454.

109. Cleveland, P. (1982). Comparison of covert conditioning, relaxation, training, biofeedback and placebo as treatments for myofacial pain (of TMJ) dysfunction syndrome (Doctoral dissertation, Boston College, 1981). *Dissertation Abstracts International, 42,* 3818B. (University Microfilms No. DA8203959.)

110. Conway, J.B. (1977). Behavioral self-control of smoking through aversive conditioning and self-management. *Journal of Consulting and Clinical Psychology, 45,* 348–357.

111. Copeman, C.D. (1977). Treatment of polydrug abuse and addiction by covert sensitization: Some contraindications. *International Journal of the Addictions, 12,* 17–23.

112. Crane, L.D. (1977, December). *Six rehearsal techniques for the public speaker: Improving memory, increasing delivery skills and reducing speech stress.* Paper presented at the annual meeting of the Speech Communication Association, Washington, DC.

113. Crits-Cristoph, P., & Singer, J.L. (1981). Imagery in cognitive-behavior therapy: Research and application. *Clinical Psychology Review, 1,* 19–32.

114. Curtis, R.H., & Presly, A.S. (1972). The extinction of homosexual behavior by covert sensitization: A case study. *Behavior Research and Therapy, 10,* 81–83.

115. Daniels, L.K. (1973). Treatment of urticaria and severe headache by behavior therapy. *Psychosomatics, 14,* 347–351.

116. Daniels, L.K. (1974). Rapid extinction of nail biting by covert sensitization: A case study. *Journal of Behavior Therapy and Experimental Psychiatry, 5,* 91–92.

117. Daniels, L.K. (1975). The treatment of psychophysiological disorders and severe anxiety by behavior therapy, hypnosis and transcendental meditation. *American Journal of Clinical Hypnosis, 17,* 267–270.

118. Daniels, L.K. (1976). Covert reinforcement and hypnosis in the modification of attitudes toward physically disabled persons and generalization to the emotionally disturbed. *Psychological Reports, 38,* 554.

119. Daniels, L.K. (1976). Effects of covert reinforcement in the modification of test anxiety. *Psychological Records, 38,* 670.

120. Daniels, L.K. (1976). The effects of covert reinforcement on reading attitude with reinforcing scenes of varying intensity. *Perceptual and Motor Skills, 42,* 810.

121. Daniels, L.K. (1976). The treatment of acute anxiety and postoperative gingival pain by hypnosis and covert conditioning. A case report. *American Journal of Clinical Hypnosis, 19,* 116–119.

122. Davidson, A.M., & Denney, D.R. (1976). Covert sensitization and information in the reduction of nailbiting. *Behavior Therapy, 7,* 512–518.

123. Davison, G.C. (1968). The elimination of a sadistic fantasy by a client-controlled counterconditioning technique: A case study. *Journal of Abnormal Psychology, 73,* 84–90.

124. Davison, G.C. (1969). Self-control through "imaginal aversive contingency" and "one-downmanship": Enabling the powerless to accomodate unreasonableness. In J.D. Krumboltz & C.E. Thoresen (Eds.), *Behavioral counseling: Cases and techniques* (pp. 319–327). New York: Holt, Rinehart & Winston.

125. DeBerry, S. (1981). An evaluation of multi-model behavior therapy, covert sensitization, and long term follow-up in the treatment of obesity. *The Behavior Therapist, 4*(5), 17–18.

126. Deitchman, P.S. (1975). The use of covert sensitization in the treatment of obesity (Doctoral dissertation, Florida State University, 1972). *Dissertation Abstracts International, 35,* 3575B. (University Microfilms No. 75-932.)

127. DeLancey, A.L. (1979). The effects of covert reinforcement and social skills training with psychiatric patients (Doctoral dissertation, Boston College, 1979). *Dissertation Abstracts International, 40,* 1358B. (University Microfilms No. 79-20, 481.)

128. DeMoor, W., & Orlemans, J.W.G. (1971). *Inleiding tot de degragstherapie* (pp. 120–135). Loghum Slaterus: Deventer.

129. Denholtz, M.S. (1973). An extension of covert procedures in the treatment of male homosexuals. *Journal of Behavior Therapy and Experimental Psychiatry, 4,* 305.

130. Denney, D.R., Sullivan, B.J., & Thiry, M.C. (1977). Participant modeling and self-verbalization in training in reduction of spider fears. *Journal of Behavior Therapy and Experimental Psychiatry, 8,* 247–253.

131. Derby, W.N., Jr. (1976). Behavioral concomitants of covert processes. (Doctoral dissertation, McGill University, 1976). *Dissertation Abstracts International, 37,* 2498B–2499B.

132. Devine, D.A. (1978). Hypnosis and covert modeling in the treatment of obesity (Doctoral dissertation, University of Montana, 1977). *Dissertation Abstracts International, 38,* 3859B–3896B. (University Microfilms No. 77-28, 775)

133. Diament, C., & Wilson, G.T. (1975). An experimental investigation of the effects of covert sensitization in an analogue eating situation. *Behavior Therapy 6,* 499–509.

134. Dougher, M.J. (1984, November). *An experimental test of Cautela's operant explanation of covert conditioning procedures.* Paper presented

at the 18th Annual Meeting of the Association for Advancement of Behavior Therapy, Philadelphia.

135. Driscoll, R. (1976). Anxiety reduction using physical exertion and positive images. *The Psychological Record, 26,* 87–94.

136. Droppa, D.C. (1973). Behavioral treatment of drug addiction: A review and analysis. *International Journal of the Addictions, 8,* 143–161.

137. Droppa, D.C. (1977). Covert conditioning in the treatment of drug addiction (Doctoral dissertation, University of California at Berkeley, 1976). *Dissertation Abstracts International, 38,* 892B–893B. (University Microfilms No. 77-15, 574.)

138. Droppa, D.C. (1978). Application of covert conditioning procedures to outpatient treatment of drug addicts: Four case studies. *International Journal of the Addictions, 13,* 657–673.

139. Duehn, W.D. (1978). Covert sensitization in group treatment of adolescent drug abusers. *International Journal of the Addictions, 13,* 486–491.

140. Duehn, W.D., & Shannon, C. (1973, May). *Covert sensitization in the public high school: Short term group treatment of adolescent drug abusers.* Paper presented (revised version) at the 100th Annual Forum of the National Conference on Social Welfare, Atlantic City, NJ.

141. Edwards, J.A. (1975). *A comparison of covert sensitization and systematic desensitization when administered to groups of hospitalized alcoholics.* Unpublished doctoral dissertation, University of Vermont and State Agricultural College.

142. Elkins, R.L. (1975). Aversion therapy for alcoholism: Chemical, electrical, or verbal imaginary? *International Journal of the Addictions, 10,* 157–209.

143. Elkins, R.L. (1976). A note on aversion therapy for alcoholism. *Behavior Research and Therapy, 4,* 159–160.

144. Elkins, R.L. (1980). Covert sensitization treatment of alcoholism: Contributions of successful conditioning to subsequent abstinence maintenance. *Addictive Behaviors, 5,* 67–89.

145. Elkins, R.L., Murdock, R.P., & Wiggins, S. (1972). Autonomic response changes associated with imaginary alcohol consumption and verbally induced nausea during covert sensitization treatment for alcoholics. *Newsletter for Research in Psychology, 14*(3), 29–31.

146. Elliott, C.H., & Denney, D.R. (1975). Weight control through covert sensitization and false feedback. *Journal of Consulting and Clinical Psychology, 43,* 842–850.

147. Elson, S.E., & Scheurer, W.E. (1975). *An experimental test of covert negative reinforcement: A constructive replication of a study by Ascher and Cautela.* Paper presented at the annual meeting of the American Educational Research Association, Washington, DC.

148. Emmelkamp, P.M.G., & Walta, C. (1978). Effects of therapy set on electrical aversion therapy and covert sensitization. *Behavior Therapy, 9,* 185–188.

149. Engum, E.S., Miller, F.D., & Meredith, R.L. (1980). An analysis of three parameters of covert positive reinforcement. *Journal of Clinical Psychology, 36,* 301–309.
150. Epstein, L.H., Parker, F.C., & Jenkins, C.C. (1976). A multiple baseline analysis of treatment for heroin addiction. *Addictive Behaviors, 1,* 327–330.
151. Epstein, L.H., & Peterson, G.L. (1973). Differential conditioning using covert stimuli. *Behavior Therapy, 4,* 96–99.
152. Euse, F.J. (1976). An application of covert positive reinforcement for the modification of attitudes toward physically disabled persons (Doctoral dissertation, Auburn University, 1975). *Dissertation Abstracts International, 36,* 5787B–5788B. (University Microfilms No. 76-10, 895.)
153. Evans, D.R., Kazarian, S.S., & Greenough, T. (1977). The illusive attention-placebo control for covert sensitization. *Behavior Therapy, 8,* 98–99.
154. Evans, J.H. (1977). Imagery training for covert conditioning procedures (Doctoral dissertation, University of Missouri, 1976). *Dissertation Abstracts International, 37,* 4674B–4675B. (University Microfilms No. 77-4906.)
155. Fagertrom, K.O., Götestam, K.G., & Melin, L. (1982). A controlled study of covert extinction and relaxation in smoking cessation. *Scandinavian Journal of Behavior Therapy, 12,* 11–20.
156. Feamster, J.H., & Brown, J.E. (1963). Hypnotic aversion to alcohol: Three-year follow-up of one patient. *American Journal of Clinical Hypnosis, 6,* 164–166.
157. Finger, R., & Galassi, J.P. (1977). Effects of modifying cognitive vs. emotionality responses in the treatment of test anxiety. *Journal of Consulting and Clinical Psychology, 45,* 280–287.
158. Finkelstein, J.N., & Carlin, A.S. (1977). Treatment of an unusual adolescent bedwetting behavior by covert sensitization: A case study. *Journal of the American Academy of Child Psychiatry, 16,* 159–164.
159. Flannery, R.B., Jr. (1970). *The use of actual and imaginary fear stimuli in the behavior modification of a simple fear with covert reinforcement.* Unpublished doctoral dissertation, University of Windsor, Ontario.
160. Flannery, R.B., Jr. (1972). Covert conditioning in the behavioral treatment of an agoraphobic. *Psychotherapy: Theory, Research, and Practice, 9,* 217–220.
161. Flannery, R.B., Jr. (1972). A laboratory analogue of two covert reinforcement procedures. *Journal of Behavior Therapy and Experimental Psychiatry, 3,* 171–177.
162. Flannery, R.B., Jr. (1972). Use of covert conditioning in the behavioral treatment of a drug dependent college dropout. *Journal of Counseling Psychology, 19,* 547–550.
163. Fleiger, D.L. (1972). *Covert sensitization treatment with alcoholics.* Unpublished doctoral dissertation, University of Alberta.

164. Fleiger, D.L., & Zingle, H.W. (1973). Covert sensitization treatment with alcoholics. *Canadian Counsellor, 7*, 269–277.

165. Foreyt, J.P., & Hagen, R.L. (1973). Covert sensitization: Conditioning or suggestion? *Journal of Abnormal Psychology, 82*, 17–23.

166. Franks, C.M. (1966). Conditioning and conditioned aversion therapies in the treatment of the alcoholic. *International Journal of the Addictions, 1*, 61–97.

167. Franks, C.M. (1980). Covert conditioning—The evidence not yet overt (Review of *Covert Conditioning*). *Contemporary Psychology, 25*(12), 1005–1006.

168. Fuhrer, R.E. (1972). The effects of covert sensitization with relaxation induction, and attention-placebo on the reduction of cigarette smoking. (Doctoral dissertation, University of Montana, 1971). *Dissertation Abstracts International, 32*, 6644B–6645B. (University Microfilms No. 72-13, 449.)

169. Gallagher, J.W., & Arkowitz, H. (1978). Weak effects of covert modeling treatment of test anxiety. *Journal of Behavior Therapy and Experimental Psychiatry, 9*, 23–26.

170. Gauthier, J., & Pellerin, D. (1982). Management of compulsive shoplifting through covert sensitization. *Journal of Behavior Therapy and Experimental Psychiatry, 13*, 73–75.

171. Gershman, L. (1970). Case conference: A transvestite fantasy treated by thought-stopping, covert sensitization and aversive shock. *Journal of Behavior Therapy and Experimental Psychiatry, 1*, 153–161.

172. Gerson, P.D. (1971). The effect of covert sensitization and modeling in treating maladaptive behavior (Doctoral dissertation, University of Pittsburgh, 1970). *Dissertation Abstracts International, 32*, 1841B. (University Microfilms No. 71-23, 654.)

173. Gerson, P., & Lanyon, R.I. (1972). Modification of behavior with an aversion-desensitization procedure. *Journal of Consulting and Clinical Psychology, 38*, 399–402.

174. Glick, B.S. (1972). Aversive imagery therapy using hypnosis. *American Journal of Psychotherapy, 26*, 432–436.

175. Goguen, L.J. (1973). Effects of over-learning on covert conditioning. Unpublished doctoral dissertation, University of Moncton.

176. Goguen, L.J. (1974, November). *Overlearning of covert conditioning as a variable in the permanent modification of smoking behavior.* Paper presented at the Eighth Annual Conference of the Association for Advancement of Behavior Therapy, Chicago.

177. Gold, S., & Neufeld, I. (1965). A learning theory approach to the treatment of homosexuality. *Behavior Research and Therapy, 2*, 201–204.

178. Gordon, S.B. (1972). Self-control with a covert aversive stimulus: Modification of smoking (Doctoral dissertation, West Virginia University 1971). *Dissertation Abstracts International, 32*, 4858B–4859B. (University Microfilms No. 72-5154.)

179. Götestam, K.G., & Melin, L. (1974). Covert extinction of amphetamine addiction. *Behavior Therapy, 5,* 90–92.
180. Götestam, K.G., & Melin, L. (1983). An experimental study of covert extinction on smoking cessation. *Addictive Behaviors, 8,* 27–31.
181. Götestam, K.G., Melin, L., & Dockens, W.S. (1972, October). *Behavioral program for intravenous amphetamine addicts.* Paper presented at the International Symposium on Behavior Modification, Minneapolis, MN.
182. Gottlieb, B.S., McNamara, J.R., Perrine, H.E., & Kropf, K.P. (1979, December). *Covert modeling: A matter of credibility.* Paper presented at the meeting of the Association for Advancement of Behavior Therapy, San Francisco.
183. Graff, S.M. (1977). An application of covert positive reinforcement to the modification of social anxiety and interpersonal behaviors in male psychiatric inpatients. (Doctoral dissertation, Auburn University, 1977). *Dissertation Abstracts International, 38,* 1880B. (University Microfilms No. 77-20, 336.)
184. Greenough, T.J. (1977). An analogue study of specific parameters of overt and covert aversive conditioning. (Doctoral dissertation, University of Western Ontario, 1976). *Dissertation Abstracts International, 37,* 5351B–5352B.
185. Groden, G., & Cautela, J.R. (1981). Behavior therapy: A survey of procedures for counselors. *The Personnel and Guidance Journal, 60,* 175–180.
186. Groden, J. (1980). *Teaching covert conditioning procedures to mentally retarded students labelled "trainable retardates."* Unpublished manuscript, Boston College, Chestnut Hill, MA.
187. Groden, J. (1982). Procedures to increase social interaction among autistic adolescents: A multiple baseline analysis (Doctoral dissertation, Boston College, 1982). *Dissertation Abstracts International, 43,* 525B. (University Microfilms No. 8215479.)
188. Groden, J., & Cautela, J.R. (1984). Use of imagery procedure with students labeled "trainable retarded." *Psychological Reports, 54,* 595–605.
189. Guidry, L.S. (1974). Covert reinforcement in the treatment of test anxiety (Doctoral dissertation, University of Southern Mississippi, 1973.) *Dissertation Abstracts International, 34,* 3497B. (University Microfilms No. 73-32, 000.)
190. Guidry, L.S. (1974). Treatment of a case of compulsive stealing by use of a covert aversive contingency and the Premack Principle. *Newsletter for Research in Mental Health and Behavioral Sciences, 16*(2), 27–28.
191. Guidry, L.S. (1975). Use of a covert punishing contingency in compulsive stealing. *Journal of Behavior Therapy and Experimental Psychiatry, 6,* 169.
192. Guidry, L.S., & Randolph, D.L. (1974). Covert reinforcement in the treatment of test anxiety. *Journal of Counseling Psychology, 21,* 260–264.

193. Haney, J.G., & Euse, F.J. (1974, May). *Autonomic correlates of visual imagery: Implications for covert reinforcement and sensitization.* Paper presented at annual conference of Midwestern Psychological Association, Chicago.

194. Haney, J.G., & Euse, F.J. (1976). Skin conductance and heart rate responses to neutral, positive, and negative imagery: Implications for covert behavior therapy procedures. *Behavior Therapy, 7,* 494–503.

195. Harbert, T.L., Barlow, D.H., Hersen, M., & Austin, J.B. (1974). Measurement and modification of incestuous behavior: A case study. *Psychological Reports, 34,* 79–86.

196. Harris, G., & Johnson, S.B. (1980). Comparison of individualized covert modeling self-control desensitization, and study skills training for the alleviation of test anxiety. *Journal of Consulting and Clinical Psychology, 48,* 186–194.

197. Harris, G.M., & Johnson, S.B. (1983). Coping imagery and relaxation instructions in a covert modeling treatment for test anxiety. *Behavior Therapy, 14,* 144–157.

198. Harris, M.B. (1969). Self-directed program for weight control: A pilot study. *Journal of Abnormal Psychology, 74,* 263–270.

199. Hay, W.M., Barlow, D.H., & Hay, L.R. (1981). Treatment of a stereotypic cross-gender motor behavior using covert modeling in a boy with gender identity confusion. *Journal of Consulting and Clinical Psychology, 49,* 388–394.

200. Hay, W.M., Hay, L.R., & Nelson, R.O. (1977). The adaptation of covert modeling procedures to the treatment of chronic alcoholism and obsessive-compulsive behavior: Two case reports. *Behavior Therapy, 8,* 70–76.

201. Hayes, S.C., & Barlow, D.H. (1977). Flooding relief in a case of public transportation phobia. *Behavior Therapy, 8,* 742–746.

202. Hayes, S.C., Brownell, K.D., & Barlow, D.H. (1978). The use of self-administered covert sensitization in the treatment of exhibitionism and sadism. *Behavior Therapy, 9,* 283–289.

203. Hayes, S.C., Brownell, K.D., & Barlow, D.H. (1983). Heterosexual skills training and covert sensitization. Effects on social skills and sexual arousal in sexual deviants. *Behavior Research and Therapy, 21,* 383–392.

204. Heavenrich, R.M. (1973). Evaluation of the effect of reward and punishment contingencies in the covert behavioral treatment of depression. (Doctoral dissertation, Wayne State University, 1972). *Dissertation Abstracts International, 33,* 5515B–5516B. (University Microfilms No. 73-12, 529.)

205. Hedberg, A.G., & Campbell, L. (1974). A comparison of four behavioral treatments of alcoholism. *Journal of Behavior Therapy and Experimental Psychiatry, 5,* 251–256.

206. Heppner, P.P. (1978). The clinical alteration of covert thoughts: A critical review. *Behavior Therapy, 9,* 717–734.

207. Hersen, M., Kazdin, A.E., Bellack, A.S., & Turner, S.M. (1979). Effects of live modeling and rehearsal on assertiveness in psychiatric patients. *Behavior, Research, and Therapy, 17,* 369–377.

208. Hoffman, M.R. (1980). The effects of non-contingent covert punishment on overt behavior (Doctoral dissertation, Temple University, 1980). *Dissertation Abstracts International, 41,* 353B. (University Microfilms No. 8014492.)

209. Horan, J.J. (1973). Obesity: Toward a behavioral perspective. *Rehabilitation Counseling Bulletin, 17,* 6–14.

210. Horton, A.M. (1978). On stopping thoughts about thought-stopping. *The Behavior Therapist, 1(2),* 15–16.

211. Hout, M.C.N. (1977). Early treatment of alcohol abuse through a brief program of covert sensitization and aversive olfactory conditioning (Doctoral dissertation, University of Oregon, 1977). *Dissertation Abstracts International, 38,* 3288A. (University Microfilms No. 77-26, 449.)

212. Hughes, R.C. (1977). Covert sensitization treatment of exhibitionism. *Journal of Behavior Therapy and Experimental Psychiatry, 8,* 177–179.

213. Hunsaker, J.H. (1977). Covert self-management: A comparative analogue study. (Doctoral dissertation, Memphis State University, 1977). *Dissertation Abstracts International, 38,* 1404B. (University Microfilms No. 77-19, 200.)

214. Hurley, A.D. (1976). Covert reinforcement: The contributions of the reinforcing stimulus to treatment outcome. *Behavior Therapy, 7,* 374–378.

215. Irey, P.A. (1972). *Covert sensitization of cigarette smokers with high and low extraversion scores.* Unpublished master's thesis, University of Southern Illinois at Carbondale.

216. Janda, L.H., & Rimm, D.C. (1972). Covert sensitization in the treatment of obesity. *Journal of Abnormal Psychology, 80,* 37–42.

217. Johnson, R.G., & Elson, S.E. (1974, April). *The modification of covert behavior: A survey of the literature.* Paper presented at the annual meeting of the American Educational Research Association, Chicago.

218. Johnson, R.G., & Scheurer, W.E., Jr. (1975, March). *Covert reinforcement: A replication of an experimental test by Wish, Cautela, and Steffen.* Paper presented at the annual meeting of the American Educational Research Association, Washington, DC.

219. Jurgela, A.R. (in press). The use of covert conditioning in the treatment of attempted suicide. *Journal of Behavior Therapy and Experimental Psychiatry.*

220. Kachorek, J.J. (1972). Imagery and pairing in the covert sensitization paradigm (Doctoral dissertation, University of Cincinnati, 1972). *Dissertation Abstracts International, 33,* 2812B. (University Microfilms No. 72-31, 745.)

221. Kapche, R. (1974). Aversion-relief therapy: A review of current procedures and clinical and experimental evidence. *Psychotherapy, 1,* 156.

222. Kato, M., & Fukushima, O. (1977). The effects of covert modeling in reducing avoidance behavior. *Japanese Psychological Research, 19*(4), 199–203.

223. Kazarian, S.S. (1975). *The treatment of obsessional ruminations, a comparative study.* Unpublished doctoral dissertation, University of Western Ontario.

224. Kazarian, S.S., & Evans, D.R. (1977). Modification of obsessional rumination: A comparative study. *Canadian Journal of Behavioral Science, 9,* 91–100.

225. Kazdin, A.E. (1973). Covert modeling and the reduction of avoidance behavior. *Journal of Abnormal Psychology, 81,* 87–95.

226. Kazdin, A.E. (1973). Effects of covert modeling and reinforcement on assertive behavior. *Proceedings of the 81st Annual Convention of the American Psychological Association, 8,* 537–538.

227. Kazdin, A.E. (1974). Comparative effects of some variations of covert modeling. *Journal of Behavior Therapy and Experimental Psychiatry, 5,* 225–231.

228. Kazdin, A.E. (1974, November). *Covert modeling: Effects of multiple models and reinforcement on assertive behavior.* Paper presented at the Eighth Annual conference of the Association for Advancement of Behavior Therapy, Chicago.

229. Kazdin, A.E. (1974). Covert modeling, model similarity and the reduction of avoidance behavior. *Behavior Therapy, 5,* 325–340.

230. Kazdin, A.E. (1974). The effect of model identity and fear-relevant similarity on covert modeling. *Behavior Therapy, 5,* 624–635.

231. Kazdin, A.E. (1974). Effects of covert modeling and model reinforcement on assertive behavior. *Journal of Abnormal Psychology, 83,* 240–252.

232. Kazdin, A.E. (1975). Covert modeling, imagery assessment, and assertive behavior. *Journal of Consulting and Clinical Psychology, 43,* 716–724.

233. Kazdin, A.E. (1976). Assessment of imagery during covert modeling of assertive behavior. *Journal of Behavior Therapy and Experimental Psychiatry, 7,* 213–219.

234. Kazdin, A.E. (1976). Effect of covert modeling, multiple models, and model reinforcement on assertive behavior. *Behavior Therapy, 7,* 211–222.

235. Kazdin, A.E. (1977). Research issues in covert conditioning. *Cognitive Therapy and Research, 1,* 45–48.

236. Kazdin, A.E. (1978). Covert modeling: The therapeutic application of imagined rehearsal. In J.L. Singer & K.S. Pope (Eds.), *The power of human imagination* (pp. 255–278). New York: Plenum.

237. Kazdin, A.E. (1979). Effects of covert modeling and coding of modeled

stimuli on assertive behavior. *Behaviour Research and Therapy, 17,* 53–61.

238. Kazdin, A.E. (1979). Imagery elaboration and self-efficacy in the covert modeling treatment of unassertive behavior. *Journal of Consulting and Clinical Psychology, 47,* 725–733.

239. Kazdin, A.E. (1980). Covert and overt rehearsal and elaboration during treatment in the development of assertive behavior. *Behavior Research and Therapy, 18,* 191–201.

240. Kazdin, A.E. (1982). The separate and combined effects of covert and overt rehearsal in developing assertive behavior. *Behavior Research and Therapy, 20,* 17–25.

241. Kazdin, A.E., & Mascitelli, S. (1982). Covert and overt rehearsal and homework practice in developing assertiveness. *Journal of Consulting and Clinical Psychology, 2,* 250–258.

242. Kazdin, A.E., & Smith, G.A. (1979). Covert conditioning: A review and evaluation. *Advances in Behaviour Research and Therapy, 2,* 57–98.

243. Kean, J.E. (1980). Modification of the self-concept of learning disabled children by covert positive reinforcement (Doctoral dissertation, Boston College, 1980). *Dissertation Abstracts International, 41,* 629B. (University Microfilms No. 8016608.)

244. Kearney, A.B. (1984). *A comparison of the relative efficacy of related versus unrelated reinforcing scenes in the use of covert positive reinforcement for the treatment of test anxiety.* Unpublished doctoral dissertation, Boston College.

245. Kearney, A.J., Jr. (1976). A comparison of systematic desensitization and covert positive reinforcement in the treatment of a fear of laboratory rats (Doctoral dissertation, Boston College, 1976). *Dissertation Abstracts International, 37,* 809A. (University Microfilms No. 76-13, 935.)

246. Kendrick, S.R. (1974). The effect of partial and continuous schedules of reinforcement of covert acquisition and covert extinction training (Doctoral dissertation, University of Southern Mississippi). *Dissertation Abstracts International, 35,* 2436B. (University Microfilms No. 74-25, 510.)

247. Kendrick, S.R., & McCullough, J.P. (1972). Sequential phases of covert reinforcement and covert sensitization in the treatment of homosexuality. *Journal of Behavior Therapy and Experimental Psychiatry, 3,* 229–231.

248. Keßler, B.H., & Jacobs, B. (1976). Covert sensitization: Eine kritische Analyses Konditionierens. *Arbeiten der Fachrichtung Psychologie,* Nr. 28. Universitat des Saarlandes, Saarbrucken.

249. King, D.L. (1973). An image theory of classical conditioning. *Psychological Reports, 33,* 403–411.

250. Kingsley, R.G. (1973). *An analysis of contingency content in covert conditioning.* Unpublished master's thesis, Rutgers University, Piscataway, NJ.

251. Kolvin, I. (1967). "Aversive imagery" treatment in adolescents. *Behavior Research and Therapy, 5,* 245-248.
252. Kostka, M.P. (1974). The effectiveness of group systematic desensitization vs. covert positive reinforcement as utilized by paraprofessionals in the reduction of test anxiety in college students (Doctoral dissertation, West Virginia University, 1973). *Dissertation Abstracts International, 4,* 4747A. (University Microfilms No. 74-202.)
253. Kostka, M.P., & Galassi, J.P. (1974). Group systematic desensitization vs. covert positive reinforcement in the reduction of test anxiety. *Journal of Consulting Psychology, 21,* 464-468.
254. Krop, H., Calhoun, B., & Verrier, R. (1971). Modification of the "self-concept" of emotionally disturbed children by covert reinforcement. *Behavior Therapy, 2,* 201-204.
255. Krop, H., Messinger, J., & Reiner, C. (1973). Increasing eye contact by covert reinforcement. *Interpersonal Development, 1973, 4,* 51-57.
256. Krop, H., Perez, F., & Beaudoin, C. (1973). Modification of "self-concept" of psychiatric patients by covert reinforcement. In R.D. Rubin, J.P. Brady, & J.D. Henderson (Eds.), *Advances in Behavior Therapy, Vol. 4: Proceedings of the Fifth Conference of the Association for Advancement of Behavior Therapy* (pp. 139-144). New York: Academic Press.
257. Ladouceur, R. (1974). An experimental test of the learning paradigm of covert positive reinforcement in deconditioning anxiety. *Journal of Behavior Therapy and Experimental Psychiatry, 5,* 3-6.
258. Ladouceur, R. (1977). Rationale of covert reinforcement: Additional evidence. *Psychological Reports, 4,* 547-550.
259. Ladouceur, R. (1978). Rationale of systematic desensitization and covert reinforcement. *Behavior Research and Therapy,16,* 411-420.
260. Lande, S.D. (1980). A combination of organic reconditioning and covert sensitization in the treatment of a fire fetish. *Journal of Behavior Therapy and Experimental Psychiatry, 11,* 291-296.
261. Lawson, D.M., & May, R.B. (1970). Three procedures for the extinction of smoking behavior. *Psychological Record, 20,* 151-157.
262. Ledoux, S. (1981, November). *Theory and practice in operant experimental control of covert behavior: Four studies.* Paper presented at the 15th annual convention of the Association for Advancement of Behavior Therapy, Toronto.
263. Ledoux, S., & Jackson, K. (1982, May). *Generality of a private event study: Covert verbalizing or covert visualizing.* Paper at the Eighth Annual Convention of the Association for Behavior Analysis, Milwaukee, WI.
264. Levin, S.M., Barry, S.M., Gambaro, S., Wolfinsohn, & Smith, A., (1977). Variation of covert sensitization in the treatment of pedophilic behavior: A case study. *Journal of Consulting and Clinical Psychology, 45,* 896-907.
265. Levine, B.A. (1976). The treatment of trichotillomania by covert

sensitization. *Journal of Behavior Therapy and Experimental Psychiatry, 7,* 75–76.

266. Lewis, B.J. (1979). Treatment of a schizoid personality using hypnoperant therapy. *American Journal of Clinical Hypnosis, 22,* 42–46.

267. Lichstein, K.L., & Hung, J.H.F. (1980). Covert sensitization: An examination of covert and overt parameters. *Behavioral Engineering, 6*(1), 1–18.

268. Lichstein, K.L., & Sallis, J.F. (1981). Covert sensitization for smoking: In search of efficacy. *Addictive Behaviors, 6,* 83–91.

269. Lick, J., & Bootzin, R. (1971, May). *Covert sensitization for the treatment of obesity.* Paper presented at the meeting of the Midwestern Psychological Association, Detroit.

270. Little, L.M., & Curran, J.P. (1978). Covert sensitization: A clinical procedure in need of some explanations. *Psychological Bulletin, 85,* 513–531.

271. Livingston, R.H., & Elson, S.E. (1975). *The need for replications of key studies in covert conditioning.* Paper presented at the annual meeting of the American Educational Research Association, Washington, DC.

272. Livingston, R.H., & Johnson, R.G. (1979). Covert conditioning and self-management in rehabilitation counseling. *Rehabilitation Counseling Bulletin, 22,* 330–337.

273. Lott, S.J. (1975). A study of covert reinforcement as a treatment of test anxiety in male and female fifth graders (Doctoral dissertation, University of Southern Mississippi, 1975). *Dissertation Abstracts International, 36,* 2028A. (University Microfilms No. 75-22, 510.)

274. Lowe, M.R. (1978). The use of covert modeling in social skills training with depressed patients (Doctoral dissertation, Boston College, 1978). *Dissertation Abstracts International, 38,* 6163B–6164B. (University Microfilms No. 7807239)

275. Lowe, S.E. (1978). The comparative effectiveness of ideal self, ideal person, and real self as models in covert modeling procedures (Doctoral dissertation, Boston College, 1978). *Dissertation Abstracts International, 39,* 988B. (University Microfilms No. 7813783.)

276. Lurie, E.S., & Steffen, J.J. (1980). Effective components of covert reinforcement. *Journal of Psychology, 106,* 241–248.

277. Mahoney, M.J. (1970). Toward an experimental analysis of covert control. *Behavior Therapy, 1,* 510–521.

278. Mahoney, M.J. (1972). Research issues in self-management. *Behavior Therapy, 3,* 45–63.

279. Mahoney, M.J. (1974). *Cognition and behavior modification.* Cambridge, MA: Ballinger.

280. Mahoney, M.J. (1978). On the rumors of my death. *The Behavior Therapist, 1*(2), 15–16.

281. Mahoney, M.J., Thoresen, C.E., & Danaher, B.G. (1972). Covert behavior modification: An experimental analog. *Journal of Behavior Therapy and Experimental Psychiatry, 3,* 7–14.

282. Maletzky, B.M. (1973). "Assisted" covert sensitization: A preliminary report. *Behavior Therapy, 4,* 117–119.
283. Maletzky, B.M. (1974). "Assisted" covert sensitization for drug abuse. *International Journal of the Addictions, 9,* 411–429.
284. Maletzky, B.M. (1974). "Assisted" covert sensitization in the treatment of exhibitionism. *Journal of Consulting and Clinical Psychology, 42,* 34–40.
285. Maletzky, B.M. (1977). "Booster" sessions in aversion therapy: The permanency of treatment. *Behavior Therapy, 8,* 460–463.
286. Maletzky, B.M. (1980). "Assisted" covert sensitization in the treatment of exhibitionism. In D.J. Cox & R.J. Daitzman (Eds.), *Exhibitionism: Description, assessment and treatment.* New York: Garland.
287. Maletzky, B.M. (1980b). Self-referred versus court referred sexually deviant patients: Success with assisted covert sensitization. *Behavior Therapy, 11,* 306–314.
288. Maletzky, B.M., & George, F.S. (1973). Treatment of homosexuality by "assisted" covert sensitization. *Behavior Research and Therapy, 11,* 655–657.
289. Mandel, K.H. (1970). Preliminary report on a new aversion therapy for male homosexuals. *Behaviour Research and Therapy, 8,* 93–96.
290. Manno, B.I. (1972). Weight reduction as a function of the timing of reinforcement in a covert aversive conditioning paradigm (Doctoral dissertation, University of Southern California, 1971). *Dissertation Abstracts International, 32,* 4221B. (University Microfilms No. 72-3789.)
291. Manno, B., & Marston, A.R. (1972). Weight reduction as a function of negative covert reinforcement (sensitization) versus positive covert reinforcement. *Behavior Research and Therapy, 10,* 201–207.
292. Marshall, W.L., Boutillier, J., & Minnes, P. (1974). The modification of phobic behavior by covert reinforcement. *Behavior Therapy, 5,* 469–480.
293. Marshall, W.L., & Christie, M.M. (1982). The enhancement of social self-esteem. *Canadian Counsellor, 16*(2), 82–89.
294. Marshall, W.L., Christie, M.M., Lanthier, R.D., & Cruchley, J. (1982). The nature of the reinforcer in the enhancement of social self-esteem. *Canadian Counsellor 16*(2), 90–96.
295. Martos Perales, F.J., & Vila Castellar, J. (1982). La validez y los modelos teoricos de la sensibilizacion encubierta: una revision (Validity and theoretical models of covert sensitization: A review) (in Spanish). *Analysis y Modificacion de Conducta, 8*(18), 165–190.
296. Marx, D.H. (1978). The effects of self-administered covert reinforcement in the reduction of test anxiety (Doctoral dissertation, University of Missouri, 1977). *Dissertation Abstracts International, 38,* 3895B–3896B. (University Microfilms No. 7731744.)
297. Mazza, J. (1972-1973). Behavioral techniques applied to covert events. *University of Maryland Counseling and Student Personnel Journal, 3,* 1–7.

298. McAndrew, J.F. (1981). The relative efficacy of covert and overt conditioning in modifying verbal and pain tolerance behavior (Doctoral dissertation, University of Minnesota, 1980). *Dissertation Abstracts International, 41,* 2771B. (University Microfilms No. 8102123.)

299. McBrearty, J., Garfield, Z., Dichter, M., & Heath, G. (1968). A behaviorally oriented treatment program for alcoholism. *Psychological Reports, 22,* 287–298.

300. McConaghy, N., Armstrong, M.S., & Blaszczynski, A. (1981). Controlled comparison of aversive therapy and covert sensitization in compulsive homosexuality. *Behavior Research and Therapy, 19,* 425–434.

301. McCullough, J.P., & Powell, P.O. (1972). A technique for measuring clarity of imagery in therapy clients. *Behavior Therapy, 3,* 447–488.

302. McCullough, L. (1978, November). *The efficacy of covert conditioning: A brief review.* Paper presented at the meeting of the Association for Advancement of Behavior Therapy, Chicago.

303. McDermott, W.F. (1976). Weight reduction through imagery therapies: An outcome study (Doctoral dissertation, Indiana University, 1976). *Dissertation Abstracts International, 37,* 1915B. (University Microfilms No. 76-21, 592.)

304. McFall, R.M., & Lillesand, D.B. (1971). Behavior rehearsal with modeling and coaching in assertion training. *Journal of Abnormal Psychology, 3,* 313–323.

305. McFall, R.M., & Twentyman, C.T. (1973). Four experiments on the relative contributions of rehearsal, modeling, and coaching to assertion training. *Journal of Abnormal Psychology, 81,* 199–218.

306. Meade, L.S. (1979). Covert positive reinforcement in the treatment of nailbiting: Target-relevant versus target-irrelevant consequences (Doctoral dissertation, University of North Carolina at Greensboro, 1978). *Dissertation Abstracts International, 39,* 3530B–3531B. (University Microfilms No. 7824896.)

307. Meynen, G.E. (1970). A comparative study of three treatment approaches with the obese: Relaxation, covert sensitization, and modified systematic desensitization (Doctoral dissertation, Illinois Institute of Technology, 1970). *Dissertation Abstracts International, 31,* 2998B. (University Microfilms No. 70-22, 122.)

308. Miller, M.M. (1976). Hypnoaversion treatment in alcoholism, nicotinism, and weight control. *Journal of the National Medical Association, 68,* 129–130.

309. Miller, P., & Barlow, D. (1973). Behavioral approaches to treatment of alcoholism. *Journal of Nervous and Mental Disease, 157,* 10–20.

310. Mills, H.L. (1974). Covert conditioning of an incidental response during paired associate learning (Doctoral dissertation, University of Southern Mississippi, 1973). *Dissertation Abstracts International, 34,* 4053. (University Microfilms No. 74-3947.)

311. Moser, A.J. (1974). Covert punishment of hallucinatory behavior in a

psychotic male. *Journal of Behavior Therapy and Experimental Psychiatry, 5,* 297–299.

312. Mullen, F.C. (1968). *The effect of covert sensitization on smoking behavior.* Unpublished manuscript Queens College, Charlotte, NC. Described in L.M. Little & J.P. Curran (1978), Covert sensitization: A clinical procedure in need of some explanations. *Psychological Bulletin, 85,* 513–531.

313. Murphy, W.D. (1977). The contribution of relaxation and relief to covert sensitization in the treatment of smoking (Doctoral dissertation, Ohio University, 1976). *Dissertation Abstracts International, 37,* 4157B. (University Microfilms No. 77-3487.)

314. Murray, D.C., & Harrington, L.G. (1972). Covert aversive sensitization in the treatment of obesity. *Psychological Reports, 30,* 560.

315. Nesse, M., & Nelson, R. (1977). Variations of covert modeling on cigarette smoking. *Cognitive Therapy and Research, 1,* 343–354.

316. Nietzel, M.T., Martorano, R.D., & Melnick, J. (1977). The effects of covert modeling with and without reply training on the development and generalization of assertive responses. *Behavior Therapy, 8,* 183–192.

317. Nigel, A.J. (1976). The use of covert reinforcements in the acquisition of dental behavior (Doctoral dissertation, University of Cincinnati, 1975). *Dissertation Abstracts International, 36,* 4172B–4173B. (University Microfilms No. 75-25, 922.)

318. O'Brien, J.S. (1971, April). *Long term trichotillomania in a non-psychotic housewife treated with self administered verbal aversion therapy and instructional control.* Paper presented at the Second Multistate Interhospital Conference of the Eastern Psychiatric Research Association, Inc., New York.

319. O'Brien, J.S., Raynes, A.E., & Patch, V.D. (1972). Treatment of heroin addiction with aversion therapy, relaxation training, and systematic desensitization. *Behavior Research and Therapy, 10,* 77–80.

320. Olson, R.P., Ganley, R., Devine, V.T., & Dorsey, G.C. Jr. (1981). Long-term effects of behavioral vs. insight-oriented therapy with inpatient alcoholics. *Journal of Consulting and Clinical Psychology, 49,* 866–877.

321. Pace, D.G. (1977). The effects of imagined scene selection and encouragement of association on covert reinforcement and covert sensitization (Doctoral dissertation, University of North Dakota, 1976). *Dissertation Abstracts International, 38,* 372B–373B. (University Microfilms No. 77-14, 564.)

322. Pace, D.G., Yager, G.G., Ochilltree, J.K., & Tepper, N.G. (1975). *The effects of type of imagery selection and multiplicity of images upon covert positive reinforcement.* Paper presented at the annual meeting of the American Educational Research Association, Washington, DC.

323. Painter, J.H. (1972). The modification of smoking behavior in a controlled public clinic (Doctoral dissertation, Arizona State University,

1972). *Dissertation Abstracts International, 32,* 4867B. (University Microfilms No. 72-6256.)

324. Paniagua, F.A., & Baer, D.M. (1981). A procedural analysis of the symbolic forms of behavior therapy. *Behaviorism, 9,* 171–205.

325. Paquin, M.J. (1977). Treatment of a nail biting compulsion by covert sensitization in a poorly motivated client. *Journal of Behavior Therapy and Experimental Psychiatry, 8,* 181–183.

326. Park, T.P. (1979). Covert positive reinforcement: The contribution of the reinforcing stimulus in reducing public speaking anxiety (Doctoral dissertation, University of South Dakota, 1978). *Dissertation Abstracts International, 39,* 5574B. (University Microfilms No. 7904903.)

327. Poetter, R.A. (1978). The effects of covert negative reinforcement on students' attending behavior (Doctoral dissertation, Ohio University, 1977). *Dissertation Abstracts International, 38,* 3901B–3902B. (University Microfilms No. 7730272.)

328. Polakow, R.L. (1975). Covert sensitization treatment of a probational barbiturate addict. *Journal of Behavior Therapy and Experimental Psychiatry, 6,* 53–54.

329. Primo, R.V. (1973). Covert avoidance learning: A refined covert sensitization method for the modification of smoking behavior (Doctoral dissertation, University of Pittsburgh, 1972). *Dissertation Abstracts International, 33,* 3958B–3959B. (University Microfilms No. 73-4992.)

330. Rachlin, H. (1977). Reinforcing and punishing thoughts. *Behavior Therapy, 8,* 659–665.

331. Ramsey, G.T. (1978). A program of weight loss and weight maintenance employing behavioral and somatic awareness training (Doctoral dissertation, Virginia Commonwealth University, 1978). *Dissertation Abstracts International, 39,* 1496B. (University Microfilms No. 7814875.)

332. Rawlings, D.A. (1974). The effects of three versions of covert sensitization on the reduction of the maladaptive behavior of smoking (Doctoral dissertation, Oklahoma State University, 1973). *Dissertation Abstracts International, 34,* 5206B. (University Microfilms No. 74-8106.)

333. Reeves, J.O. (1973). Covert sensitization and weight control: An analysis of escape and imagery variables (Doctoral dissertation, Texas A. & M. University, 1973). *Dissertation Abstracts International, 34,* 1283B–1284B. (University Microfilms No. 73-21, 695.)

334. Rehm, L.P., & Rozensky, R.H. (1974). Multiple behavior therapy techniques with a homosexual client: A case study. *Journal of Behavior Therapy and Experimental Psychiatry, 5,* 53–57.

335. Rhodes, R.S. (1978). Covert positive reinforcement: A test of the experimental paradigms (Doctoral dissertation, University of Mississippi, 1978). *Dissertation Abstracts International, 39,* 3002B–3003B. (University Microfilms No. 7824062.)

336. Ripstra, C.C., Elson, S.E., Johnson, R.G., Rate, L., Schnickley, U.G., & Yager, G.G. (1974, April). *Covert reinforcement: A partial replication.*

Paper presented at the annual meeting of the American Educational Research Association, Chicago.

337. Rochios, J.S. (1976). A comparison of the three types of imagery used in covert sensitization to treat obesity (Doctoral dissertation, Southern Illinois University, 1973). *Dissertation Abstracts International, 36* 4176B–4177B. (University Microfilms No. 76-3345.)

338. Rohan, W.A. (1970). A comparison of two aversive conditioning procedures for problem drinking. In D. Upper & D.S. Goodenough (Eds.), *Proceedings of the First Annual Brockton Symposium and Workshop on Behavior Therapy.* Nutley, NJ: Roche Laboratories.

339. Romancyzk, R.G., Tracey, D.A., Wilson, G.T., & Thorpe, G.L. (1973). Behavioral techniques in the treatment of obesity: A comparative analysis. *Behavior Research and Therapy, 11,* 629–640.

340. Rosenthal, T.L., Linehan, K.S., Kelley, J.E., Rosenthal, R.H., Theobald, D.E., & Davis, A.F. (1978). Group aversion by imaginal, vicarious and shared, recipient-observer shocks. *Behavior Research and Therapy, 16,* 421–427.

341. Rosenthal, T.L., & Reese, S.L. (1976). The effects of covert and overt modeling on assertive behavior. *Behavior Research and Therapy, 14,* 463–469.

342. Rotatori, A.F., Switzky, H., & Fox, R. (1981). Behavioral treatment approaches to obesity: Successes with the nonretarded and retarded. *Obesity and Metabolism, 1*(2), 140–158.

343. Roth, W.L. (1977). *Covert positive reinforcement—ein Konditionierungsverfahren? Ubenblick, Analyse, Kritik und eine experimentelle Testung der theoretischen Grundlagen* (in German). Unveroff. Diplomarbeit, Fachrichtung Psychologie, Universitat des Saarlandes, Saarbrucken.

344. Roth, W.L., & Keßler, B.H. (1979). Verdeckte positive Verstarkung: Analyse und Kritik klinischer Therapieexperimente. (Covert positive reinforcement: Analysis and criticism of clinical therapy experiments) (in German). *Mitteilungen der DGVT, 11,* 677–712.

345. Rutner, I.T. (1967). *The modification of smoking behavior through techniques of self-control.* Unpublished master's thesis, Wichita State University.

346. Sachs, L.B., Bean, H., & Morrow, J.E. (1970). Comparison of smoking treatments. *Behavior Therapy, 1,* 465–472.

347. Sachs, L.B., & Ingram, G.L. (1972). Covert sensitization as a treatment for weight control. *Psychological Reports, 30,* 971–974.

348. Sanders, S.H. (1978). An empirical test of four theoretical explanations for covert reinforcement effects (Doctoral dissertation, Memphis State University, 1977). *Dissertation Abstracts International, 38,* 3414B. (University Microfilms No. 77-28, 801.)

349. Sanders, S.H., & Hammer, D. (1979). An empirical test of three alternative explanations for covert reinforcement effects. *Psychological Reports, 44,* 611–622.

350. Sank, L.I. (1976). Counterconditioning for a flight phobia. *Social Work*, *21*, 318–319.

351. Sarkisian, R.A. (1975). The use of ideal models in covert rehearsal to influence self-concept (Doctoral dissertation, University of California, Berkeley, 1974). *Dissertation Abstracts International, 35*, 3596B. (University Microfilms No. 75-917.)

352. Scher, S.S. (1978). Overt versus covert modeling with overcontrolled youthful offenders (Doctoral dissertation, Florida State University, 1978). *Dissertation Abstracts International, 39*, 1499B–1500B. (University Microfilms No. 7815480.)

353. Schmickley, V.G. (1974, April). *Covert operant reinforcement of remedial reading learning tasks*. Paper presented at the annual meeting of the American Educational Research Association, Chicago.

354. Scott, A.J. (1978). The effects of covert modeling and written material on the acquisition of a counseling strategy (Doctoral dissertation, West Virginia University, 1978). *Dissertation Abstracts International, 39*, 4066A. (University Microfilms No. 7900874.)

355. Scott, D.S., & Leonard, C.F. (1978). Modification of pain threshold by covert reinforcement procedure and a cognitive strategy. *Psychological Record, 28*, 49–57.

356. Scott, D.S., & Rosenstiel, A.K. (1975). Covert positive reinforcement studies: Review, critique, and guidelines. *Psychotherapy: Theory, Research and Practice, 12*, 374–384.

357. Schwartz, G.E., & Higgins, J.D. (1971). Cardiac activity preparatory to overt and covert behavior. *Science, 173*, 1144–1146.

358. Secter, I.I. (1963). Tongue thrust and nail biting simultaneously treated during hypnosis: A case report. *American Journal of Clinical Hypnosis, 6*, 164–166.

359. Segel, B., & Sims, J. (1972). Covert sensitization with a homosexual: A controlled replication. *Journal of Consulting and Clinical Psychology, 39*, 259–263.

360. Shatus, E.L. (1974). Treatment of disruptive classroom behavior in male, hospitalized delinquents using two covert procedures (Doctoral dissertation, University of Southern Mississippi, 1973). *Dissertation Abstracts International, 34*, 4057B–4058B. (University Microfilms No. 74-3958.)

361. Shefrin, R.N. (1977). A study of covert reinforcement with children (Doctoral dissertation, State University of New York at Buffalo, 1976). *Dissertation Abstracts International, 37*, 4166B–4167B. (University Microfilms No. 77-3585.)

362. Simone, S.S., & Long, M.A.D. (1985). Marital cognitive behavioral treatment for chronic tension headache: A case study. *The Behavior Therapist, 8*, 26, 36–37.

363. Singer, J.R. (1974). *Imagery and daydream methods in psychotherapy and behavior modification*. New York: Academic Press.

364. Sipich, J.F., Russell, R.K., & Tobias, L.L. (1974). A comparison of covert

sensitization and "nonspecific" treatment in the modification of smoking behavior. *Journal of Behavior Therapy and Experimental Psychiatry, 5*, 201–203.

365. Small, M.M. (1977). Covert discrimination training: An experimental test of the assumed functional equivalence between covert and overt conditioning. *Psychological Reports, 41*, 715–720.

366. Smith, G.S., & Delprato, D.J. (1976). Stimulus control of covert behaviors (urges). *Psychological Record, 26*, 461–466.

367. Smith, R.E., & Gregory, P.B. (1976). Covert sensitization by induced anxiety in the treatment of an alcoholic. *Journal of Behavior Therapy and Experimental Psychiatry, 7*, 31–33.

368. Snowden, L.R. (1975). Heroin abuse modification through sensitization tailored to locus of control (Doctoral dissertation, Wayne State University, 1975). *Dissertation Abstracts International, 36*, 2484B–2485B. (University Microfilms No. 75-25, 265.)

369. Snowden, L.R. (1978). Personality tailored covert sensitization of heroin abuse. *Addictive Behaviors, 3*, 43–49.

370. Steffen, J.J. (1971). *Covert reinforcement with schizophrenics.* Paper presented at the annual meeting of the Association for Advancement of Behavior Therapy, Washington, DC.

371. Steffen, J.J. (1974). Covert reinforcement: Some facts and fantasies. In G. Baron (Chair), *Experimental analysis of covert reinforcement.* Symposium presented at the meeting of the Association for Advancement of Behavior Therapy, Chicago.

372. Steffen, J.J. (1977). Covert reinforcement: Two studies and a comment. *Psychological Reports, 40*, 291–294.

373. Steinfeld, G.J. (1970). The use of covert sensitization with institutionalized narcotic addicts. *International Journal of the Addictions, 5*, 225–232.

374. Steinfeld, G.J., Rautio, E.A., Rice, A.H., & Egan, M.J. (1974). Group covert sensitization with narcotic addicts: Further comments. *International Journal of the Addictions, 9*, 447–464.

375. Stevens, M.J. (1982). The effects of covert positive reinforcement in modifying cold-pressor pain (Doctoral dissertation, University of Missouri-Columbia, 1981). *Dissertation Abstracts International, 43*, 81A. (University Microfilms No. DA8213876.)

376. Stevens, T.G. (1974). The effects of varying covert reinforcement and covert behavior rehearsal instructions on friendly assertive behavior: An automated self-control procedure (Doctoral dissertation, University of Hawaii, 1973). *Dissertation Abstracts International, 34*, 4678B. (University Microfilms No. 74-7514.)

377. Stuart, R.B. (1967). Behavioral control of overeating. *Behaviour Research and Therapy, 5*, 357–365.

378. Tearnan, B.H., & Graziano, W.G. (1980). Covert modeling and children's fears: A methodological critique of Chertock and Bornstein. *Child Behavior Therapy, 2*(3), 73–77.

379. Tearnan, B.H., Lahey, B.B., Thompson, J., & Hammer, D. (1982). The role of coping self-instructions combined with covert modeling in specific fear reduction. *Cognitive Therapy and Research, 6*, 185–190.

380. Tearnan, B.H., Thompson, J., & Hammer, D. (1979, December). *The role of covert modeling in the reduction of fear*. Paper presented at the meeting of the Association for Advancement of Behavior Therapy, San Francisco.

381. Teixeira, R.M. (1970). *The experimental control of covert seeing.* Unpublished master's thesis, California State University, Sacramento.

382. Tepfer, K.S., & Levine, B.A. (1977). Covert sensitization with internal aversive cues in the treatment of chronic alcoholism. *Psychological Reports, 41*, 92–94.

383. Thase, M.E., & Moss, M.K. (1976). The relative efficacy of covert modeling procedures and guided participant modeling on the reduction of avoidance behavior. *Journal of Behavior Therapy and Experimental Psychiatry, 7*, 7–12.

384. Thompson, M.S., & Conrad, P.L. (1977). Multifaceted behavioral treatment of drug dependence: A case study. *Behavior Therapy, 8*, 731–737.

385. Tilker, M.A., & Meyer, R.G. (1972). The use of covert sensitization in the treatment of an overweight person: A case report. *American Journal of Clinical Hypnosis, 15*, 15–21.

386. Tondo, T.R., & Cautela, J.R. (1974). Assessment of imagery in covert reinforcement. *Psychological Reports, 34*, 1271–1280.

387. Tondo, T.R. (1976). The effects of real vs. imagined (covert) reinforcement of specific inter-response times (Doctoral dissertation, University of Mississippi, 1975). *Dissertation Abstracts International, 36*, 3632B. (University Microfilms No.76-472.)

388. Tondo, T.R., Hayden, R., & Cautela, J.R. (1971). *Imagery ability and differential effects of covert reinforcement and imagery practice.* Unpublished manuscript, Boston College, Chestnut Hill, MA.

389. Tondo, T.R., Lane, J.R., & Gill, Jr., K. (1975). Suppression of specific eating behaviors by covert response cost: An experimental analysis. *Psychological Record, 25*, 187–196.

390. Tooley, J., & Pratt, S. (1967). An experimental procedure for the extinction of smoking behaviour. *Psychological Record, 17*, 209–218.

391. Trent, J.T. (1978). Human preference for covert reinforcement compared to overt reinforcement (Doctoral dissertation, University of Mississippi, 1977). *Dissertation Abstracts International, 38*, 3420B. (University Microfilms No. 77-28, 979.)

392. Trey, P.A. (1972). *Covert sensitization of cigarette smokers with high and low extraversion scores.* Unpublished master's thesis, Southern Illinois University at Carbondale.

393. Turkat, I.D., & Adams, H.E. (1978). Issues in pain modification: The Cautela model. *Journal of Behavior Therapy and Experimental Psychiatry, 9*, 135–138.

394. Turkat, I.D., & Adams, H.E. (1982). Covert positive reinforcement and

pain modification: A test of efficacy and theory. *Journal of Psychosomatic Research, 26,* 191–201.

395. Uchiyama, K., & Maeda, M. (1983, December). *The effects of vicarious reinforcement on the formation of assertive behavior in covert modeling.* Paper presented at the Seventeenth Annual Meeting of the Association for Advancement of Behavior Therapy, Washington, DC.

396. Upper, D., & Cautela, J.R. (1977). *Covert conditioning.* New York: Pergamon.

397. Van Wyke, P.E. (1981). Covert modeling in the context of storytelling: Observational learning in therapy with children. In E. Klinger (Ed.), *Imagery, Vol. 2: Concepts, results and applications* (pp. 335–345). Plenum.

398. Venters, W.C. (1973). Generalization of covert reinforcement of a covert response to its overt manifestation (Doctoral dissertation, University of Southern Mississippi, 1972). *Dissertation Abstracts International, 33,* 4531B. (University Microfilms No. 73-5590.)

399. Viernstein, L. (1968). *Evaluation of therapeutic techniques of covert sensitization.* Unpublished manuscript, Queens College, Charlotte, NC. Described in L.M. Little & J.P. Curran (1978), Covert sensitization: A clinical procedure in need of some explanations. *Psychological Bulletin, 85,* 515–531.

400. Wadden, T.A., & Flaxman, J. (1981). Hypnosis and weight loss: A preliminary study. *International Journal of Clinical and Experimental Hypnosis, 29,* 162–173.

401. Wagner, M.K. (1968). *A self-administered programmed recording for decreasing cigarette consumption.* Paper presented at the meeting of the Association for Advancement of Behavior Therapy, San Francisco.

402. Wagner, M.K., & Bragg, A. (1970). Comparing behavior modification approaches to habit decrement—Smoking. *Journal of Consulting and Clinical Psychology, 34,* 258–263.

403. Walker, C.E., Hedberg, A., Clement, P.W., & Wright, L. (1981). *Clinical procedures for behavior therapy* (pp. 239–264). Englewood Cliffs, NJ: Prentice-Hall.

404. Walsh, K.J. (1973). Promoting investigation of occupational alternatives in students with problems in unrealism of vocational choice: A comparison of two counseling methods (Doctoral dissertation, Boston College, 1973). *Dissertation Abstracts International, 33,* 6103A. (University Microfilms No. 73-11, 375.)

405. Wasserman, T.H. (1978). The elimination of complaints of stomach cramps in a 12-year-old child by covert positive reinforcement. *The Behavior Therapist, 1*(3), 13–14.

406. Watson, L.J. (1977). The effects of covert modeling and covert reinforcement on acquisition of job interview skills by youth offenders (Doctoral dissertation, West Virginia University, 1976). *Dissertation Abstracts International, 37,* 4229B–4230B. (University Microfilms No. 77-2556.)

407. Weedman, S.H. (1973). An investigation of factors relating to covert

sensitization (Doctoral dissertation, University of Montana, 1973). *Dissertation Abstracts International, 34,* 430B. (University Microfilms No. 73-15, 746.)

408. Weiner, H. (1965). Real and imagined cost effects upon human fixed-interval responding. *Psychological Reports, 17,* 659–662.

409. Weis, J.I. (1974). An experimental examination of Cautela's covert sensitization as a smoking reduction technique. (Doctoral dissertation, University of North Dakota, 1974). *Dissertation Abstracts International, 35,* 2454B. (University Microfilms No. 74-24, 540.)

410. Welt, K.A. (1973). The maintenance of behavior changes following intervention by covert sensitization (Doctoral dissertation, University of Montana, 1973). *Dissertation Abstracts International, 34,* 431B. (University Microfilms No. 73-15, 747.)

411. Wilkins, W. (1974). Parameters of therapeutic imagery: Directions from case studies. *Psychotherapy: Theory Research, and Practice, 11,* 163–171.

412. Williams, R.F. (1971). Effects of covert sensitization with nausea and anxiety imagery (Doctoral dissertation, Northwestern University, 1971). *Dissertation Abstracts International, 32,* 5463B–5464B. (University Microfilms No. 72-7860.)

413. Wilson, G.T. (1974, January). *Aversive control of maladaptive behavior.* Paper presented at Pennsylvania State University. Described in L.M. Little & J.P. Curran (1978), Covert sensitization: A clinical procedure in need of some explanations. *Psychological Bulletin, 85,* 515–531.

414. Wilson, G.T. (1978). Alcoholism and aversion therapy: Issues, ethics and evidence. In G.A. Marlatt & P.E. Nathan (Eds.), *Behavioral approaches to alcoholism.* New Brunswick, NJ: Rutgers Center of Alcohol Studies.

415. Wilson, G.T., & Tracey, D.A. (1976). An experimental analysis of aversive imagery versus electrical aversive conditioning in the treatment of chronic alcoholics. *Behavior Research and Therapy, 14,* 41–51.

416. Wish, P.A., (1975). The use of imagery-based techniques in the treatment of sexual dysfunction. *The Counseling Psychologist, 5,* 52–55.

417. Wish, P.A., Cautela, J.R., & Steffen, J.J. (1970). Covert reinforcement: An experimental test. *Proceedings of the 78th Annual Convention of the American Psychological Association, 5,* 513–514.

418. Wisocki, P.A. (1970). Treatment of the obsessive-compulsive behavior by covert sensitization and covert reinforcement: A case report. *Journal of Behavior Therapy and Experimental Psychiatry, 1,* 233–239.

419. Wisocki, P.A. (1971). An application of covert reinforcement for the treatment of test anxiety (Doctoral dissertation, Boston College, 1971). *Dissertation Abstracts International, 32,* 1229B–1230B. (University Microfilms No. 71-19, 792.)

420. Wisocki, P.A. (1972). The empirical evidence of covert sensitization in the treatment of alcoholism: An evaluation. In R.D. Rubin, H. Fensterheim, J.D. Henderson, & L.P. Ullman, (Eds.), *Advances in behavior*

therapy: Proceedings of the Fourth Conference of the Association for Advancement of Behavior Therapy. New York: Academic Press.

421. Wisocki, P.A. (1972). The successful treatment of heroin addiction by covert conditioning techniques. *Proceedings of the Third Annual Brockton Symposium on Behavior Therapy, 3,* 25–34.

422. Wisocki, P.A. (1973). A covert reinforcement program for the treatment of test anxiety: A brief report. *Behavior Therapy, 4,* 264–266.

423. Wisocki, P.A. (1973). The successful treatment of heroin addiction by covert conditioning techniques. *Journal of Behavior Therapy and Experimental Psychiatry, 4,* 55–61.

424. Wisocki, P.A. (1976). A treatment program for social inadequacy. Multiple methods for a complex problem. In J. Krumboltz & C. Thoresen (Eds.), *Counseling methods* (pp. 287–301). New York: Holt, Rinehart, & Winston.

425. Wisocki, P.A. (1976). Instructions, exposure, rehearsal feedback as elements in imagery-based techniques. *Behaviorism: A Critical Focus, 4,* 189–193.

426. Wisocki, P.A. (1977). The successful treatment of a heroin addict by covert conditioning techniques: An updated report. In D. Upper (Ed.), *Perspectives in behavior therapy* (pp. 31–44). Kalamazoo, MI: Behaviordelia.

427. Wisocki, P.A., & Rooney, E.J. (1974). A comparison of thought stopping and covert sensitization techniques in the treatment of smoking: A brief report. *Psychological Record, 24,* 191–192.

428. Wisocki, P.A., & Telch, M.J. (1980). Modifying attitudes toward the elderly with the use of sampling procedures. *Scandinavian Journal of Behavior Therapy, 9,* 87–96.

429. Wolfinsohn, L.S. (1974). Modification of eating patterns in the obese through covert sensitization: An integration of learning and dynamic positions (Doctoral dissertation, Wayne State University, 1973). *Dissertation Abstracts International, 34,* 3513B–3514B. (University Microfilms No. 73-31, 793.)

430. Woolfolk, R.L., Parrish, M.W., & Murphy, S.M. (1983, December). *The effects of positive and negative imagery on motor skill performance.* Paper presented at the Seventeenth Annual Meeting of the Association for Advancement of Behavior Therapy, Washington, DC.

431. Workman, E.A. (1977, March). *The use of covert behavioral self control procedures in a program for intellectually gifted children.* Paper presented at the Annual Convention of the National Association of School Psychologists, Cincinnati, OH.

432. Workman, E.A. (1978). The effect of a covert behavioral self-control procedure on the on-task behavior of elementary school children: A time series analysis (Doctoral dissertation, University of Tennessee, 1977). *Dissertation Abstracts International, 38,* 4495B. (University Microfilms No. 78-2048.)

433. Workman, E.A., & Dickinson, D.J. (1979). The use of covert con-

ditioning with children: Three empirical case studies. *Education and Treatment of Children, 2,* 245–259.

434. Workman, E.A., & Dickinson, D.J. (1979). The use of covert positive reinforcement in the treatment of a hyperactive child: An empirical case study. *Journal of School Psychology, 17,* 67–73.

435. Yager, G.G. (1974, April). *Covert conditioning: Case studies in self-management.* Paper presented at the Annual Meeting of the American Educational Research Association, Chicago.

436. Yager, G.G. (1974). The effect of the covert behavior of visual imagery, self-monitoring, and self-evaluation upon the overt expression of emotional words (Doctoral dissertation, Michigan State University, 1973). *Dissertation Abstracts International, 34,* 5648A–5649A. (University Microfilms No. 74-6170.)

437. Yager, G.G. (1975, April). *The effect of the covert behavior of visual imagery, self-monitoring, and self-evaluation upon the overt expression of emotional words.* Paper presented at the Annual Meeting of the American Educational Research Association, Chicago.

438. Yager, G.G. (1975). A new behavioral emphasis: Turning the inside out. *Personnel and Guidance Journal, 53,* 585–591.

439. Yager, G.G., Pace, D.G., & Tepper, N.G. (1975, March). *Differential covert conditioning: A replication of an experiment by Wish, Cautela, and Steffen.* Paper presented at the Annual Meeting of the American Educational Research Association, Washington, DC.

440. Yaremko, R.M., & Werner, M. (1974). Cognitive conditioning: Imagerial stimulus contiguity and third interval conditional GSR. *Pavlovian Journal of Biological Science, 9,* 215–221.

441. Zemore, R., Ramsay, B., & Zemore, J. (1978). Success of covert negative reinforcement is not the result of operant conditioning. *Psychological Reports, 43,* 955–961.

442. Zielinski, J.J., & Williams, L.J. (1979). Covert modeling vs. behavior rehearsal. The training and generalization of assertive behavior: cross-over design. *Journal of Clinical Psychology, 35,* 855–863.

Index